Dyslexia in Higher Education:
policy, provision and practice

◆

Report of the National Working Party on
Dyslexia in Higher Education

Chris Singleton (Chair)

Stella ní Ghallchóir Cottrell	Lindsay Peer
Dorothy Gilroy	Peter D. Pumfrey
Vicki Goodwin	Gavin Reid
Julia Hetherington	Ginny Stacey
Melanie Jameson	Judith Waterfield
David Laycock	Dorota Zdzienski
David McLoughlin	

◆

Funded by the
Higher Education Funding Councils for
England and Scotland

THE
ITY

Published by

The National Working Party on Dyslexia in Higher Education
Department of Psychology
University of Hull
Hull HU6 7RX
UK

E-mail: *dyslexia@hull.ac.uk*

ISBN 1 898862 99 0

THE
UNIVERSITY
OF HULL

Printed by the University of Hull

Outline Contents

Full List of Contents

Dyslexia in Higher Education:
policy, provision and practice

◆

The Report of the National Working Party on Dyslexia in Higher Education

Chris Singleton (Chair)

Funded by the

Higher Education Funding Councils for England (HEFCE) and Scotland (SHEFC)

January 1999

Executive Summary

Introduction

Intellectual potential, represented by the abilities of individuals, is a social, cultural and economic asset that no nation can afford to neglect. Equal opportunities and anti-discrimination legislation encourage the entry of talented but disabled students into higher education. When the existence of a legally-recognised disability such as dyslexia obscures the recognition of able individuals by institutions of higher education, the individual, educational institutions and the nation lose.

Dyslexia is a complex neurological condition that occurs in approximately 4% of the population, and which primarily affects acquisition and use of written language, memory and organisational skills. It is a legally recognised disability, and there is strong evidence that supports a genetic causation of the condition.

This report addresses the questions:

- *Is higher education responding adequately to the challenges represented by students with dyslexia, who may require support in order to learn and study effectively and take their places in the work force?*

- *How best might higher education respond to these challenges, taking into account the imperative to maintain academic standards, the ethics of equal opportunities and the exigencies of economics?*

Contexts

The *Disability Discrimination Act 1995* established, *inter alia*, a mechanism whereby the Higher Education Funding Councils have become the guardians of provision for disabled students in higher education. A key feature is the requirement that each institution of higher education produce a Disability Statement setting out its policy and provision for disabled students. The Act gives the Funding Councils powers to impose conditions upon HEIs regarding provision for disabled students.

In 1996, the Higher Education Quality Council (HEQC) published a discussion paper entitled *What are graduates? Clarifying the attributes of 'graduateness'*. This initiative formed part of the

Graduate Standards Programme (GSP) instigated by the Committee of Vice-Chancellors and Principals (CVCP). Its purpose was to stimulate debate concerning the nature of the core attributes denoted by the award of a first degree in the UK. The discussion on 'graduateness' within higher education nationally impinges directly on the admission to higher education of students with dyslexia, who have specific difficulties in literacy skills. Should talented students with dyslexia be excluded from higher education because of their literacy difficulties? Evidence that dyslexic students can satisfactorily complete first (and higher) degree courses and that a significant proportion (40% or greater) obtain 'good' degrees (i.e. first or upper second class honours) suggests that, in principle, the answer must be 'No'. In practice, this means that higher education institutions (HEIs) need to consider how such students can be identified and enabled to demonstrate their intellectual abilities.

Widening access to higher education is a key recommendation of the Report of the National Committee of Inquiry into Higher Education, chaired by Sir Ron Dearing, *Higher Education in the Learning Society* (Dearing, 1997). Specific reference is made to applicants with disabilities, including a call for increased funding to enable HEIs to provide for such students. The Report also recommends widening of application of the Disabled Student's Allowances (DSA) to support individual students with disabilities.

The implications of the *Disability Discrimination Act 1995*, the observations and recommendation of the Dearing Report (1997) and the government's response to that report (DfEE, 1998), confirm that, in principle, all HEIs have a duty to provide equal opportunities for students with disabilities, including those with dyslexia. But the provisions required to assure equal opportunities inevitably have costs attached to them, and HEIs are under many pressures, including financial ones.

Since 1993, the Higher Education Funding Council for England (HEFCE) has financially supported a series of initiatives on disability in higher education. These included a variety of research and development projects in individual HEIs, specifically linked to dyslexia. While these initiatives have done a great deal to establish improved provision and to promote good practice, staff working in disability support in HEIs have expressed continuing concerns about dyslexia. In particular, concern has been expressed about inconsistencies in procedures for identification of students with dyslexia, maintenance of institutional support for students with dyslexia in the face of increasing numbers and financial constraints, and about the effective operation of the DSA system in dyslexia cases.

Objectives

The serious and growing professional and political concerns described above signalled the need for:

- *a national survey of policies, provision and practices bearing on the identification, assessment and support of students with dyslexia in higher education*

- *the formulation of national guidelines on identification and support of students with dyslexia that could assist the development of unified mechanisms of provision across the sector.*

Following a HEFCE funded conference on Dyslexia and Higher Education held in November, 1994, a National Working Party on Dyslexia in Higher Education was established. Financial support for its work was agreed by the Higher Education Funding Councils of England (HEFCE) and Scotland (SHEFC) as from September, 1995. The National Working Party comprised fourteen members.

Focusing on higher education and students with dyslexia, the National Working Party was concerned with all phases of the student's progress from the application stage to the completion of their course in higher education and entry to a career.

The National Working Party had five major objectives:

1) To carry out a national survey of policy, provision and practice in relation to the identification and support of students with dyslexia in higher education.

2) To identify the concerns of providers of higher education services and their students with dyslexia.

3) To describe promising practices concerning the assessment and support of students with dyslexia.

4) To investigate the operations of the Disabled Student's Allowance in relation to students with dyslexia.

5) To make recommendations on policy and national guidelines for HEIs on the assessment and support of students with dyslexia.

Method

A questionnaire was developed for circulation to all 234 HEIs in the UK. These institutions were categorised as: 'Traditional universities' (N = 44); 'New universities' (i.e. those which had been established as universities since 1990; N = 48); and 'colleges offering higher education courses' (N = 142). The questions asked included ones on: admissions policy; the identification of dyslexia; its incidence; support provision for students with dyslexia in HEIs; specialist counselling facilities and staff development; technological support; the operation of the Disabled Students Allowance (DSA); and examination and assessment arrangements.

A series of five regional consultative meetings, to which representatives of all HEIs were invited, was held in London, Birmingham, Manchester, Bristol and Edinburgh. A national consultation was organised for Local Education Authority (LEA) Awards Officers with responsibility for the administration of the Disabled Students' Allowances (DSA). Their concerns regarding the DSA for students with dyslexia were considered in relation to the Awards Officers' overall brief.

Information was obtained from national organisations having an involvement in the identification and support of students with dyslexia in higher education, whether in professional or voluntary capacity. Such groups included the Association of Educational Psychologists, Adult Dyslexia Organisation, British Dyslexia Association, British Psychological Society, Dyslexia Institute, National Federation of Access Centres and the National Bureau for Students with Disabilities (Skill). As a consequence of an article in the *Times Higher Educational Supplement* in 1996, the regional and national consultations, plus presentations made by members of the National Working Party at more than two dozen academic and professional conferences (several of which were international), additional representations and documentation were also submitted for the National Working Party's consideration.

Selected findings

The national survey

All 234 institutions offering higher education courses in Britain were sent a specially devised questionnaire. 195 responses were received (83% response rate). The responses were broken down as follows: traditional universities (41 responses; 93% response rate), new universities (45 responses; 94% response rate, and colleges (109 responses; 77% response rate).

94% of institutions claim to admit students registered as dyslexics to all courses. Those institutions reporting that students with dyslexia were not admitted to certain courses referred mainly to courses leading to professional qualifications in teaching and courses connected with medicine and/or pharmacy.

HEIs provided information regarding the total number of current students at the institution who had declared themselves to be dyslexic on the UCAS form and the total number of current students identified as dyslexic after admission. From these data the overall incidence of dyslexia in the student population was estimated to be 1.35%. Incidence figures varied across the categories of HEIs, from 0.95% in traditional universities, 1.31% in the new universities to 1.54% in the colleges. These figures are consistent with data published by the Higher Education Statistics Agency (HESA). Allowing for a margin of error, the incidence of dyslexia in higher education may be estimated at between 1.2% and 1.5% of all students.

57% of students with dyslexia are already known to be dyslexic on entry to higher education. The traditional universities and the colleges report that dyslexic students are more likely to be spread equally across different subject areas than is the case in the new universities.

Almost 75% of HEIs reported that they had a support service for students with dyslexia. More of the new universities reported having such a facility (79%) in comparison with 68% of the traditional universities. On a range of additional indices, there appeared to be more adequate provision for students with dyslexia in the new universities than in the traditional universities.

45% of HEIs reported that they employed a dyslexia-trained tutor to support students with dyslexia. In the new universities this figure was 57%. In contrast, in the traditional universities the figure was 27% and in the colleges 48%. In the colleges the vast majority of such tutors were employed by the institution. In the universities only about half of such professionals were employed by the institution; the others were employed on a consultancy basis.

On the basis of the analyses of the questionnaire data, the differences noted in the range of provision in HEIs concerning the identification and support of students with dyslexia are sufficiently marked to suggest that action is required to reduce the manifest variability across the sector.

Consultations

The five regional meetings were attended by a total of 121 individuals representing HEIs, plus members of the National Working Party. Those attending were provided with briefing papers covering key issues. During those meetings, a record was kept of points of concern made during the group discussions and plenary sessions. The total number of points collated from the five consultations was 440. Because of overlaps, these were subsequently reduced to 65 concerns, which may be summarised as follows. Widening access to higher education for students with dyslexia raised concerns about equal opportunities and academic standards. Obtaining official recognition of a student's dyslexia through a diagnostic assessment is sometimes found to be problematic. The subsequent identification of the special needs of students with dyslexia, and the provision of the support that they require, often creates resourcing problems. Students identified as having dyslexia, or considered as possibly having dyslexia, often face more than academic stresses. Problems of equity arise in the organisation of examination and assessment arrangements. Finally, are the legitimate interests of students and potential employers compatible?

The consultation with LEA Awards Officers having responsibility for the management of the DSA programme was attended by 22 Awards Officers and 7 members of the National Working Party. Because of the Awards Officers particular concerns, their observations were recorded separately. Under similar reporting arrangements to those operating at the regional meetings, a total of 67 concerns were identified and subsequently condensed to 21 points. A major point raised was that the Awards Officers are not experts in dyslexia. For them to operate the DSA programme effectively, it is administratively essential that they are provided with a diagnostic assessment carried out by a qualified professional, normally a Chartered Psychologist, experienced in the assessment of adolescents and adults. This raises important questions concerning the variety of ways whereby a previously undiagnosed and possibly dyslexic student obtains an assessment. Awards Officers were also concerned at what some saw as considerable variability in the nature, structure and content of diagnostic reports.

Proposals on good practice

In many respects, HEIs are autonomous bodies. In relation to disabled students in general, and those with dyslexia in particular, individual institution's policies and practices will typically reflect their particular academic and professional priorities and circumstances. During the study, examples of good practice in HEIs were noted under each of the eight headings specified above. Details are presented in Chapters 5 to 12. They demonstrate how certain institutions have developed policies, provision and practice to meet more effectively the many and complex reciprocal challenges presented to HEIs and faced by students with dyslexia aspiring to study at this level.

The Working Party wishes to draw particular attention to its guidelines on diagnostic assessment of students with dyslexia, which are to be found in Section 8.3 of the report. These specify in some detail the qualifications of personnel suitable to carry out such assessments, and the nature of the information that should be provided in assessment reports.

There are a number of important reasons why guidelines on diagnostic assessment are necessary, of which the first and foremost is that it is imperative to have *objective and professionally acceptable evidence* that the poor literacy skills or poor studying skills displayed by the individual being assessed are due to dyslexia. If satisfactory evidence is not available, application for the DSA would be fraudulent and the allocation of special provision such as additional time in examinations would be grossly unjust. Meeting these requirements calls for evidence (obtained by means of appropriate standardised tests and professionally established procedures) of a *significant discrepancy* between the student's abilities reading, writing, spelling (and mathematics or number work, if necessary) and the level of those abilities that would reasonably be expected of the student, based on the student's general intellectual ability and other relevant factors, such as educational history. In addition, there should be evidence of limitations in memory or other cognitive domains that impact significantly on studying and performance in examinations.

Key recommendations

It is the explicit intention of the Working Party that the complete set of 101 recommendations presented in Chapters 5 to 12 of the full report will provide guidelines for the development of more consistent policy, provision and practice across the higher education sector nationally. Recommendations are based on evidence obtained during the inquiry bearing on eight aspects of higher education policy, provision and practice. For each of the eight areas, a small number of key recommendation are presented here. The total number of recommendations in each of the sections in the full report is shown below in square brackets.

1. Institutional and national policy [13 recommendations]

- Dyslexia should be explicitly recognised by all HEIs both as a disability and as a special educational need. *(5.3 Recommendation 1)*

- Each institution should have a clear general policy setting out regulations, procedures and guidelines, as appropriate, for the identification and support of students with dyslexia. The general policy should make reference to, but not necessarily provide detail in every respect of, all the following basic areas of concern: staff development and awareness, admissions, identification, evaluation of needs, provision of learning support (including technological support), counselling, examinations and assessments, and careers advice. *(5.3 Recommendation 2)*

2. Staff development and awareness [10 recommendations]

- All appropriate staff of each HEI, including academic, academic-related, and administrative staff, should become aware of the institution's policy on dyslexia, of the needs of students with dyslexia, and of the support that is available within the institution. *(6.3 Recommendation 1)*

- There should be a member of the academic staff within each faculty and/or sub-faculty unit (e.g. school or department) with explicit responsibility for students with dyslexia within that area. *(6.3 Recommendation 2)*

- There should be a programme of staff development and awareness within the institution that (a) relates explicitly to provision for students with dyslexia; (b) should be referred to in the institution's general policy on provision for students with dyslexia; and (c) has been constructed with the advice of a professional with understanding and experience of dyslexia support. *(6.3 Recommendation 4)*

3. Admission to higher education [14 recommendations]

- Each HEI should maintain and publish an admissions policy that does not discriminate against students with dyslexia, except in those subjects and areas of study for which a clear, explicit and published justification is given by the institution. *(7.3 Recommendation 1)*

- When dealing with the admission of students with dyslexia, admissions tutors or officers should endeavour to understand the educational problems and needs of students with dyslexia. *(7.3 Recommendation 3a)*

4. Identification of students with dyslexia [15 recommendations]

- All HEIs should formulate a clear policy on identification of dyslexia which embodies the National Working Party's *Guidelines on diagnostic assessment of dyslexia. (8.4 Recommendation 1)*

- When considering applications for Disabled Students' Allowances from students with dyslexia, all LEAs should expect such applications to be accompanied by reports of diagnostic assessments that conform to the *Guidelines on diagnostic assessment of dyslexia* given in this report. *(8.4 Recommendation 5)*

5. Evaluation of needs and support provisions [16 recommendations]

- All HEIs should have a policy and set of procedures for evaluation of the learning and support needs of students with dyslexia. *(9.3 Recommendation 3a)*

- All HEIs should have, either on the staff or otherwise available to students, at least one tutor with training and/or experience in supporting students with dyslexia and all students with dyslexia should be made aware of that tutor. *(9.3 Recommendation 4a)*

6. Counselling [6 recommendations]

- Every HEI should have at least one student counsellor available who has specific knowledge and/or experience of dyslexia counselling. *(10.3 Recommendation 1)*

7. Examinations and assessment [16 recommendations]

- Every HEI should have a written policy on the examination and assessment of students with dyslexia ('the examinations policy'). *(11.3 Recommendation 1)*

- The examinations policy should: (a) acknowledge that academic standards are paramount and that special arrangements in examinations and assessments are for the purpose of creating a level playing field for these disabled students; and (b) be compiled having due regard to the Working Party's proposals on good practice given in Section 11.2 of this report. *(11.3 Recommendations 2a and 2b)*

8. Careers Advice [11 recommendations]

- At least one careers adviser in every HEI should have explicit knowledge and/or experience of dyslexia as it relates to the employment of graduates. *(12.3 Recommendation 1)*

Costs

All of the recommendations and proposals made in this report have been put forward with the awareness that the majority of HEIs have to manage very tight budgets and have little excess income over already-committed expenditure that can be devoted to the support of disabled students.

Utilising all available data, the Working Party has estimated that if an average-sized university, with about 15,000 students, wished to implement the recommendations of this report, the annual overall expenditure would be in the region of £66,500. This amount should cover about 50% of a disability officer's time, a full-time dyslexia tutor, half-time secretary or clerical assistant, overheads and recurrent costs, and provision for dyslexia screening and diagnostic assessments. The average cost to the institution per each dyslexic student (estimated at about 200 per institution) would be about £330 per annum. This figure does not include cost of special technology or other support that should be available through DSAs.

With appropriately skilled staff and efficient administration, a fair proportion of those costs should be recoverable from DSAs. The estimates given here are not recommendations but should serve as a useful starting point for discussion within any institution that is considering establishing or improving provisions for students with dyslexia.

Conclusions

Talented students with dyslexia legitimately aspire to undertake courses in higher education. It is known that such students can be successful. The evidence in this report demonstrates the marked variability across HEIs in institutional efforts and effectiveness in developing and implementing policies that facilitate the identification and support of dyslexic students.

The information provided on existing good practice, taken in conjunction with the full set of recommendations, provides a basis whereby each HEI can consider the adequacy of its current provision and consider means whereby this can be improved. The costs of establishing and maintaining a satisfactory service for students with dyslexia that is consistent with the recommendations made in this report are not inconsiderable, although in many cases a proportion of costs should be recoverable from DSAs. The benefits to dyslexic students, in terms of the quality of their educational experience and their academic and occupational outcomes should be significant. Above all, this expenditure should be seen as an integral and essential part of the institution's general commitment to securing equal opportunities for all disabled students and honouring its implied responsibilities under the *Disability Discrimination Act 1995*.

The membership of
The National Working Party on Dyslexia in Higher Education

(in alphabetical order)

Dr Stella ní Ghallchóir Cottrell

Dr Stella Cottrell is Senior Lecturer in Educational Development at the University of East London. Her role is to contribute to the improvement of learning and teaching in the university, with particular responsibility for study skills development and co-ordinating services for students with dyslexia. Dr Cottrell is a qualified teacher and lectured at Somerville College, Oxford, for four years. She has published many articles on dyslexia and is author of *Skills for Success* (University of East London, 1990). In recent years she has acted as consultant to several HEIs on establishing or extending support for students with dyslexia. She presented a paper at the First International Conference on Dyslexia in Higher Education organised by the University of Plymouth, held in 1994.

Dorothy Gilroy

Dorothy Gilroy is Support Tutor in the Dyslexia Unit, University of Wales at Bangor. She was nominated as a member of the Working Party by the Higher Education Funding Council for Wales. She has worked for many years with dyslexic people, individually and in groups, in teaching, support and counselling capacities. She is co-author (with Professor Tim Miles) of the book *Dyslexia at College* (Routledge, 1986, 1996), which has become the international standard in its field. She has also published articles on the effects of stress in college students with dyslexia.

Vicki Goodwin

Vicki Goodwin is Senior Counsellor for the West Midlands region of the Open University. She has worked with dyslexic students for many years and is co-author of the book *Adult Students and Dyslexia* (Open University, 1995). She has presented papers on study skills support and counselling students with dyslexia at a number of important research conferences in this field, including the Skill National Conference on Dyslexia in Higher Education held at Huddersfield University in 1996, the Second International Conference on Dyslexia in Higher Education organised by the University of Plymouth, also in 1996, and the Fourth BDA International Conference, held at the University of York in 1997.

Julia Hetherington

Julia Hetherington is a consultant in adult dyslexia based in East Sussex, with many years' experience of teaching and supporting students and other adults with dyslexia. Formerly she was Learning Support Tutor in the Department of Students Services at the University of Brighton, and was involved in HEFCE Special Initiative projects on dyslexia and other disabilities at Brighton during 1993–95. She has made a particular study of the self-esteem of young people with dyslexia and how they come to terms with their disability in the higher education setting, a subject about which she presented a workshop at the Skill National Conference on Dyslexia in Higher Education, held at Huddersfield University in 1996.

Melanie Jameson

Melanie Jameson is the Education Adviser of the Adult Dyslexia Organisation. She has worked for several years as a support tutor to students with dyslexia in various institutions of higher education, including the University of Lancaster and Bolton Institute of Higher Education. She has also acted as a consultant on dyslexia to several colleges and universities, and has made many presentations on supporting students with dyslexia, including a paper delivered at the Fourth BDA International Conference, held at the University of York in 1997, on running an adult dyslexic support group, which was based on her own experiences of co-ordinating the Lancaster Adult Dyslexics/Dyspraxics group since 1993. She has particular interests in the assessment and treatment of visual discomfort, technology for supporting students with dyslexia, and self-management techniques for adults with dyslexia and dyspraxia.

David Laycock

David Laycock is Head of the Computer Centre for People with Disabilities at the University of Westminster, which provides support for disabled undergraduates as well as those who are employed or unemployed. He is also Chair of the National Federation of Access Centres. He specialises in assessment of disability in adulthood, particularly for higher education, and in the use of assistive technology to support dyslexia and other disabilities. He has given many presentations on technology support for dyslexic adults, including an invited paper at the First International Conference on Dyslexia in Higher Education organised by the University of Plymouth and held in 1994. He has been an advisor to DfEE and HEFCE on matters concerning disability and in 1997 he was awarded the MBE for services to the disabled.

Dr David McLoughlin

Dr David McLoughlin is a Chartered Psychologist, qualified in educational and occupational psychology. He has been in professional practice for over 25 years, both in the UK and in Australia. He has specialised in dyslexia for the past 15 years and works with dyslexic people of all ages. He is a director of the Adult Dyslexia and Skills Development Centre in London, and principal author of the book *Adult Dyslexia: Assessment, Counselling and Training* (Whurr, 1993), which has become one of the standard works in this field. Dr McLoughlin is an Associate Fellow of the British Psychological Society. He has given many presentations at conferences, including an invited paper on assessment and counselling of the adult dyslexic at the First International Conference on Dyslexia in Higher Education, University of Plymouth (1994), and a paper on enhancing the metacognitive strategies of adult dyslexics, delivered at the Fourth BDA International Conference, University of York (1997).

Lindsay Peer

Lindsay Peer is Education Director of the British Dyslexia Association. She has been involved in teacher training for many years, including a period in Israel during 1989–91, when she was responsible for specialist teacher training and establishing centres for the assessment, remediation and support of people with dyslexia. As well as publishing many articles on dyslexia, she is author of *Dyslexia: The training and awareness of teachers* (BDA, 1994), *Winning with Dyslexia: A guide for secondary schools* (BDA, 1996), and *A Young Person's Guide to Dyslexia* (BDA, 1997). She has given presentations at numerous conferences, including the Skill National Conference on Dyslexia in Higher Education, held at the University of Huddersfield in 1994. She was a member of the organising committee of the Fourth BDA International Conference, held at the University of York in 1997, and is an Executive Editor of *Dyslexia: An International Journal of Research and Practice* (BDA/Wiley).

Professor Peter D. Pumfrey

Professor Peter Pumfrey is Emeritus Professor of Education at the University of Manchester and also affiliated to the Centre for Special Educational Needs at University College, Worcester. He is a qualified and experienced teacher, having been employed in mainstream schools and remedial services for 14 years prior to training and working as an LEA educational psychologist. In 1969 he became a lecturer in education at the University of Manchester, rising to become Professor in 1990 and Dean of Education for the final two years before his retirement in 1998. He is a Chartered Psychologist and a Fellow of the British Psychological Society. He is a member of the Council of the Dyslexia Institute and a vice-president of the British Dyslexia Association. Professor Pumfrey has numerous publications to his name, including more than 60 papers in refereed academic journals, several hundred other chapters and articles, and over 20 books and monographs, of which the volume *Specific Learning Difficulties (Dyslexia): Challenges and Responses* (Routledge, 1991) has become one of the most widely respected and cited works in the field and has been reprinted many times. Throughout his distinguished academic career, Professor Pumfrey has given numerous presentations at conferences throughout the world, including at the Second World Congress on Dyslexia held in Greece in 1998, where he represented the Working Party. In 1995 he was invited to give the 15th Vernon-Wall Lecture to the Education Section of the British Psychological Society, which was subsequently published as the monograph *Specific Developmental Dyslexia: Basics to Back?* (BPS, 1996).

Dr Gavin Reid

Dr Gavin Reid is a lecturer at Moray House Institute of Education in Edinburgh and Course Leader for the Postgraduate Awards in Specific Learning Difficulties (Dyslexia). He was nominated as a member of the Working Party by the Scottish Higher Education Funding Council (SHEFC). He has many years' experience as a class teacher and an educational psychologist. He is a Chartered Psychologist, an Associate Fellow of the British Psychological Society and a member of the British Dyslexia Association's Accreditation Board for Teacher Training. Dr Reid's many publications on dyslexia include *Dyslexia: A practitioner's handbook* (Wiley, 1998), and he is editor of the two-volume text *Dimensions of Dyslexia* (Moray House, 1996). He has made numerous keynote conference presentations on dyslexia throughout the world, including a paper on study skills for students with dyslexia, given at the First International Conference on Dyslexia in Higher Education, University of Plymouth (1994), and papers delivered at the Fourth BDA International Conference, held at the University of York in 1997.

Dr Chris Singleton (Chair)

Dr Chris Singleton is Senior Lecturer in Educational Psychology at the University of Hull, and a Chartered Psychologist with over 20 years' experience of assessment and research in the fields of educational difficulties and dyslexia. He heads a research team that has created three pioneering computer-based assessment systems now used in education in many parts of the world. He is also currently directing two HEFCE Special Initiative projects on disability at Hull, where he is also Vice-Chair of the Disability Committee. Dr. Singleton has been an invited keynote speaker at many international conferences, and is author of over 100 publications on dyslexia, the development of literacy, and computer-based assessment. He is co-author/editor of several books, including *Computers and Dyslexia: Educational Applications of New Technology* (British Dyslexia Association, 1994) and *Psychological Assessment of Reading* (Routledge, 1997). He is Editor of the *Journal of Research in Reading* (UKRA/Blackwell) and a member of the Editorial Board of *Dyslexia: An International Journal of Research and Practice* (BDA/Wiley). Dr. Singleton is an Associate Fellow of the British Psychological Society and a member of the BPS Steering Committee on Test Standards. He is also a member of the Computer Committee of the British Dyslexia Association, and of the Publications Board of the United Kingdom Reading Association.

Dr Ginny Stacey

Dr Ginny Stacey is Support Tutor for Dyslexic Students at Oxford Brookes University where, for the past five years, as well as providing individual support for students, she has taught an accredited module that helps dyslexic undergraduates to improve their skills in English and to develop learning strategies. For several years she has studied the learning strengths and limitations of the dyslexic mind, based initially on her experiences of her own dyslexia and subsequently by working with other dyslexic adults. Her ideas have been disseminated in numerous articles and presentations at many conferences, including the Skill National Conference on Dyslexia in Higher Education (Huddersfield University, 1994), the Fourth BDA International Conference (University of York, 1997), and both of the international conferences on dyslexia in higher education (University of Plymouth, 1994; 1996). In 1998 Dr Stacey represented the National Working Party and presented two invited papers at an international conference on dyslexia held in Israel. She also produced the video programme *A Taste of Dyslexia* (Oxfordshire Dyslexia Association, 1992) which aims to show non-dyslexic people what it is like to have dyslexia.

Judith Waterfield

Judith Waterfield is Adviser for Special Learning Needs at the University of Plymouth and manager of the South West Regional Access Centre for students with disabilities and dyslexia. She has a Masters Degree in Education from the University of Bristol and a postgraduate qualification in dyslexia from the University of Bangor. For the past 25 years she has been teaching in the areas of education and health, and educational therapy, and has published several articles in these fields. She has organised two international conferences on dyslexia in higher education, held in 1994 and 1996, and edited the published proceedings of these conferences (*Dyslexia in Higher Education: Learning along the continuum,* University of Plymouth, 1995, 1998). She has also made many presentations herself, including an invited workshop on a whole-institution approach to provision for dyslexic students in higher education, given at the Skill National Conference on Dyslexia in Higher Education held at Huddersfield University in 1996. She had a managerial role in two HEFCE Special Initiative projects on dyslexia and disabilities at Plymouth during 1993–95.

Dorota Zdzienski

Dorota Zdzienski is a qualified teacher with a diploma in specific learning difficulties, who has more than 18 years' experience of teaching and counselling in the dyslexia field. She has ran diploma courses in specific learning difficulties (dyslexia) for the RSA (Royal Society of Arts) and has worked in conjunction with many professional bodies in this field, including the Hornsby International Dyslexia Centre and the Dyslexia Institute. She has published many articles and given numerous conference presentations on dyslexia, including an invited paper on study skills for students with dyslexia, given at the First International Conference on Dyslexia in Higher Education organised by the University of Plymouth in 1994. During 1993–95 she was employed on the HEFCE Special Initiative project at Kingston University, in which she carried out research on assessment procedures for identifying students with dyslexia in higher education. The resulting computerised system that she developed has now been published under the name *StudyScan* (Interactive Services, 1997), and the research behind this was presented at the Skill National Conference on Dyslexia in Higher Education held at Huddersfield University in 1994 and also at the Fourth BDA International Conference, held at the University of York in 1997.

Preface

With widening access to higher education it is inevitable that more students with dyslexia will appear in lecture rooms and tutorial groups – it is not a large number, but it is a significant minority. Although a few may have outstanding talents which any society would wish to foster, most of those with dyslexia will probably appear to be similar to other students – except that they find some aspects of studying unusually difficult. In level of intelligence, general ability and interests they will usually be no different to other students, although some may display exceptionally high motivation, despite – or perhaps because of – their dyslexic difficulties.

Provided they have the necessary aptitude, students with dyslexia have just as much right to participate in higher education as have any other able and motivated adults, but their disability can be a barrier. We cannot simply brush aside all questions concerning the relevance of good literacy skills to the concept of 'graduateness'. Nevertheless, the overwhelming desire of most teachers in higher education is to promote equal opportunities for *all* students who have sufficient ability, show a keen interest and who are committed to their studies. The key question is – how to achieve this? Academic and administrative staff are becoming increasingly aware that students with dyslexia can be found in all institutions of higher education (HEIs). The educational provision for such students may have to be differentiated in some respects, and practical solutions for meeting the needs of these students are required. Lack of knowledge and of resources – both financial and human – remain major obstacles to enabling students with dyslexia to address their problems.

These were the issues confronting a number of professionals who came together at a conference on dyslexia in higher education held at Dartington Hall, Devon, in November 1994. The outcome was the establishment of the National Working Party on Dyslexia in Higher Education, which set as its objectives the consideration of policy and provision for students with dyslexia in higher education in the UK and the formulation of recommendations and guidelines which would assist HEIs in meeting the needs of such students. The provision of financial support for the project by the Higher Education Funding Council for England (HEFCE) and the Scottish Higher Education Funding Council (SHEFC) enabled the activities of the Working Party to commence in September 1995.

The task proved to be far more difficult and much more time-consuming that we had at first imagined. The projected time scale of one year to carry out data collection and consultation turned out to be almost two. During that period the fourteen members of the Working Party put in an enormous amount of time and effort, examining the issues as widely and as comprehensively as possible, including considering evidence from various sources and consulting with a large number of representatives from HEIs across the country. Following that, the members of the Working Party had to formulate specific recommendations for policy and practice that would enable all HEIs to address the problems in this area in a fair, cost-effective and consistent manner. Because many of the issues are highly contentious a considerable amount of time has had to be devoted to their resolution.

As well as making recommendations, the Working Party also wanted to provide the personnel having responsibility for students with dyslexia with practical guidance on *how* those recommended policies should be implemented. The task of formulating proposals on good practice is the principal cause of the further delay in completing this report, but we believe that this course of action was necessary in order to maximise the prospects of the recommendations being implemented.

In this report we have tried to address all the issues in a fair and balanced manner. Where good evidence is lacking we have sought to obtain it. In our recommendations we have been mindful of the fact that HEIs have very restricted funds and that provision for students with dyslexia cannot be permitted to take undue resources away from other students. In this respect our report is *not* special pleading for a minority group within higher education, but rather the advocacy of equality and fairness for all, including those who happen to have dyslexia.

This report has been written in a manner that is designed to be accessible to professionals working in higher education and related fields. Although technical terminology has been kept to a minimum, is has not been possible to exclude all technical terms because dyslexia is a topic that has been the subject of considerable scientific research. Consequently, where scientific terms are used, a brief explanation is given in the text and appropriate references have been provided.

At the request of the HEFCE and SHEFC, copies of this report have been sent to the Secretary of State for Education and Employment, to the Vice Chancellors or Principals of all HEIs, and to the Directors of Education for all LEAs. Further copies are available from the publishers.

As Chair, I would like to take this opportunity to thank my colleagues on the Working Party sincerely for their enthusiasm, commitment, diligence and sheer hard work over the past three years. The process of reaching agreement between fourteen very experienced individuals each with their different professional and personal perspectives on this often contentious subject has not been without its fireworks. But our common objective to produce a report which will be of real value to HEIs – and thereby potentially to help all students with dyslexia to achieve their personal goals in higher education – has sustained us through the inevitable battles and I am grateful for everyone's perseverance. Although the contents of this report represent a joint effort by all the members of the Working Party, the Chair has taken responsibility for collating and organising the material, for the greater part of the writing and for imposing consistencies of style. In addressing that considerable task, and especially in the final stages of editing, I have been particularly encouraged and supported by Working Party members Ginny Stacey and Peter Pumfrey, to whom I extend my special thanks.

On behalf of the Working Party and myself I would like to thank HEFCE and SHEFC for their financial support and also for their patience in waiting rather longer for this report than at first they envisaged. We would also like to thank those representatives of HEIs and LEAs and others who participated in our various consultations and fact-gathering exercises, and the many individuals and organisations that have taken the trouble to communicate with the Working Party. Finally, I would like to express my gratitude to Joanna Horne (research assistant), Brenda Smith (administrative assistant) and Christine Mallet (secretary), for their vital contributions to this endeavour.

The very existence of the Working Party and the work in which it has been engaged during the last three years has heightened awareness of the issues. In consequence, the vast majority of HEIs are now actively seeking ways to provide more effectively for their dyslexic students. Enquiries received from HEIs suggest that our recommendations are eagerly awaited by many in higher education. This report, which goes beyond the making of recommendations, has tried to distil the wide-ranging concerns of all parties and offer encouragement as well as practical solutions to the challenges which confront HEIs in meeting the needs of students with dyslexia. If our recommendations are widely accepted and implemented then the foundations will have been firmly laid for a more equitable, effective and consistent provision for students with dyslexia across the higher education sector in this country.

Chris Singleton *(Chair)*

1 Introduction

1.1 Dyslexia in higher education: current issues and contexts

1.1.1 Access, awareness and support issues

Widening access to higher education matters (HEFCE, 1996a). The potential represented by the human resources of individuals is a social, cultural and economic asset that no nation can afford to neglect. When a disability such as dyslexia prevents the recognition of talent by educational institutions, the nation and the individual lose. There are plenty of instances where this unnecessary loss has taken place. Much can be done to redress the situation in higher education (Friel, 1997; Stephens, 1996).

While public awareness of dyslexia has increased in recent years, public understanding of the condition appears to have developed little. Other than a minority of specialists within education, psychology and some branches of the medical profession, few people know very much about this puzzling and often controversial syndrome. Such a state of affairs may seem surprising in view of the fact that for over 25 years, dyslexia has been a registered disability (under the provisions of the *1970 Chronically Sick and Disabled Persons Act*). Since the *1981 Education Act,* dyslexia has been implicitly recognised in the school system by the issue of *Statements of Special Educational Need* by Local Education Authorities (LEAs) for some (but by no means all) pupils with dyslexia. More recently, dyslexia has been explicitly recognised as a form of specific learning difficulty in the school system (*Code of Practice for the Identification and Assessment of Special Educational Needs* [DfE, 1994][1]. Within higher education, some students with dyslexia are entitled to apply for the Disabled Students Allowance (DSA), which is a system of special allowances to enable them to purchase technology and other materials, and to pay for support which they may need in their studies. There is still widespread concern about the manner in which the DSA system operates in practice and its adequacy in providing for the needs of all students with dyslexia.

Dyslexia is therefore recognised legally and educationally, both as a disability and as a special educational need. Yet at all levels of the education system, students with dyslexia[2] have found themselves experiencing difficulties in the learning situation of which their teachers have little or no understanding. In the primary and secondary sectors the problem is now beginning to be addressed because the *Code of Practice* (DfE, 1994) places an obligation on schools in England and Wales to identify special educational needs. In England and Wales and also in Scotland, the school programme has been accompanied by an increase in specific policies issued by LEAs on practice and provision for dyslexia (Crombie and Reid, 1994; Reid, 1998).

In further and higher education sectors, these matters have not yet been properly addressed and the issues pertaining to the educational needs of students with dyslexia have yet to be fully discussed, although a start has been made (see Pumfrey, 1998). In colleges and universities – compared with the situation in schools – understanding of dyslexia is still rather limited, especially at senior management level. Few of those administrators who are called upon to formulate and implement policy for dyslexia in further and higher education know much about the nature of the condition for which they are allocating provision.

---

[1] Issued by the Secretary of State for Education under the requirements of the 1993 Education Act (now consolidated in the 1996 Education Act).

[2] In common with changes in terminology in other areas of disability, the term 'students (or persons) with dyslexia' is now generally preferred to 'dyslexics'. However, by no means all persons with dyslexia object to the use of the term 'dyslexic', and in those cases where repeated use of the term 'students with dyslexia' is would be unnecessarily cumbersome, the term 'dyslexic students' may be substituted without causing offence.

1.1.2 Increase in numbers of students with dyslexia in higher education

Many representatives of higher education institutions (HEIs) who contributed to the consultative process carried out by the Working Party (see Section 4.1.2) have observed that the number of students with dyslexia in higher education has been steadily increasing over recent years. One of the questions asked in the Working Party's national questionnaire survey of all HEIs was *'In your experience, what is the biggest problem confronting your Institution at the present time in relation to dyslexic students?'* It was found that 'Increasing numbers of dyslexic students' was the fourth most frequent answer, after (1st) finance, (2nd) lack of staff awareness, and (3rd) lack of qualified staff (see Appendix 14.3, question 46). In a subsequent survey of 93 HEIs that carry out routine pre-assessment screening for dyslexia, 73% of institutions reported that the number of students coming forward for dyslexia assessment was rising steadily (Singleton, Trotter and Smart, 1998).

The overall numbers of students entering higher education has also increased in recent years. From 1994 to 1996, the overall number of students entering HEIs in the UK increased from 271,000 to 296,000: a 9% increase. Over the corresponding period, the number of students declaring they have dyslexia on entry to higher education courses increased by 47%, and the incidence of such students increased from 0.74% of all students entering higher education in 1994 to 1.00% in 1996 (Dearing, 1997). Many students with dyslexia only obtain formal diagnosis after entry to higher education; if these students are also taken into account, the increase in recent years is more marked. One university (in Wales) was able to supply the Working Party with data for the period 1990–91 to 1996–97. These data showed that although overall student numbers had slightly less than doubled, there was a corresponding *seven-fold increase* in numbers of students identified as having dyslexia during the same period, representing a jump from 0.6% to 2.6% of the student population in that institution.

Another strand of evidence may be drawn from statistics regarding awards of DSA to students with dyslexia. The overall number of students in higher education who are in receipt of DSAs has been steadily increasing in recent years (DfEE, 1995) and the proportion of DSA awards to students with dyslexia is over 50% (Computer Centre for People with Disabilities, 1996).

What reasons may be brought forward to explain this increase in numbers of students with dyslexia in higher education? The general widening of access to higher education that has been seen in recent years is doubtless a major factor. There is increasing public awareness of 'dyslexia' and so students are probably more willing to acknowledge that they have dyslexia. Evidence from a national survey of HEIs carried out by the National Working Party suggests that these phenomena alone are unlikely to be able to account for the increase (see Section 3.2). Amongst alternative explanations the following appear most likely:

- *Earlier identification and provision for school children with dyslexia.* During the past twenty years or so, there has been a slow but steady increase in the availability of specialist teaching for pupils with dyslexia at primary and secondary school level. As a result, more students with dyslexia are likely to be able to master the literacy and learning skills that are necessary to achieve success in GCSE and 'A' level examinations. There is also increased availability of special provision for these pupils, such as additional time in exams. Consequently, more pupils with dyslexia are progressing to higher education.

- *Increased support for students with dyslexia within higher education.* In the past, students with dyslexia who were successful in gaining admission to higher education often would not have realised that they had dyslexia, and many will probably have failed or withdrawn because, without support, they were unable to manage. Now, with increased availability of various forms of support (including DSA) students with dyslexia are in a better position to cope with the demands of higher education.

- *Wider access for mature students.* In recent years there have been particularly improved opportunities for mature students wanting to enter higher education. Many of these students, although intellectually capable, left school without the formal qualifications required for application to higher education at the time. It often turns out that such students were not very successful at school because they had dyslexia but this was not appreciated then. By means of Access courses and other 'non-traditional' routes, these students can now accumulate the credits required to qualify for entry to higher education without necessarily having to demonstrate the traditional 'A' level competencies. Sometimes, mature students only come forward for dyslexia assessment after their school-aged children have been identified as having dyslexia.

1.1.3   The impact of the Disability Discrimination Act 1995

The *Disability Discrimination Act 1995* established, *inter alia*, a mechanism by which the Funding Councils for Higher Education have become the guardians of provision for disabled students in higher education. In order to ensure that a general improvement in disability provision does come about, the Act gives the Funding Councils power to impose conditions upon HEIs regarding provision for disabled students. In theory, therefore, the Funding Councils could impose financial penalties on institutions that do not make adequate provision for students with disabilities. This is unlikely in the short term, because the Funding Councils want to encourage HEIs to improve disability provision rather than to impose penalties.

A key feature of the Act is the requirement for all HEIs to publish *Disability Statements*, which must set out their policy and provision for all students with a disability. The purpose of these Disability Statements is twofold: (a) to provide information for disabled students regarding facilities, and (b) to keep the Funding Councils informed, since it is their job to ensure that institutions of higher education are doing their best to make appropriate provision. The expectation is that facilities for students with disabilities will steadily improve because institutions will be under greater scrutiny than before. Although the guidelines do not compel institutions to detail their provision for any given disability (such as dyslexia) it is already clear that those HEIs who have good disability provision are generally proud to proclaim that provision in their Disability Statements. In November 1998, HEFCE issued new guidelines on the content and style of Disability Statements (HEFCE, 1998), which are intended to make such Statements more informative and more accessible to prospective students with disabilities.

In 1996, the Higher Education Funding Council for England (HEFCE) instigated a three-year programme of special funding for disability projects in HEIs, which was the third of such initiatives (HEFCE, 1996b). The hope is that these projects will provide models of good practice on disability that other HEIs will be able to emulate. In the long term, however, establishments that fail to provide appropriately for students with disabilities (including dyslexia) could find that their negligence has unfortunate repercussions. Hence there is a further problem now confronting administrators in HEIs — what provision should they make for students with dyslexia and how should that provision be reflected in the institution's Disability Statement?

1.1.4   The recommendations of the Dearing Report 1997

The Report of the National Committee of Inquiry into Higher Education, *Higher Education in the Learning Society* (Dearing, 1997), embodies a number of recommendations relating to disability. The Report commented:

> *'Despite the welcome increase in overall participation, there remain groups in the population who are under-represented in higher education, notably those from socio-economic groups III to V, people with disabilities and specific ethnic minority groups. ... We believe that the best progress will be made if funding of expansion is targeted on institutions which can demonstrate a commitment to widening participation in the recent past, and have a robust strategy for doing so in the future.'* (Dearing, 1997, Executive Summary, Point 29; see also Recommendation 2).

If this recommendation is adopted by the Government, there should be a further stimulus for HEIs to improve provision for disabled students. More specifically, in order to promote widening access for students with disabilities, the Dearing Committee recommended that the funding bodies *'provide funding for institutions to provide learning support for students with disabilities'* and that the Government *'extends the scope of the Disabled Students Allowance so that it is available without a parental means test and to part-time students, postgraduate students and those who have become disabled who wish to obtain a second higher education qualification.'* (Dearing, 1997, Recommendation 6).

The Dearing Report also put forward proposals that all HEIs should develop programmes of training for higher education teachers (Recommendation 13) and that to this end there should be established a professional Institute for Learning and Teaching in Higher Education which would accredit such programmes (Recommendation 14). In Recommendation 6 it advocates that the learning needs of students with disabilities should be incorporated within the activities of such an Institute, including being a component of accredited teacher training courses in higher education. If accepted, these proposals would go a considerable way towards enhancing awareness of higher education teaching staff about disability and enabling them to make learning more accessible for students with disabilities.

In line with much current thinking, the Dearing Report advocates both *individual* provision (through the continuance and extension of the DSA) as well as *institutional* provision (in the form of learning support for students with disabilities). Yet one of the categories of the DSA (the Non-medical Helper's Allowance) *already covers* provision of learning support where that can be shown to be a special requirement of a student with a disability. If such support can be obtained through the mechanism of the DSA and the range of recipients of the DSA is extended as the Dearing Report suggests, why is it also necessary to recommend that HEIs provide such support? It may well be the case that in future the DSA will be extended in its *range* of recipients (e.g. to cover part-time and postgraduate students), but its *categories* of provision will be more restricted (e.g. to more severe types of individual disability). At the same time, provision of disability services that can be extended to a number of disabled students within an institution (e.g. study skills support for students with dyslexia) could become increasingly an institutional responsibility. The maximum amounts for various categories of allowance and/or types of disability could be restricted to a greater extent than at present. Indeed, there are indications in Chapter 7 of the Dearing Report that a sliding scale of allowances may have to be introduced because different disabilities have different resource implications.

There are already indications that developments are moving in this direction. In 1998, HEFCE commissioned an investigation of 'basal level' provision in HEIs – i.e. provision for disabled students that the institution might reasonably be expected to make from its own resources, independently of the DSA. The results of this investigation were expected as this report went to press.

How far the Government will ultimately go in adopting the recommendations of the Dearing Committee must remain a matter for speculation at the present time. However, the removal of means testing for DSAs will take effect from September 1998. The administration of the DSA will remain with LEAs at least until 1999, after which a unitary administrative body is expected to be established. This should resolve many of the concerns about inconsistencies between LEAs in the administration of the DSA, which have been expressed by many HEIs (see Sections 3.2.9 and 4.1.2.5).

Recommendation 5 of the Dearing Report also calls for a doubling of the amount of Access Funds that HEIs can use to provide for full-time students in need. Access funds are already being used by many HEIs to cover the costs of dyslexia assessments and provision of technology and other support for students with dyslexia who are not in receipt of a DSA. If Access Funds are increased and extended to apply to part-time students and postgraduate students, then this would help to provide for the needs of dyslexic students in these categories.

1.1.5 Current controversies

Although scientific understanding of dyslexia is growing steadily, it would be improper not to acknowledge that dyslexia has been, and to some extent can still be, the subject of legitimate scientific controversy. The principal issues and developments concerning these controversies have already been documented elsewhere (Pumfrey and Reason, 1991; Pumfrey, 1996). As far as higher education is concerned, the major controversy does not surround the issue of whether dyslexia (i.e. a type of specific learning difficulty of constitutional origin) *exists*, but rather the issues of:

- whether students with difficulties in literacy rightfully belong in higher education, and
- how students with dyslexia may be reliably and consistently identified and supported.

1.1.5.1   The concept of 'graduateness'

The first of these controversies identified above relates to the concept of 'graduateness'. In 1996 the Higher Education Quality Council (HEQC) produced a discussion paper entitled *What are graduates? Clarifying the attributes of 'graduateness'* (HEQC, 1996). This initiative formed part of the Graduate Standards Programme (GSP) instigated by the Committee of Vice-Chancellors and Principals (CVCP). The purpose was to explore what core attributes are denoted by the award of a first degree in the UK – i.e. the attributes of 'graduateness'. The paper refers to:

> '...ancillary qualities that would be expected of a graduate, but which had not previously been regarded as the responsibility of higher education to teach. These ancillary qualities would be likely to include such things as the ability to write in grammatically acceptable and correctly spelt English (or Welsh), a certain level of numeracy, a range of general knowledge, a basic familiarity with information technology, and so on.' (HEQC, 1996, Para. 14).

The paper concludes:

> 'There seem to be irresistible arguments that no-one should graduate who lacks such ancillary skills; but there is anecdotal evidence that this can occur. If this is so, it is to be condemned – and should be remedied – not least because the absence of such ancillary attributes must impede the exercise of those higher-level qualities that are regarded as central to degree study.' (HEQC, 1996, Para. 15).

If such a proposition were to be implemented, it would probably have the effect of banning most, or all, students with dyslexia from higher education. It is difficult to see how this can be compatible with the Dearing Committee's call for increased access for students with disabilities (including dyslexia) and for provision of learning support to such students to help them to become graduates. Only in medically-related courses and programmes of teacher training do we find some HEIs specifically denying access to students with dyslexia (see Sections 7.1.1 and 7.1.2). Nevertheless, it is apparent that in higher education in the UK today, a tension still exists between the concerns of quality and of access, and that this tension is heightened when it comes to participation of students who are likely to have poor literacy skills. The increasing 'league table' pressure on HEIs could also disadvantage students with dyslexia.

These concerns may be addressed by considering the quality of graduates with dyslexia. Statistics supplied to the Working Party by the Higher Education Statistics Agency (HESA) on the degree classes of students with dyslexia graduating from HEIs in the UK in 1996/97 (see Table 1) reveal that despite their difficulties in literacy and various aspects of studying, students with dyslexia attain standards that are not radically different from other graduates. A more detailed break-down of these data, including analysis by gender and length of course (3 year or 4 year) is provided in Section 14.2.

From Table 1 it can be seen that students with dyslexia achieve a somewhat lower proportion of first class and upper second class honours degrees, when compared with other groups, including 'Other disabilities' and 'No known disabilities'. This can be most easily summarised as follows. While the proportion of 'good' degrees (i.e. first class and upper second class honours) for students with no known disabilities is about 52%, and for students with other disabilities is only slightly lower (51%), in the dyslexia category this proportion is significantly lower, at about 41%. [3] This difference can be partly attributed to the significant gender imbalance within the dyslexia category. In the overall student population for this cohort, 53% were females and 47% males. In the 'Other disabilities' group there is a slightly higher proportion of females (56% as opposed to 44% males), whereas in the dyslexia group there is only 39% females and 61% males. This imbalance is unsurprising: the research literature on dyslexia is consistent in finding female : male ratios between 1:3 and 1:5 (see Section 2.1). The interesting feature of these data is that the ratio is only 1:1.6. This suggests that females with dyslexia stand a better chance of entering higher education than males with dyslexia, possibly because males tend to be more seriously affected and/or females are better able to compensate for the disabling effects of the condition.

---

[3] Dyslexia group compared with 'No known disabilities' group: $\chi^2 = 74.43$, df = 1, p < 0.001. Dyslexia group compared with 'Other disabilities' group: $\chi^2 = 45.43$, df = 1, p < 0.001.

Table 1. Students graduating from HEIs in the UK in 1997 by class of degree and disability status (source: HESA, 1998).

Disability category		First	Upper Second	Lower Second	Third / Pass	Unclass -ified	Total
				Degree class			
Dyslexia	Number	57	581	695	163	73	1,569
	Percent	3.63	37.03	44.30	10.39	4.65	**0.80**
Other disabilities	Number	367	2,494	2,164	440	199	5,664
	Percent	6.48	44.03	38.21	7.77	3.51	**2.90**
No known disabilities	Number	11,475	72,349	61,162	11,598	5,765	162,349
	Percent	7.07	44.56	37.67	7.14	3.55	**83.02**
Unknown	Number	2,139	11,806	8,707	2,235	1,089	25,976
	Percent	8.23	45.45	33.52	8.60	4.19	**13.28**
Total	Number	14,038	87,230	72,728	14,436	7,126	195,558
	Percent	7.18	44.61	37.19	7.38	3.64	100.00

Notes to Table 1:

1. 'Other disabilities' includes all HESA disability categories other than dyslexia, i.e. blind and partially sighted; deaf and hearing impaired; wheelchair user and mobility difficulties; personal care support; mental health difficulties; unseen disabilities (e.g. diabetes, epilepsy, asthma); multiple disabilities; and miscellaneous disabilities.

2. The category 'Unknown' refers to students for whom information on disability status is not available.

3. Figures include all students graduating from 3-year and 4-year first degree courses, whether on a full-time, part-time or sandwich basis. Data from students on postgraduate courses are not included.

4. 'Unclassified' refers to degrees that are not subject to a classification, e.g. medical and general degrees.

5. In HEIs where second class honours are undivided, these figures have been amalgamated with the lower second category.

6. In the percent rows under the 'degree class' columns, the figures are for each degree class as percentages of the *category total*; in the 'total' column, the figures are for each disability category as percentages of the *overall total* number of students graduating.

7. The category 'Dyslexia' does not include students with dyslexia whose condition has been diagnosed *after* entry to higher education (see Section 3.2.3).

In the student population overall, females tend to achieve a significantly higher proportion of 'good' degrees than males (in this cohort, 55% of the female group obtained 'good' degrees, compared with 48% of the male group). The gender imbalance in the dyslexia category, therefore, will be a factor in the differential proportion of 'good' degrees found in this group. This conclusion is supported by the fact that in the dyslexia category, the females achieved results that were rather better than the males: 45% obtained 'good' degrees, while only 38% of the males did so. However, the performance of the females in the dyslexia category still does not reach that of the females in other categories, so the gender factor *only partially* accounts for the finding that students with dyslexia are less likely to achieve 'good' degrees.

In Chapter 3 it will be seen that the quality of provision for students with dyslexia across the higher education sector is not uniform. Some universities provide much better support for such students, including – most notably – giving tuition in study strategies that can help to compensate for the adverse effects of dyslexia. In this report, we are concerned not simply with the extant performance of students with dyslexia in higher education, but also with the issue of how such students *could perform* given appropriate support. Unfortunately, not all HEIs maintain proper annual records on the degree classes of graduating disabled students, or, if this is done, they are difficult to obtain. (HESA calculates its statistics based on disability information given on the UCAS form.) However, the Working Party obtained degree class data for students with dyslexia graduating in 1997 from three well-established English universities, one in the North, one in the South, and one in the Midlands. One of these was a 'new' university – i.e. it attained university status since 1990. At each of these institutions there are established procedures for provision for students with dyslexia, including study skills support from a trained tutor. These data (which includes students who have been identified as having dyslexia after entry) are shown in Table 2.[4]

Table 2. Degree class result for students with dyslexia from three UK universities, 1997.

	First	Upper Second	Lower Second	Third / Pass	Unclass-ified	Total
Number	7	38	40	5	7	97
Percent	7.22	39.17	41.24	5.15	7.22	100

It can be seen that 46% of these students obtained 'good' degrees (i.e. first or upper second classifications). This suggests that where appropriate support provision is available for students with dyslexia, their degree class performance is nearer to that of the sector as a whole and by no means discredits the institution.

Perhaps the most important conclusion that can be drawn from these data is that dyslexia is not necessarily a barrier to success in higher education. For although the proportion of students obtaining 'good' degrees is somewhat lower in the dyslexia category, very substantial numbers of students with dyslexia *do* obtain 'good' degrees. Furthermore, the evidence suggests that this proportion is increased in institutions where appropriate provision is made for students with this disability. Further evidence that support this view is given in Section 2.5, where mention is made of the 'positive' features that students with dyslexia can bring to higher education. The fact that a considerable number of talented and highly successful persons with dyslexia can be found in many professions suggests that higher education has nothing to fear from opening its doors to able applicants with dyslexia.

1.1.5.2   Identifying students with dyslexia

The second controversy arises because of the lack of established criteria for the identification of dyslexia. Under these circumstances the concept of dyslexia can all too easily become diluted so that it encompasses *any* sort of difficulty with literacy or learning. The result is a diffuse category frequently referred to as 'learning disabilities', especially in the United States (McGuire et al, 1996). It is often a small step from there to the assumption that *all* difficulties with literacy or studying are essentially of neurological origin, with the result that possible environmental, cultural and educational causes of learning problems may be neglected.

A similar predicament concerning the identification of dyslexia can currently be found in higher education. In a recent national conference on dyslexia in adults, the principal concern was not with whether dyslexia existed but rather with *how* dyslexia can be identified amongst the higher education population, given that such individuals are most 'literate' in the accepted sense of the word (Beaton, McDougall and Singleton, 1997a). Many students experience problems with studying at some time, and not all of them have dyslexia. Many may never have had the opportunity to acquire the skills that are necessary for learning at higher education level – in other words, their difficulties may have environmental, cultural or educational causes rather than neurological ones. If there are perceived 'benefits' of being categorised as having dyslexia, then there is a danger that the system for disability support may be abused. Hence there is uncertainty concerning how we should distinguish those

---

[4] To make the data in Table 2 comparable with those produced by HESA and shown in Table 1, those dyslexic students in the three universities categorised as 'Fail, Withdrew or Deferred' had to be omitted. They were N = 15/112, approximately 13%, which is believed to be not dissimilar to the rate found for other first degree students.

students with dyslexia from those with other learning problems. This also raises a further dilemma: if any student is found to be experiencing a problem in studying that is not attributable to dyslexia, should the institution necessarily take some of the responsibility for addressing that problem?

McGuire et al (1996) reported similar concerns about identification of dyslexia or learning disabilities in university students in the US. Specifically, they allege that '...serious problems exist in the type and quality of evaluation reports' and refer to '...flaws in the comprehensiveness of the assessments, and the use of questionable instruments for this population' (p. 297). There is a striking similarity between these concerns and those expressed by Singleton in the UK in 1994 (Singleton, 1995) and the rationale for establishing the Working Party in the first place (see Section 1.2.1). Hence on both sides of the Atlantic there has been a growing awareness of the need to establish guidelines for acceptable documentation of dyslexia amongst university students, especially when this is being used to obtain special examination arrangements or financial or other support. Issues connected with identification of dyslexia are considered in some detail in Chapter 8 of this report.

In principle, the system of identifying and alleviating dyslexia (and other special educational needs) in compulsory education could be extended to both further and higher education, providing a consistent policy throughout. The *Code of Practice* (DfE, 1994) gives a staged model of intervention, specifying the various responsibilities for identification and support through the school system. It recognises that special educational needs vary in severity and that some may be able to be addressed at a basic level (i.e. within the classroom) whereas more severe difficulties may require intervention of a more specialist kind from elsewhere within or outwith the school. Teachers at all levels have their parts to play in this process. A similar approach is worthy of consideration in further and higher education, where the individual lecturer or tutor would represent the first line of support and not all needs would necessarily require specialist intervention from elsewhere in the institution. Such a system presupposes a substantial training input for academic staff concerning the support needs of students with disabilities, but some HEIs are already implementing schemes that embody these principles. These ideas are developed elsewhere in this report (see Section 13.2.2).

1.2   Aims and activities of the National Working Party

1.2.1   *The creation of the National Working Party*

The *National Working Party on Dyslexia in Higher Education* was established because of serious concerns about the lack of national standards on the identification, assessment and support for students with dyslexia at the level of higher education. There are increasing numbers of students with dyslexia being admitted to higher education, but there are widespread and highly unsatisfactory variations between establishments on how students with this disability are supported. Pressure upon the Disabled Students' Allowances (DSA) has been increasing steadily. There are current concerns about how students with dyslexia should be properly identified and how the DSA should be applied in cases of such students.

The Working Party originated at a conference on *Dyslexia and Higher Education* organised by the University of Plymouth, and held at Dartington Hall, Devon, in November 1994. At that conference, which was funded by the Higher Education Funding Council for England (HEFCE), important issues relating to the assessment of, and support for, dyslexics in Higher Education were discussed. Although it was acknowledged that there have been a number of HEFCE funded projects which involved dyslexia-related issues, these are individual solutions, and the need for a co-ordinated overall approach to the problem was stressed. It became clear that many HEIs are currently seeking guidance on this matter and the following issues were highlighted:

1. The wide variation across HEIs in *identification* arrangements for dyslexics. These range from those HEIs that make arrangements (and sometimes pay) for students to be assessed by psychologists, through HEIs that use their own staff for this purpose, to HEIs that leave students to make their own private arrangements outside the institution.

2. The wide variation across HEIs in the *content of dyslexia assessments*. In particular, issues of (i) how dyslexia should be assessed in adults, (ii) distinguishing the dyslexic from other students with

literacy problems, and (iii) the varying severity of the condition in relation to the student's academic and learning needs in the context of a given course of study.

3. The grave concerns of *LEA Awards Officers* regarding the provision of satisfactory information in psychological assessment reports, on the basis of which decisions are made regarding the award of the DSA.

4. The *consequences of identification of dyslexia*. In particular, issues of (i) appropriate technological support of students with dyslexia (including the increasing number of applications for the DSA by students with dyslexia), (ii) appropriate learning support within the institution, and (iii) appropriate examination provision for students with dyslexia.

A number of interested persons who attended the Dartington Conference, all of whom had considerable experience in this area, formed the nucleus of the Working Party, and resolved to address the above issues, with the intention of creating guidelines to assist HEIs in making provision for students with dyslexia. A planning meeting of this group was held at the University of Westminster, London, in February 1995, at which Dr. Chris Singleton of the Department of Psychology, University of Hull, was asked to act as Chairperson of the group. An application for funds to carry out the tasks of the Working Party was subsequently made by Dr. Singleton on behalf of the group to the bodies responsible for funding higher education in England, Scotland, and Wales, as well as to the Department for Education and Employment (DfEE). In August 1995, the Working Party received funding for its activities from HEFCE and from the Scottish Higher Education Funding Council (SHEFC). The Welsh Higher Education Funding Council and the DfEE wrote to the Working Party giving moral support but declined to provide funding. The main thrust of the Working Party's activities therefore began in September 1995.

1.2.2   The objectives of the Working Party

The principal objectives of the Working Party were as follows.

1. To survey existing provision for identification and support of students with dyslexia in higher education.

2. To evaluate different methods of identification and varied approaches to support.

3. To consult as widely as possible with HEIs.

4. To investigate the operation of the DSA in cases of dyslexia.

5. To formulate recommendations in a published report which can serve to establish national guidelines for HEIs on identification and support of students with dyslexia.

In order to achieve those objectives, the Working Party undertook the following activities.

a) Carrying out a survey of existing provision for identification and support of students with dyslexia, and compiling a report, with appropriate statistical analysis.

b) Consulting with HEIs across the country, and with other bodies and appropriate individuals with expertise or concerns in this matter.

c) Reviewing existing practices for the identification of dyslexia and pointing out where there are gaps, ambiguities and anomalies.

d) Addressing issues of relative degrees of severity of dyslexia in relation to academic needs of the student.

e) Considering issues relating to the up-to-date evaluation of the learning needs of students who enter higher education after already having been identified as having dyslexia.

f) Considering and formulating recommendations on a variety of models of, and factors involved in, an institutional approach to dyslexia, including admissions policy and procedures; assessment; individual student support needs; modular course approaches; counselling and technological needs; examination and assessment policy and provision.

g) Considering issues concerning identification of dyslexia, including the credentials of assessors; the nature and components of screening and diagnostic assessments; the stages of assessment;

the criteria for identification of dyslexia; the various types of recommendation required from an assessor; payment for assessments; recommendations made by psychologists and others for examination provision.

h) Considering the operation and effectiveness of the DSA system from the point of view of the student, the LEA, and the institution and, where appropriate, proposing amendments to the DSA system.

i) Formulating a range of recommendations and publishing its findings as a final report to the Higher Education Funding Councils, the DfEE, all HEIs and all LEAs.

1.2.3   *Composition of the Working Party*

In the interests of efficiency and cost of meetings, the membership of the Working Party has been kept reasonably small. All members were invited because their experience and expertise in this area is nationally recognised. The total membership of the group is 14, comprising representation from all parts of the country (including Scotland and Wales), and includes some members who are dyslexic. The final composition of the Working Party consists of:

- Four psychologists who all have professional experience of the identification of dyslexia in adults (one from outside higher education and three from within, one of the latter being the director of a nationally-recognised specialist training course for teachers of people with dyslexia, provided within an HEI).

- Seven professionals who are (or recently have been) actively involved in providing learning support and/or counselling to students with dyslexia in HEIs.

- The chairperson of the National Federation of Access Centres, who has been professionally involved in the assessment of disability, including assessment of technology needs, for many years and who works within an HEI.

- One representative (the Education Director) of the British Dyslexia Association (BDA).

- One representative of the Adult Dyslexia Organisation (ADO), who is also a dyslexia support tutor in an HEI.

Dr. Chris Singleton was formally confirmed as Chairperson of the group. Further details of the membership are given in the Section on *Membership of the Working Party* which can be found at the beginning of the report, immediately after the Executive Summary.

1.2.4   *The activities of the Working Party*

During the period October 1995 to March 1996 the Working Party conducted a survey of current policy and provision with regard to students with dyslexia in all HEIs in the UK. Joanna Horne, a psychologist, was appointed as Research Assistant in order to assist Dr. Singleton and to carry out this work. The response to this was extremely encouraging, and detailed information was obtained from 83% of HEIs (see Chapter 3).

During the spring of 1996 five regional consultative meetings were held, to which representatives of all HEIs were invited. These were held in London, Birmingham, Manchester, Bristol, and Edinburgh. These meetings were attended by representatives from approximately 120 HEIs and by a selection of members of the Working Party, who chaired discussion groups. Issues connected with diagnosis, assessment, support and institutional policy and planning were all considered. These meetings were widely regarded as being extremely rewarding, both from the point of view of the members of the Working Party, and also of the representatives from the HEIs (4.1.2).

In May 1996 a further consultative meeting was held in London, to which LEA Awards Officers were invited to discuss their concerns regarding the DSA for students with dyslexia. This meeting was attended by officers representing 22 different LEAs, as well as by several members of the Working Party. The discussion was extremely helpful (see Section 4.1.3).

In addition, seven full meetings and several subsidiary meetings of the Working Party were held during the period November 1995 to August 1997, including one residential meeting over two days.

As well as these full meetings, the Working Party sub-divided itself into three groups dealing with (i) identification, (ii) evaluation of needs, and (iii) support and institutional policy. These sub-groups have met on various occasions and produced working documents within their remit. These documents were considered at the full meetings of the Working Party, where the points raised in the consultative meetings and the results of the National Survey were also under consideration.

The findings of the Working Party have been progressively distilled and consolidated to create this report, produced during the period August 1997 to November 1998. All members of the Working Party contributed to the contents of the report, which has been edited through several drafts by Dr Singleton. At each stage of the process, drafts have been circulated and comments and amendments by the members incorporated. The final version and its recommendations has been approved by all 14 members of the Working Party.

1.3   The structure of this report

Having first discussed the background to the establishment of the Working Party and outlined the nature and extent of the Working Party's remit (Chapter 1), this report turns its attention to the question: *What is dyslexia?* and, in particular, the ways in which dyslexia can affect students in higher education (Chapter 2).

The report then considers the evidence that has been available to the Working Party about current policy and provision for students with dyslexia in higher education. This evidence derives from the findings of the national survey carried out on behalf of the Working Party (Chapter 3) and also from others sources, including the various consultative processes in which the Working Party has been engaged (Chapter 4).

The report goes on to consider the issues in greater depth and to put forward the recommendations of the Working Party. To present these as clearly as possible, they are sub-divided into the following eight key areas of higher education activity:

- Institutional and national policy (Chapter 5)

- Staff development and institutional awareness (Chapter 6)

- Admission to higher education (Chapter 7)

- Identification of students with dyslexia (Chapter 8)

- Evaluation of needs and provision of support (Chapter 9)

- Counselling of students with dyslexia (Chapter 10)

- Examinations and assessment (Chapter 11)

- Careers advice for students with dyslexia (Chapter 12)

Within each of these areas, we have first outlined the issues, problems and challenges that must be confronted. Then we have offered proposals on good practice that the Working Party believes can help to address the issues, resolve the problems and meet the various challenges. Finally, the Working Party's recommendations are listed for that area.

In the final chapter, we draw our conclusions regarding dyslexia in higher education, together with our suggestions for further research and development that we believe is still required (Chapter 13). The appendices contain various supporting materials.

2   What is dyslexia?

2.1   The syndrome of dyslexia

The popular image of dyslexia is that it is a difficulty with reading – something to do with the misperception of printed words. This image may to some extent have been perpetuated by the continuing fondness of the media for the use of the antiquated and misleading term 'word blindness', which in the early part of this century was often used synonymously with 'dyslexia'. In fact, although people with dyslexia typically do have some problems with reading, the condition is much broader than this, and for students with dyslexia, reading may be the least of their troubles. Some individuals with dyslexia may have problems of visual perception, but their difficulties are more likely to be due to limitations in memory and anomalies in processing certain types of language-related information (Frith, 1997).

There are actually two forms of dyslexia – *developmental* dyslexia and *acquired* dyslexia. Developmental dyslexia is properly recognised as a form of *specific learning difficulty* – that is, a problem with particular aspects of learning despite adequate intelligence and general learning skills. Current evidence suggests that developmental dyslexia is neurologically based and in many cases is inherited – although the precise genetic mechanisms have yet to be identified (DeFries, Alarcón and Olson, 1997). In some instances it may be due to pre-natal or peri-natal difficulties (Fleming and Singleton, 1997). In many cases the term 'specific learning difficulty' has often been used synonymously with (or in preference to) 'developmental dyslexia' but, since there are other types of specific learning difficulty[5], this practice is not strictly correct. Acquired dyslexia is a condition characterised by significant loss of literacy skills (wholly or partially) as a result of some neurological trauma (such as stroke or head injury) illness or brain disease. It is most commonly seen in older people and although there may be some students with acquired dyslexia in higher education, the vast majority of students with dyslexia are clearly in the developmental category. In this Report we shall be referring mainly to developmental dyslexia and therefore will omit the adjective 'developmental' unless it is necessary to make a distinction with the acquired form of the disorder.

Dyslexia is properly described as a *syndrome*: a collection of associated characteristics that vary in degree and from person to person. These characteristics encompass not only distinctive clusters of *problems* but sometimes also distinctive *talents*. Miles (1993) comments that dyslexia is typically characterised by "an unusual balance of skills". The syndrome of dyslexia is now widely recognised as being a specific learning disability of neurological origin that does not imply low intelligence or poor educational potential, and which is independent of race and social background (Pumfrey and Reason, 1991).

Although dyslexia seems to be more prevalent amongst males than females, the exact ratio is unknown: the most commonly quoted figures are between 3:1 and 5:1. The evidence suggests that in at least two-thirds of cases, dyslexia has a genetic cause, but in some cases birth difficulties may play an aetiological role. Dyslexia may overlap with related conditions such as dyspraxia, attention deficit disorder (with or without hyperactivity) and dysphasia. In childhood, its effects can be mis-attributed to emotional or behavioural disorder. By adulthood, many dyslexics will have developed sophisticated compensating strategies that may mask their difficulties. The majority of experts and professional bodies in the field concur that about 4% of the population are affected to a significant extent (American Psychiatric Association, 1994; Thomson, 1993). This figure is based on the incidence of pupils who have received normal schooling and who do not have significant emotional, social or medical aetiology, but whose literacy development by the end of the primary school is more than 2 years behind levels which would be expected on the basis of chronological age and intelligence.

---

[5] Such as dyspraxia, developmental coordination disorder or specific language disorder.

The question 'What is dyslexia?' may be more fully addressed from a number of different perspectives, including (but not exclusively) the following:

- the neurological bases of dyslexia

- the cognitive characteristics of dyslexia

- the educational and behavioural outcomes for the person with dyslexia

- the positive aspects of dyslexia.

2.2   The neurological bases of dyslexia

The neurological bases of dyslexia are now well established and reflected in current definitions of the condition. For example, in 1994 the International Dyslexia Association[6] published the following definition of dyslexia:

> *"Dyslexia is a neurologically-based, often familial disorder which interferes with the acquisition of language. Varying the degrees of severity, it is manifested by difficulties in receptive and expressive language, including phonological processing, in reading, writing, spelling, handwriting and sometimes arithmetic. Dyslexia is not the result of lack of motivation, sensory impairment, inadequate instructional or environmental opportunities, but may occur together with these conditions. Although dyslexia is life-long, individuals with dyslexia frequently respond successfully to timely and appropriate intervention"* (ODS, 1994).

The Research Committee of the International Dyslexia Association also produced the following definition of dyslexia, couched in more scientific terminology:

> *"Dyslexia is one of several distinct learning disabilities. It is a specific language-based disorder of constitutional origin characterised by difficulties in single-word decoding, usually reflecting insufficient phonological processing abilities. These difficulties in single word decoding are often unexpected in relation to age and other cognitive and academic abilities: they are not the result of generalised developmental disability or sensory impairment. Dyslexia is manifest by variable difficulty with different forms of language, often including, in addition to problems of reading, a conspicuous problem with acquiring proficiency in writing and spelling."* (ODS, 1994)

The British Dyslexia Association has also published a definition of dyslexia that reflects the neurological bases of the condition:

> *"Dyslexia is a complex neurological condition which is constitutional in origin. The symptoms may affect many areas of learning and function, and may be described as a specific difficulty in reading, spelling and written language."* (British Dyslexia Association, 1995).

The biology of dyslexia has been investigated in a range of studies that have confirmed a difference in brain anatomy, organisation and functioning. Research has also shown that the effects of dyslexia are due – at least, in part – to heritable influences (DeFries and Alarcón, 1996; DeFries, Alarcón and Olson, 1997). The latest brain imaging techniques, as well as encephalographic recording of the electrical activity of the brain, and even post-mortem examination, all reveal a range of functional and structural cerebral anomalies of persons with dyslexia (Frith and Frith, 1996; Galaburda, 1993; Hynd and Heimenz, 1997). On the other hand, we should beware the temptation to 'pathologise' normality – in other words, to assume that individuals whose skills in certain domains are at the lower end of the ability spectrum necessarily reflect clinical abnormality rather than normal variation in abilities.

Despite the neurological dimension, medical terms such as 'diagnosis' and 'symptom' are regarded by many as inappropriate to discuss the specific ways in which dyslexia affects people. Although it is a disability, dyslexia is not a 'disease' nor can it be 'cured'. Indeed, the neurological differences found in dyslexia may confer advantages for some individuals (e.g. in visual or perceptual skills), which may to some extent explain the apparent paradox that some individuals who have

---

[6] Formerly the Orton Dyslexia Society.

problems with elementary skills such as reading and writing can nevertheless be highly gifted in other areas.

The *deficit model of dyslexia* is now steadily giving way to one in which dyslexia is increasingly recognised as a *difference in cognition and learning*. In this report we will therefore generally refer to *identification* (rather than 'diagnosis') and concentrate on exploring *the pattern of strengths and weaknesses* manifested by students with dyslexia (rather than dwelling on their 'deficits').

2.3   The cognitive characteristics of dyslexia

Dyslexia is a variable condition and not all people with dyslexia will display the same range of difficulties or characteristics. Nevertheless, the following characteristics have been widely noted in connection with dyslexia.

- A marked inefficiency in the *working or short-term memory system,* which is regarded by many experts in the field as the fundamental underlying difficulty experienced by people with dyslexia (e.g. Beech, 1997; McLoughlin, Fitzgibbon and Young 1993; Rack, 1997). Memory difficulties may result in problems of retaining the meaning of text (especially when reading at speed), failure to marshall learned facts effectively in examinations, disjointed written work or in omission of words and phrases in written examinations, because students have lost track of what they are trying to express.

- Inadequate *phonological processing abilities*, which affects the acquisition of phonic skills in reading and spelling so that unfamiliar words are frequently misread, which may in turn affect comprehension. Not only has it been clearly established that phonological processing difficulties are seen in the majority of children with dyslexia (e.g. Snowling, 1995), but recent research has also indicated that this occurs in many adults with dyslexia (see Beaton, McDougall and Singleton, 1997a).

- *Difficulties with motor skills or coordination.* Nicolson and Fawcett (1990, 1994) have noted that people with dyslexia can show a particular difficulty in *automatising skills*. Examples of failure to automatise skills in the student situation might be the inability to listen with understanding while taking adequate notes, or the inability to concentrate on both the spelling and the content of written work. *Dyspraxia* is the generic term used to cover a heterogeneous range of disorders affecting the initiation, organisation and performance of action (Ayres, 1985; Fisher et al, 1991; Ripley et al, 1997). In childhood it is sometimes referred to as developmental coordination disorder. Students with dyspraxic difficulties are likely to have problems with handwriting, especially for lengthy periods or under conditions of time pressure. It should be noted that by no means all students with dyslexia will necessarily have dyspraxic difficulties.

- A range of problems connected with *visual processing,* which can affect reading generally, but especially when dealing with large amounts of text (Lovegrove, 1994; Willows et al, 1993). Such problems can include *binocular instability* (Cornelissen et al, 1991, 1992, 1993, 1994; Evans, 1997; Stein, 1991) and susceptibility to *visual discomfort* (see Evans, 1997; Evans, Drasdo and Richards, 1996; Wilkins, 1995). *Visual discomfort* is a generic term for the effects of hypersensitivity to the irritating effect of strong visual contrast or rapid flicker (e.g. where parallel lines of text create the appearance of a black-and-white grating or consciously or subconsciously perceived flicker of fluorescent lighting or some computer monitors). Movement and colour illusions can be perceived, or the text may appear unstable or obscured. Reading for any length of time may cause headaches and eyestrain, and so can be done only in short bursts, which can disrupt the comprehension process. In some medical conditions (e.g. epilepsy and migraine) susceptibility to visual discomfort is generally more extreme than is usually seen in cases of dyslexia (Wilkins, 1995). It should be noted, however, that although there appears to be a statistical association between dyslexia and visual discomfort, *not all* persons with dyslexia are highly susceptible to visual discomfort and *not all* persons who suffer from visual discomfort will necessarily exhibit the typical characteristics of dyslexia outlined above. There evidence that use of coloured overlays or filters (e.g. by use of acetate sheets or tinted lenses) can be beneficial in alleviating the symptoms of visual discomfort in a fair proportion of cases (Irlen, 1991; Wilkins et al, 1994).

2.4   Educational and behavioural outcomes for the person with dyslexia

Although significant discrepancies between obvious ability and unexpectedly poor academic performance should alert teachers to the presence of dyslexia at an early age, the problem may go unnoticed for several years. Under-achievement in literacy despite normal schooling and satisfactory oral and intellectual skills may persist through childhood. Because of the development of compensatory strategies, by adulthood, literacy skills of many dyslexics can appear superficially adequate. A closer investigation, however, will often reveal underlying difficulties that can seriously affect learning at the higher education level (see Riddick, Farmer and Sterling, 1997).

2.4.1   Reading and perceptual difficulties

These can include:

- difficulty in extracting the sense from written material without substantial re-reading
- slow reading speed
- inaccurate reading, omission of words
- frequent loss of the place when reading
- an inability to skim through or scan over reading matter
- a high degree of distractibility when reading
- perceived distortion of text (words may seem to float off the page or run together)
- a visually irritating glare from white paper or white-boards.

2.4.2   Writing problems

These can include:

- an intractable spelling problem, often concealed by the use of an automatic spell-checker
- confusion of small words such as which/with
- omission of words, especially when the writer is under pressure
- awkward handwriting and/or slow writing speed
- an unexpected difference between oral and written expression, with oral contributions being typically of a much higher quality than written accounts of the same subject matter in terms of structure, self expression and correct use of words.

2.4.3   Other difficulties

Reliance on the surface manifestations (derived from the 'literacy framework') to describe dyslexia, has had two serious repercussions. First, it has caused a relative neglect of other issues that are fundamental to educational success (e.g. ability to memorise). Second, it has often resulted in misguided rejection of dyslexia as the underlying cause of difficulty in those students whose problems are no longer primarily with reading, writing or spelling (e.g. in the case of the 'compensated' dyslexic who has developed successful coping strategies for reading and writing, but who may still experience major difficulties with examinations).

Further factors in dyslexia which merit consideration include the following.

- *Numeracy.* In many cases, dyslexia affects numeracy skills. This can take the form of unexpected inaccuracy in calculation or a failure to grasp mathematical or computational course components, such as statistics in the social sciences. Gifted dyslexic mathematicians and scientists are sometimes found to have unusually weak computational skills despite the originality and validity of their theories (Miles and Miles, 1992).

- *Oral skills.* Although many dyslexic people are highly articulate, others demonstrate a lack of logical structure in oral presentations as well as in writing. Oral skills can be further compromised by difficulties in word retrieval or by mispronunciation and spoonerisms (Miles, 1993). A delay in producing a response may actually be due to a slight lapse between hearing what is said and understanding it – an inefficiency in aural processing possibly connected with the working memory system (Beech, 1997).

- *Attention span, distractibility and energy levels.* A range of characteristics, under the general heading of attentional dysfunction or attention deficit disorder, can have a significant overlap with dyslexia. A short attention span and/or a high level of distractibility can undermine the whole educational process. Associated characteristics are an inability to get started when faced with certain mental activities and also trouble switching from one type of activity to another (Stacey, 1997, 1998).

- *Social and emotional factors.* High levels of anxiety and stress have been identified as the most indicative behavioural correlates of dyslexia; these are bound to affect performance (Miles and Varma, 1995). A debilitating panic reaction is experienced by some dyslexic people when placed in academic situations where they cannot cope (McLoughlin, Fitzgibbon and Young 1993). The cumulative effect of tiredness, necessitated by additional effort at every level, should not be underestimated: *"The organisational differences in handling information apply to everything in life and the fatigue arising from it therefore also happens all the time. This aspect of dyslexia is not obvious but it is important"* (Hales, 1994). The secondary effects of dyslexia undoubtedly include loss of confidence, low self-esteem and frustration (Edwards, 1994). Mature students in particular find that years of humiliation in the classroom and constant fear of being 'shown up' take their toll (Gilroy and Miles, 1996).

- *Organisation.* Disorganisation, a poor sense of clock time and a poor awareness of space (again, associated with underlying memory problems) tend to make effective time management very difficult for many people with dyslexia (Stacey, 1997, 1998). An individual whose chaotic behaviour is not only damaging to himself, but causes inconvenience to others, can forfeit the goodwill of peers and staff (Gilroy and Miles, 1996).

2.4.4 *Compensating strategies*

By the time they reach adulthood, most individuals with dyslexia have acquired some awareness of their strengths and limitations, and have developed an array of compensatory strategies to enable them to manage their lives (McLoughlin, Fitzgibbon and Young, 1993). In times of stress and anxiety, however, they can still be vulnerable. Coping strategies that are particularly valuable in the higher education environment include:

- special technical skills

- detailed personal reminder systems

- colour coding and other methods of organisation

- visualisation as an aid to storing and recalling information

- carefully evolved back-up systems

- the use of information technology.

Typically, when compared with non-dyslexic students in higher education, the student with dyslexia has to invest much more time and effort in order to cover the course material and demonstrate the appropriate levels of academic competence. For students with dyslexia, academic success demands a very high level of persistence.

2.5   Positive aspects of dyslexia

What conspicuously sets dyslexia apart from most other disabilities in the higher education sector is the associated range of talents which dyslexic students often display, although not *all* students with dyslexia will necessarily show exceptional talents. There are numerous prominent and highly successful persons with dyslexia working in many different professions (Aaron, Phillips and Larsen, 1988). In professions such as art and graphic design, architecture, engineering and computer design –

in which visual thinking and creative skills are especially important – it has been suggested that dyslexia may offer career advantages (West, 1997).

The following list comprises those characteristics which are most often mentioned in connection with the positive aspects of dyslexia (West, 1997).

- Good powers of visualisation, including three-dimensional realisation, now increasingly important in computer graphics.

- Creative thinking skills, including lateral reasoning and intuition. Students with dyslexia may well demonstrate their intelligence by creating 'new knowledge' rather than by retaining 'old knowledge'.

- A range of artistic talents, especially those requiring visuospatial skills.

- A holistic rather than analytical approach, resulting in an aptitude for making unexpected links, associations and applications. In many cases, these students demonstrate their understanding as a refreshing overview rather than the culmination of a carefully structured, logical argument.

- Good, practical and problem-solving skills, including a strong understanding of the operation of mechanical systems.

These talents are difficult to evaluate using conventional examination or assessment procedures. It should also be noted that the same characteristic may be perceived as a strength in one situation but a weakness in another, for example an appreciation of a valid but unexpected cross-curricular link could be dismissed as a failure to keep to the point! Students with dyslexia need to recognise, value and develop their particular learning style in order fully to utilise their strengths and circumvent their weaknesses. Sometimes a personal involvement or link with a topic is needed for the student to become constructively engaged. Appropriate tuition by support tutors should be targeted at the point where the demands of the course impinge on areas of weakness and should point to solutions that take the student's learning style into account.

2.6   The experiences of students with dyslexia in higher education

2.6.1   Six vignettes

There are many difficulties encountered in higher education by students with dyslexia, but simply to list them fails to give any insight into the whole experience of any individual. Therefore, six vignettes are presented in this report to give glimpses into quite different experiences. Similar vignettes can be found in a recent anthology by Riddick, Farmer and Sterling (1997) and in Gilroy and Miles (1997).

The students that were chosen have been drawn from the population of students with dyslexia. These five students have very different stories, so the vignettes do not follow a definite pattern. The names are fictional, but the other biographical details are accurate. The picture of each student was based on an interview that covered the following:

- information about the students' experiences of education before university

- facts about their courses

- their attitudes to dyslexia at the time of the interview and in the past

- what they felt about any diagnostic or screening assessments which they had received

- how dyslexia has been personally experienced at university, including the responses of tutors, fellow students and other people

- how the students view the future.

The material included was chosen to be as representative as possible of each individual as well as of this population of students as a whole. Early experiences of the students have been included because they strongly influence the reactions of the students while at university. The terminology and description employed is largely the students' own. The vignettes are fairly detailed in order to illustrate the diversity of experience of students with dyslexia as well as common features. For those readers who do not wish to consider these vignettes in detail, summaries are given in Section 2.6.2.

2.6.1.1   Tanya

When interviewed, Tanya was 22 and in her final year at university, reading music and science. She had been identified as having dyslexia at the age of nine. Before that she had remedial lessons for two years because she wrote in mirror writing. The same lessons continued afterwards. Some teachers were more supportive; some no longer embarrassed her over her mistakes, but she did not receive any help specifically for her dyslexia at school. Tanya emotionally felt better as a result of the identification, there was an explanation for her lack of achievement. She learnt some coping strategies through many activities out of school. Tanya does not easily accept her dyslexia. Too many people have patronised her. 'Don't worry dear, you're dyslexic and it's too hard for you' sums up an attitude that she has met too often. Her response is that people did not understand that tasks were usually hard because they had not been explained adequately.

Tanya came to university having known for ten years that she has dyslexia and still wanting to deny it. Tanya indicated on her UCAS form that she has dyslexia. She went to a workshop about dyslexia in the induction week and half way through the first term she registered officially as a student with dyslexia. The university has some individual support available, but most of the support is given through group sessions. Tanya did not go to the first sessions of the term because she couldn't cope with anything extra. Having missed the first ones, she was too shy to come to later ones. If she could have found someone to go with, she would have felt comfortable about going to sessions and she could then have avoided later problems. Tanya used her own computer, which she obtained during her second term through the DSA. She does not use any other equipment, such as a tape recorder for lectures, because they are all too obvious and she would find them embarrassing.

Tanya was allowed extra time for exams, but she did not always use it. The fact that it was available meant she did not panic. Exam papers induced panic in her because she can misread the questions and the instructions, and answer the wrong question. On one occasion, her exam arrangements went wrong; there was no exam paper for her. She had to sit for some considerable time in the exam room doing nothing. The invigilators were well meaning and concerned, but their lack of understanding made the situation worse for her. She struggled even more with exams after that experience.

Tanya needed constructive feedback in order to make progress with her studies. The tutors in the music department, a small department, had time and interest to give her the necessary help. Tutors in the larger science department gave Tanya the feeling that helping dyslexic students was yet another burden. In her final year Tanya was a 'buddy' (a popular term for a mentor) to a fresher who had dyslexia. She said it was beneficial for her to be able to help someone else through the early stages of being at university.

Tanya did have some serious problems as a result of her dyslexia; specialist knowledge from the support tutor was necessary to resolve them. Tanya has noticed a change in attitude in the university as more students with dyslexia are willing to acknowledge their dyslexia. Tanya now recognises dyslexia as something you have to live with, but she is still careful about being open about it.

2.6.1.2   Keith

Keith was 57 when interviewed and in his final year reading a humanities subject. At school, numeracy and literacy were closed books and he was in the bottom class for everything. Being in the bottom class conveyed to him the message that he was of low intelligence. He chose jobs on the basis of this poor self-image. He has had three different jobs each lasting ten years and he left the first two because of boredom. Being 'illiterate' affected Keith's social life too because he couldn't keep up normal social contact through letters or Christmas cards. When Keith was made redundant and because he felt under utilised, he decided to do a two-year college course. During the course, a tutor suggested he might have dyslexia.

During his first term at university, Keith was identified as having dyslexia. He was delighted with this identification; it accounted for so much in his past life. He is now quite open about dyslexia and has taken on several roles that he previously would not have considered. However, he is irritated that the identification of dyslexia is so late. He is bitterly angry that the system rejected him as a boy.

He takes care with his writing in official letters but his memos have a disclaimer that 'the author is dyslexic and eccentricities in spelling should be enjoyed for their own sake'.

Keith is immensely interested in his subject. For him, it deals with issues in a way that no other discipline does. He feels that there is a beauty in the literature of his field and that students with dyslexia should not be barred from it. He finds a computer invaluable. He uses the thesaurus by using a synonym he can spell to find the word that he wants. He had problems in the library when the search program had no spell checker. Libraries are difficult for him because guidance information isn't presented in visual ways. Keith's university department was initially against having any student with dyslexia. Keith was only accepted because he was transferring from another field within the university. The quality of Keith's work has persuaded his tutors that it is possible for a dyslexic person to be a good student of humanities. The contrast between his course work and his exam performance has been another piece of evidence that helps tutors take dyslexia seriously. Keith seems to have been one of those students who was responsible for the change in attitudes of staff which Tanya noticed. After six years in higher education, he plans to take a year off to do photography and ceramics, and after that he has been invited back to do an M.A.

2.6.1.3   *Laura*

Laura was 33 when interviewed. She was at the end of her first year reading two humanities subjects. At school she was in the bottom class and was often told she was stupid because she was unable to learn languages or maths. Even at the age of 16, she was told she was an 'imbecile' because she couldn't do French dictation. Several times she was made to stand on a desk in front of the whole class because of her failures. She felt there was some extra reason why she could not succeed, as if the rest of the class 'had something' which she did not. She has to find strategies to deal with tasks she finds particularly difficult, such as multiplication tables.

Laura's friends went to university from school; it added to her humiliation that she was unable to do this and instead attempted a secretarial course. She found employment with friends and used her skills with people to good effect, but her humiliation was increased when she was sent on a refresher secretarial course. She had several jobs and was successful in some areas of them but her continuing problems and lack of self-esteem ended in deep depression.

The slow process of working out of her depression led Laura to enrol at a university. At the beginning of her first year, she met a person with dyslexia, Joanne, at work. Joanne discussed her dyslexic experiences openly and Laura recognised similarities with her own experiences. She consulted the university's dyslexia tutor. A screening test and interview gave a high positive score of dyslexic characteristics. Laura took advantage of the study skills help at the university. Meeting other students with dyslexia has made sense of many things that happen to her and she is gaining confidence. She can now recognise when the style of a book makes reading difficult and does not blame herself for this as she would have done in the past.

Using the library is particularly difficult for Laura because of the classification system. Sometimes she plucks up courage to approach a member of the library staff for help, but she would not dare to say she has dyslexia even if she had been formally identified. When Laura had a positive score on the dyslexia screening test, she told her parents. They still gave her no support. Her father does not want to know. Her mother's attitude is that other people get by and so Laura must too. Laura's dyslexia regularly causes problems in the family. For Laura, her family's attitude reinforces the stigma of dyslexia and the stereotype of stupidity and failure.

There are several reasons why Laura has not sought formal identification. Firstly, she cannot afford the fee. Secondly, she has got a long way already and has a strong urge to 'go it alone' without special provisions. Finally, she has a deep fear. The characteristics of dyslexia explain so much for her personally, but she is worried that the psychologist might decide she does not have dyslexia after all. He might finally confirm that she is stupid – then her stupidity would be 'official'. Laura cannot believe she is intelligent. She knows she was extremely competent at some parts of her jobs; she is getting A-grades for some of her work; yet she dismisses these achievements as flukes. She finds getting her ideas down on paper very difficult and is afraid of the next exams she has to do. She would like to have the extra time in exams that is provided for students formally identified as having dyslexia.

Laura has had access to a computer, but she is nervous about using the shared computer facilities within the university. She even finds great difficulty in putting her ID number into the university machines. It is possible that her need for extra time in exams and for a computer of her own funded by the DSA, will eventually give her the courage to seek a psychologist's assessment. Like so many, she might then find great relief from the formal identification: she could begin trusting in her abilities and enjoy fulfilling her potential.

2.6.1.4   Duncan

Duncan was 21 when interviewed. He was in the last year of his course, reading two humanities subjects. This was his second attempt at university, having withdrawn from the first because it provided very little support for dyslexic students. He had experienced problems beyond those attributable to dyslexia and pulled out of the course.

Duncan's G.P. had recently read his early history to him. Pre-school, he was thought to be hyperactive and educationally subnormal. He was treated regularly for a while at a hospital. It was suggested that he might have Down's Syndrome. His family were well aware of dyslexia as his uncle had been identified as having dyslexia as a child. At about 5, Duncan was identified as having dyslexia and from then on he received all the appropriate help he needed. All of his schooling was chosen in order to help with his dyslexia and there were only two brief occasions when this help was restricted in anyway. At his last school, there was a special unit for pupils with dyslexia. English was taught in groups of 6 and the syllabus covered was the same as for pupils without dyslexia; it was just taught differently. There were sufficient pupils in the unit that it was 'no big deal' to have dyslexia. Duncan feels this accepting atmosphere lets him accept his dyslexia more easily than several students he knows. He does not have the strong desire to 'go it alone' which leads other students to deny their dyslexia and refuse to face problems until they are practically insurmountable. As well as all the other support, Duncan had a scribe for both GCSE and Scottish Higher.

After withdrawing from his first university he spent some of the year teaching English from grammar books in India, an experience that enabled him to 'lay a grass-roots foundation' for himself. This time Duncan has thoroughly enjoyed himself at university. He has enjoyed the academic challenges. He has made full use of the administrative support, such as extra time in exams and library provisions. He used the teaching support available as much as he could during the first two terms. After that, he treated it as a 'safety net', should he be stuck for a solution to a study problem. With that knowledge, he felt confident in responding to the teaching and advice from his academic tutors. In one field, his tutors were understanding and approachable – they knew when to take the initiative to provide appropriate conditions. In the other field, although the tutors were not so understanding, they were not altogether dismissive. He has never encountered a member of staff who made him feel uncomfortable.

Duncan found using the library was not really problematic. He liked to work there because he had more space and was less likely to be distracted. He would have liked a dyslexic-friendly dictionary; he commented that it is hard to find words like 'erudite' when you are looking under 'au'. But Duncan had no awkwardness about asking for help with spelling.

Duncan's last school had given the pupils guidance about skills they would need at university. Duncan had needed the practical and psychological support to continue from school to university. It was not available at the first one he went to and it was with a big sense of relief that he found there was so much support and understanding at the second one. Small details, such as how to fill in exam forms for special provisions, showed that the needs of students with dyslexia were being accurately recognised. He has also met and made friends with several other students who have dyslexia and found their support encouraging.

At university Duncan is quite open about having dyslexia, but he is concerned about the next stage. Having experienced one university that did not have a comprehensive and supportive understanding of dyslexia, he was worried about employers' attitudes to dyslexia. Even with all his positive experience of having dyslexia, he does not want to prejudice his job prospects by admitting that he has dyslexia.

2.6.1.5   Ruth

When interviewed Ruth was 21 years old. She is an exceptionally bright and highly motivated student who had recently graduated with a first class honours degree in psychology and was proceeding to research for a Ph.D.

Ruth's father and older sister both have significant problems in reading and writing but neither has been assessed for dyslexia. Teachers at school were aware of Ruth's difficulties in reading, writing and numeracy, and noted that this was in marked contrast to her academic potential. However, she was never formally assessed and the term 'dyslexia' was not mentioned. She was diagnosed as being 'clumsy' at the start of secondary school. Extra support was provided by her family, which used every available resource to aid her learning, and largely because of this she did very well in GCSE and 'A' level exams.

Ruth found the first year at university very difficult. She missed the support she had received at school and home, especially not having anyone to discuss her work with. She contemplated leaving university but decided to persevere. At the beginning of the second year, her tutors noted that she was experiencing substantial problems when working with numbers in the statistics module. Subsequently, Ruth was formally identified as having dyslexia. Although she applied for the DSA this was turned down by her LEA. The LEA accepted that she had 'significant difficulties' but since she had coped quite well up to that point it decided that she could be expected to cope adequately at university without further support. Undaunted, she took out a loan to purchase her own computer and she found that it changed both her approach to studying and the standard of her work radically. The computer helped to organise the structure of her work, and she found the facility to develop each piece of work through several drafts invaluable.

Looking back at the three years of her degree course, Ruth admits it has been a 'struggle' but the outcome has made it all worthwhile. She believes that if her university had a disability support worker on the staff, this would have saved her much time and energy. She spent a lot of time fruitlessly seeking support in the university and (more beneficially) experimenting with ways of improving her own studying techniques but says that it would have been quicker for someone to have taught her these. Despite using the computer, she found that fundamental difficulties did persist, particularly with organisation of work and preparation for exams. The turning point came when she realised she needed to improve her support network. She found a work 'partner' with whom to share notes, ideas and revision. She also made good use of friends who were willing to check the spelling, punctuation and the grammar of her work, and most importantly to spend time helping her revise verbally for exams. She gave up trying to take notes in lectures but concentrated on mind-mapping the main ideas. She photocopied everything she could, and her department helpfully allowed her free use of the photocopier.

Ruth's lecturers tried to be supportive, but they needed more information about how to help. She was permitted to have an amanuensis to oversee her use of numbers in statistics exams, and she was allowed additional time in exams. She reports that the main benefit of extra time was the opportunity to organise her thoughts in a more structured and coherent way, and still have the time to write them down. Not being penalised for poor spelling allowed her to develop a much freer writing style. The allowances the university gave allowed her to compete on an even playing field with her fellow students, but she often felt annoyed that other students and staff only saw the results and failed to appreciate the hard work which was necessary to achieve them. She is optimistic about the future but does not underestimate the mammoth task that she now faces in her Ph.D. research.

2.6.1.6   Sarah

Sarah was identified with dyslexia when she was twelve years old on her school's recommendation because of continuing severe difficulty with spelling and reading and despite superior intellectual ability. She received extra support in small classes and received 'A' level provision of extra time, and was in receipt of an up-to-date educational psychology report. She came to university following a gap year out for travelling.

Sarah approached the dyslexia support service two months after entry to her science course. She had a good sense of her own abilities and difficulties, and an understanding of the circumstances which caused her to panic, e.g. examinations and deadlines, although she was already working long hours of study to keep up to date with notes and reading. She was also enjoying her course and university social life.

At the end of her first semester Sarah began the process of DSA application endorsed by the dyslexia service and discussions with the university computer department and received a computer with word processing packages and a hand held spellchecker. She was allowed 20 minutes per hour extra time in written examinations at the end of her first year. During her second year it was recommended that Sarah applied for money for core texts only available on short loan, and for additional photocopying to meet the additional work load.

Sarah's coping, friendly personality, dedication to her subject and willingness to explain her difficulties to academic and support staff allowed her to make the most of her three years at university both educationally and socially. At the end of her three years, she gained employment as a research assistant at another university in the UK.

2.6.2 *Vignettes – summaries and conclusions*

- **Tanya** was identified as having dyslexia when she was a child. The diagnosis was a relief to her as it explained her difficulties; however she did not get appropriate teaching help. The attitude 'Don't worry dear, it's too difficult for you' left her frustrated. Her progress through university was hampered by her unwillingness to face the problems caused by dyslexia. She used the administrative support available but she did not feel free to approach dyslexia as a challenge to be managed with her own particular strengths. Her attitude was changing towards the end of her course; she was becoming more accepting of her dyslexia through she remains cautious about telling others.

- **Keith**, a mature student aged 54, who was only diagnosed as having dyslexia during his first year at university. He had made wrong decisions about his jobs based on a very low self-worth. He had received no help at school and had been in the bottom stream. The diagnosis of dyslexia was very welcome as it explained so much about his life. He managed to get on to the course he really wanted to do and the quality of his work convinced sceptical tutors that dyslexic students could do very well on humanities courses. He is very open about having dyslexia and he has gone on to help others.

- **Laura** also had a difficult time at school. She was made to feel stupid because she couldn't learn maths and language the same as other pupils. She felt they had something she didn't. She had difficulty with courses, such as secretarial training, and got her jobs through friends and acquaintances rather than through qualifications. At university, she went through a screening process which indicated that she has dyslexia. Laura is afraid to be formally assessed and can't afford it anyway. She uses what help she can; she finds libraries very daunting. She would like the benefits of a formal diagnosis – e.g. extra time in exams – but she has to find the nerve and money to go to a psychologist.

- **Duncan** was treated for a variety of suspected problems before he was identified at the age of 5 as having dyslexia. He had appropriate teaching throughout his schooling. At one stage, he was at a school with a small dyslexia unit and having dyslexia was not regarded as an issue. He left school able to accept his dyslexia and he has noticed quite a difference between his attitude and that of other university students. He had a false start at one university and re-started his studies at a second. He has used the support available and thoroughly enjoyed his progress through the university. Even with his positive attitude to dyslexia, he still has reservations about telling employers about it.

- **Ruth** was a well-compensated, high achieving student who entered university straight from school after completing A levels. She had been fortunate to have understanding teachers at school and very supportive parents, but her dyslexia was not formally identified until the second year of her university studies. Her application for DSA was rejected by the LEA on the grounds that her difficulties were 'not severe enough', which upset her but did not discourage her. She retained her determination to succeed but she had to struggle every step of the way. She graduated with a first class honours degree and is now working as a research assistant in a university, where she is also registered for a Ph.D.

- **Sarah** was identified as having dyslexia when her school recommended assessment because her reading and spelling were poor in contrast to her obvious intelligence. At school, she had help for dyslexia and she had extra time in examinations. She contacted the support services early in her university career. She knew her abilities and difficulties. The amount of extra time for exams was set with the understanding it would be reviewed. At the review, the extra time wasn't changed, but other provisions were organised to help her. Her application for the DSA to buy a computer and to meet the costs of her other needs was successful.

The experiences of these six students with dyslexia are markedly different, yet the first four are all from the same university. The fifth and sixth vignettes are of students from two other universities. Each of the six students whose experiences have been related above is an individual with their own story and their own potential. Similar experiences are related many times by students with dyslexia, but there are also considerable differences. The ease or unease with which they approached staff and studying seems to depend to a large extent on their previous experiences, and whether these have been favourable or unfavourable. For those students who appear to have been 'damaged,' by their past experiences, the understanding and the usefulness of the support they receive at university can do a great deal to redress the balance and restore self-esteem. Even those with good self-esteem are vulnerable to unaccepting attitudes. When self-esteem is high, the latent potential of students with dyslexia can be utilised to the benefit of the student, the community at university and society at large when they enter the workforce.

There are also a number of common threads running through the experiences of students with dyslexia and reported by their tutors. To some extent, there are reflected in the vignettes. These common threads include the following.

- Difficulty in knowing what to expect, in adapting past learning to new situations or developing new skills.

- Difficulty in locating and understanding information and in deciding how to prioritise it. This difficulty applies to course information, the organisation of life and study.

- Difficulty in organising themselves. A lack of prioritising skills is noticeable, and studying, responses to college administration and general living are affected.

- Frequently there will be difficulties in managing time or space or both; many a student will expend a lot of time planning only to find he/she is at the wrong place at the wrong time.

2.7   The impact of dyslexia on students and staff in higher education

The six vignettes in the previous section illustrate the variety of difficulties encountered by students with dyslexia in higher education. This section attempts to provide an overview of how the difficulties created by dyslexia can affect the various aspects and stages of higher education. It should be noted that these observations are not based on systematic research reported elsewhere, but have been compiled from the comments of a number of dyslexia tutors at different universities who contributed to the national survey on dyslexia in higher education (see Chapter 3).

2.7.1 Admissions

Students with dyslexia often want to enter higher education but at the same time they may fail to anticipate the difficulties which they will encounter in higher education. Because they have been successful in gaining entry, they may assume that they are therefore deemed to be capable of doing the course to which they have been admitted. Many students with dyslexia enter via unconventional routes (i.e. other than 'A' level). They may assume that the practical vocational or supported-study type of entry qualification, e.g. Access, BTEC, GNVQ, will not only qualify them for higher education but also enable them to tackle the demands of studying at this level. The reality of the situation often comes as a shock. In addition, many students with dyslexia choose to study with the

Open University, which although imposing no entry requirements, places particularly heavy demands on independent learning.

2.7.2 *Communication and organisation*

Higher education demands a much higher level of organisation than most students have ever needed before. Many students with dyslexia have never acquired good organisational skills. The notice board is usually the main source of information about courses, lecture rooms and other activities, but many students with dyslexia often fail to obtain information from notice boards because:

- the form of presentation of the information creates difficulties for them
- they are unable to distinguish relevant notices from less relevant (or irrelevant) ones
- they have difficulties in copying information down in that situation
- notice boards are typically in noisy places, which affects concentration
- their poor short term memory affects recall of information.

Students with dyslexia typically experience difficulty in getting to know their new environment, its systems and its personnel. For example, the way in which libraries are laid out and organised can seem excessively complicated. Students with dyslexia often cannot judge time and so are regularly late. Their disorientation may extend to finding classrooms and offices, finding resources in an unfamiliar town, and dealing with unfamiliar people. Students with dyslexia often do not know who their tutors are, what their functions or even their names are. The feelings of alienation that this can cause in the student may be misconstrued by them as indifference on the part of the staff. Their confidence will almost certainly be affected by this experience. Their strategies for coping with these problems will be dependent on their personality. The most successful will be self-aware and develop appropriate strategies. However, some will try to cover and evade. Some will be apologetic and deferential, but others may be over-assertive and excessively demanding.

2.7.3 *Lectures*

Many students with dyslexia report that they find lectures useful provided that they can listen without having to do anything else. Taking notes in lectures is a peculiarly difficult task for them because their writing is slow and their organisational skills weak. In addition, their writing speed may be slow and they may be further slowed down by considerations of spelling. There are particular problems in combining the three tasks of listening to complex information, identifying key points, and making a written record. These students often prefer to tape record lectures and write them up afterwards. Lecturers may be reluctant about students taping their lectures and about providing notes in the form of hand-outs in case students stop attending lectures. Students with dyslexia can become dependent on the notes of other students, a practice that is sometimes resented and can damage relationships.

A few students with dyslexia have discovered that taking notes helps them to concentrate and focus on the lecture; this suggests that training in note-taking strategies may be particularly beneficial for students with dyslexia (see Section 9.2.5).

2.7.4 *Reading and writing*

Although most students with dyslexia will be adequate readers by the time they reach university, many will still tend to be rather slower at reading than other students. This will mean that getting through the reading required for a course will usually take much longer for these students. In addition, some persons with dyslexia are very susceptible to *visual discomfort* when reading for prolonged periods, which can create unpleasant reactions such as headaches and eyestrain (see Section 2.3). For most students with dyslexia, reading is not a satisfying experience: extracting adequate meaning from written materials and retaining the sense of what they have read can take inordinate amounts of time. Essay writing also typically takes much longer for students with dyslexia than for other students.

2.7.5   Examinations and assessments

Written examinations are particularly stressful for students with dyslexia because they usually have few methods which are appropriate for this situation. Because their note-taking in lectures has been deficient, they typically have inadequate material from which to revise, in a form which they can absorb. They find rote-learning ineffective and so need quite different ways of revising. Their spontaneous recall is usually very limited, and so however hard they have prepared, they may feel that they know little. Their speed of writing may be much slower than that of other students and they may be acutely aware of their problems in spelling, grammar and vocabulary. In the examination situation itself, panic can quickly set in and may immobilise them.

Departments can be reluctant to make appropriate special provision for examinations, even when it is requested through official channels. Some staff and some other students may resent a student with dyslexia being given special provision in examinations, and view this as an unfair advantage. The dyslexic student can find it embarrassing to be singled out or stigmatised in this way, which can make them even more conscious of being different and disadvantaged.

2.7.6   Attitudes of staff

The level of awareness and/or understanding on the part of academic staff seems to be a significant factor in most cases. Some members of staff may be understanding about the difficulties experienced by a student with dyslexia, others totally unaware, while still others may be perceived as hostile. Tutors tend to have least patience with those students who fail to attend lectures or tutorials or who do not ask for help. Dyslexic students are often reluctant to approach staff for help because they feel that they are being a nuisance and their impression may be that staff will not have much help to offer. Students may have a difficult decision about confidentiality – when (and who) to tell that they have dyslexia and when to stay quiet, and this is a decision that, in the end, only they can make because of the 'costs' and 'benefits' involved.

2.7.7   Employment

Many students with dyslexia express concerns about their employment prospects and, in particular, whether or not they should declare to prospective employers that they have dyslexia. In addition, there is a conviction among many students that dyslexia is a barrier to entering certain professions (e.g. teaching) and that, consequently, declaring that one has dyslexia will seriously impair one's chances of being accepted on a further course of training or study for those professions. There is some evidence that this is indeed the case. The wider issues associated with professional training of students with dyslexia are addressed in Section 7.1.

Although the *Disability Discrimination Act 1995* makes it unlawful to discriminate against candidates for employment on grounds of disability, students with dyslexia still have anxieties about whether being forthright about their dyslexia will harm their chances of obtaining the job they seek. They also worry that if their dyslexia is not declared and they succeed in gaining employment, the effects of their dyslexia (e.g. spelling errors, inaccuracies in taking down telephone messages) will create practical difficulties in the workplace, which could harm their career progress or even result in dismissal.

For the tutor or lecturer who is asked to. supply an academic reference for a student with dyslexia, whether for purposes of application for employment or for admission to a further course of study, there are dilemmas. Persons giving academic and professional references have a duty to be honest and truthful. Does that extend to making it known – regardless of the student's wishes on the matter – that the student has dyslexia and that he or she completed their degree with special support and special examination provision such as additional time? Or should the student's permission be sought before mentioning their dyslexia in the reference? In the latter case, is the referee morally entitled to decline to give a reference unless the student accepts that their dyslexia will be mentioned in that reference? It should be borne in mind that the referee in question may be the student's head of department, and that this person's reference may be the deciding factor. A refusal to provide a reference at this stage may affect the course of that student's whole career.

These, and other, issues concerning career and employment of students with dyslexia are discussed in Chapter 12.

2.7.8   Conclusions

University staff will recognise that many of the features described above are not necessarily peculiar to students with dyslexia. Individual students who do not have dyslexia may from time-to-time manifest similar problems in the organisation of their work, in coping with lectures, in keeping up with reading work, in producing good written work and in dealing with examinations. What characterises students with dyslexia, however, is the clustering of a variety of difficulties which all appear to have their origins, directly or indirectly, in the perceptual and cognitive features of the condition which have been well-reported in the scientific literature and which have been outlined in Section 2.3.

The next Chapter considers the ways in which HEIs have been responding to the needs of students with dyslexia.

3   Results of the national survey on dyslexia provision

3.1   Background to the survey

In order to investigate provision for identification and support of students with dyslexia in Higher Education in Britain the National Working Party constructed a questionnaire that was sent to all institutions offering higher education courses (HEIs). This survey was carried out on behalf of the Working Party by Joanna Horne, a Research Assistant in the Psychology Department at the University of Hull. The total number of HEIs was 234, which were categorised as follows: 44 in the category 'traditional universities'; 48 in the category 'new universities' (i.e. those which have been established as universities since 1990); and 142 in the category 'colleges offering higher education courses' (hereinafter referred to simply as 'colleges').

A total of 195 responses were received (an overall 83% response rate). The responses were broken down as follows: traditional universities (41 responses; 93% response rate), new universities (45 responses; 94% response rate), and colleges (109 responses; 77% response rate). Wherever possible, at each HEI a named person with responsibility for students with dyslexia (or for disabled students in general) was identified before the questionnaire was sent out. The questionnaire was kept as brief as possible in order to encourage a satisfactory response rate. Questionnaires were dispatched early in 1996 and responses were received back during that year. A copy of the questionnaire and the detailed results are given in Appendix 14.3.

3.2   Overview of principal findings

3.2.1   Admissions policy

It was reported that 94% of institutions claimed to admit students registered as dyslexic to all courses. Those institutions which reported that students with dyslexia were *not* admitted to some courses referred mainly to courses which led to a professional qualification in teaching and courses connected with medicine and/or pharmacy. (For discussion of these issues, see Section 7.1)

3.2.2   Identification of dyslexia

Approximately half of all HEIs reported that internal assessments for dyslexia were administered. There were slight, but non-significant, differences across the three categories in this respect (see Figure 1).

In the majority of cases (approximately 60%) these assessments were funded by the institution itself. Only in about 10% of cases was the student expected to pay for the assessment. In the remainder of cases, funds were obtained from a variety of other sources. In those institutions that did not provide internal assessments the vast majority of cases reported that the student obtained an assessment from an independent psychologist, whether through the services of the Dyslexia Institute, or by some other means. Of the remainder, the majority (10%) obtained their assessment from another HEI. The vast majority of professionals responsible for these assessments were qualified psychologists (77%), the next largest category being professionals holding a recognised diploma in specific learning difficulty.

There were some differences between the categories in this respect. Those HEIs in the 'colleges' category were rather more likely to be able call upon the services of a professional with a diploma in specific learning difficulty, presumably because such persons were employed within the learning support sector of the college. The majority of HEIs (70%) reported that they carried out a screening or preliminary assessment before students were referred for full psychological assessment. This was slightly more common in the new universities, in comparison with the traditional universities and the colleges.

Figure 1. Percentage of HEIs administering internal assessments for dyslexia (Q3, N=195).[7]

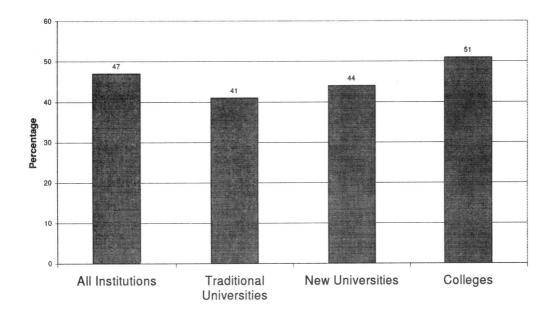

3.2.3   *Incidence of dyslexia in HEIs*

HEIs were asked to supply figures regarding the total number of current students at the institution who declared themselves to be dyslexic on the UCAS form, and the total number of current students who have been identified or diagnosed as dyslexic after admission.

Figure 2. Incidence of dyslexia (percentage) in HEIs (Q9–11, N=variable[8]).

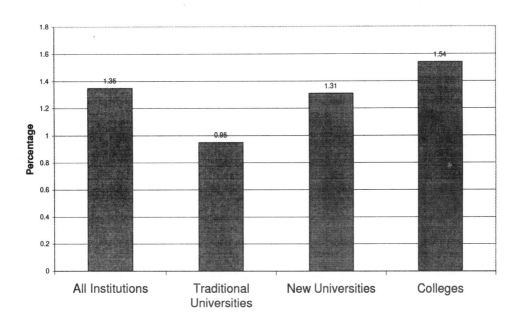

---

[7]   In the captions to the Figures in this Chapter, Q refers to the question number in the questionnaire (see Appendix 14.3) and N refers to the number of HEIs providing an answer to this question.

[8]   Q9, N=112; Q10, N=135; Q11, N=161.

These data enabled a calculation of the overall incidence of dyslexia in the student population. This was found to be 1.35%. Incidence figures varied across the categories, from 0.95% in traditional universities, 1.31% in the new universities and 1.54% in the colleges (see Figure 2). 57% of these students had already declared themselves to have dyslexia on entry to higher education; the remainder (43%) being identified or diagnosed as dyslexic after admission.

The results obtained in this survey may be compared with other available data. HESA statistics show a total of almost 1.7 million students enrolled in higher education courses in the UK in the 1996/97 academic year – this includes full-time, part time and postgraduate students. If the overall incidence of dyslexia in higher education is 1.35%, we would expect a total of about 23,000 students with dyslexia in higher education. To check these figures we can consider the number of students entering higher education in the UK that declare themselves to have dyslexia *on entry*. In the academic year 1996/97 this was 4,300 students (approximately 0.7% of all students entering that year).[9] If that figure is extrapolated to include the estimated number of students subsequently identified as having dyslexia *after* entry to higher education (based on the 43% revealed in the findings of the Working Party's national survey), the total number of students with dyslexia entering in 1996/97 was actually over 7,500. Since most higher education courses have a three-year duration, an annual figure of about 7,500 students with dyslexia would become 22,500 over three years, which is not significantly different from the 23,000 estimated previously. These calculations all lead us to similar conclusions, for if the 0.7% reported in HESA statistics is similarly extrapolated in the 57:43 ratio, the result is an estimate of 1.23% overall incidence of dyslexia in higher education, which is not remarkably different from the 1.35% reported in this survey. Allowing for a margin of error and for the fact that in all probability, a few students with dyslexia in higher education are *never* properly identified as having dyslexia, we may reasonably conclude that the *true incidence* of dyslexia in higher education in the UK at the present time lies is somewhere between 1.2% and 1.5% of all students, i.e. about 20,400 – 25,500 students in total. A university of average size (with about 15,000 students) may therefore expect to have to provide for the academic needs of between 180 and 225 students with dyslexia.

Nevertheless, the estimate that between 1.2% and 1.5% of students in higher education are dyslexic falls far short of the accepted 4% incidence of dyslexia in the general population. The implications of these findings are that although there has been a reported increase in numbers of students with dyslexia entering higher education (Singleton, Trotter and Smart, 1998) this category of disabled students is still under-represented in HEIs. This conclusion supports the verdict of the Dearing Committee that, in general, people with disabilities are under-represented in higher education (Dearing, 1997).

3.2.4   *Distribution across subject areas*

In the traditional universities and in the colleges, it was more common for the dyslexic students to be reported to be distributed about equally across different subject areas. In the new universities it was more common for these dyslexic students to be reported as being distributed unequally across different subject areas (see Figure 3). These differences may stem from a somewhat different balance of courses offered in the new universities.

3.2.5   *Support provision for students with dyslexia in HEIs*

Almost three quarters of institutions reported that they had a support service of some sort for dyslexic students. There were some differences across the different categories in this respect: rather more of the new universities (79%) reported this facility compared to the traditional universities (68%). Over those HEIs as a group the average number of students with dyslexia currently using such a service on a regular basis was found to be 34 per institution. A little less than half of HEIs reported that they had a dyslexia-trained tutor who could provide support for students with dyslexia. The new universities were much better off in comparison with the traditional universities in this respect – 57% compared with 27% (see Figure 4).

---

[9] Higher Education Statistics Agency Data Report: *Students in Higher Education Institutions,* 1996/97.

Figure 3. Percentage of HEIs which reported dyslexia to be distributed about equally across different subject areas (Q12, N=167).

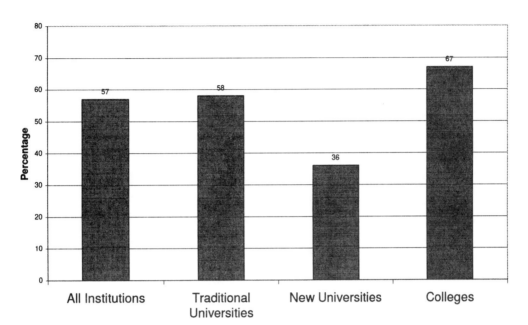

Figure 4. Percentage of HEIs which have a dyslexia-trained tutor (Q15, N=191).

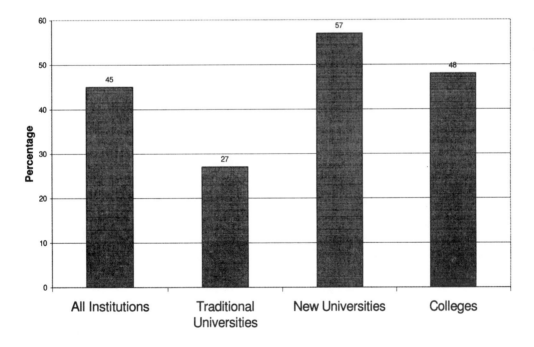

In the case of colleges offering higher education courses, the vast majority of such tutors were employed by the institution. In the universities, only about half of such professionals were actually employed by the institution, the remainder being employed on a consultancy basis. 40% of institutions reported organising group activities for dyslexic students, such as special courses, modules or workshops. Again, the students in new universities were rather better served in this respect than either students in the traditional universities or the colleges. Approximately two thirds of new universities reported such facilities, compared with approximately a third of the other categories (see Figure 5). Similar findings were reported in connection with special support to enable dyslexic students to use library facilities. Virtually all HEIs reported that dyslexic students were permitted to use tape recorders in lectures.

Figure 5. Percentage of HEIs which organise group activities for students with dyslexia (Q17, N=190).

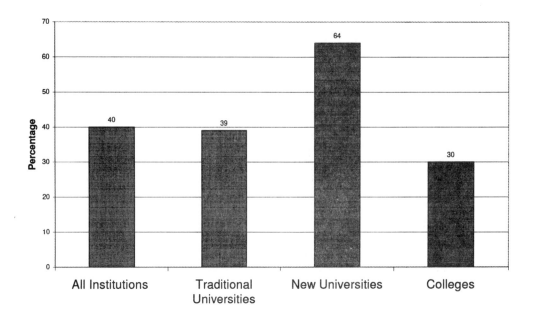

3.2.6   *Provision of specialist counselling facilities and staff development*

Approximately 40% of institutions reported that they provided *specialist* counselling facilities for dyslexic students, there being no significant differences across the categories in this respect. Approximately half of institutions reported giving all academic staff information on dyslexia. New universities reported rather better provision of staff development courses on dyslexia – 59% as opposed to 39% of traditional universities and 43% of colleges (see Figure 6).

Figure 6. Percentage of HEIs which run staff development courses on dyslexia (Q22, N=191).

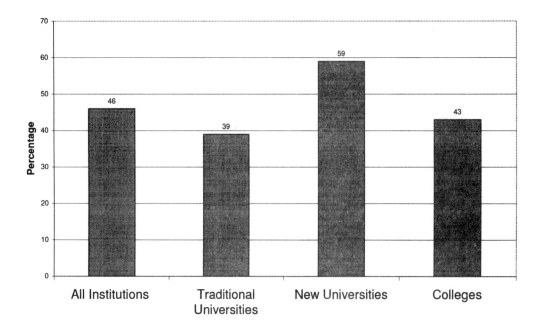

3.2.7   *General awareness raising*

Part 7 of the survey addressed general awareness-raising within the institution. Only about one third of institutions reported displaying posters to raise general awareness about dyslexia among students.

Almost two thirds of institutions did make special information available to students about support services for students with dyslexia.

3.2.8 Provision of technological support for students with dyslexia

Slightly fewer than half of institutions reported having special computer facilities at the institution to which dyslexic students could have open access. This type of provision was reported to be slightly more common in the new universities (see Figure 7). Specialist equipment, specifically referred to in response to this section of the survey, included scanners, talking word processors, and other specialist software for use by dyslexic students. Only approximately a third of institutions reported having any tutors or technicians with special responsibility for advising or assisting dyslexic students in the use of such technology.

3.2.9 Operation of the Disabled Students Allowances (DSA)

Almost all institutions (91%) claimed to help students to apply for the DSA but less than a third of institutions were able to answer in the affirmative the question *"Do you know how many dyslexic students at your institution are currently in receipt of the DSA?"* Of those who *were* able to answer "Yes" to this question, the mean number of students was 18. This may appear somewhat surprising, but probably reflects the fact that many students with dyslexia do not inform their institutions about the final outcome of their DSA applications.

Figure 7. Percentage of HEIs with specialist computer facilities for students with dyslexia (Q26, N=192).

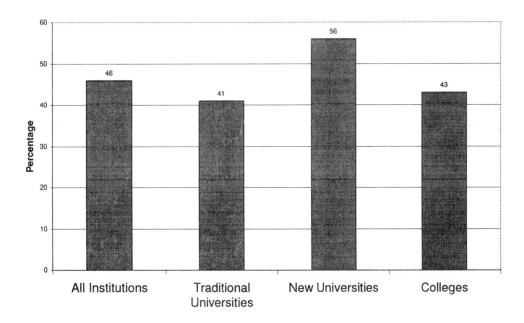

Over two thirds of institutions maintained that the DSA system was "unsatisfactory" in relation to applications by dyslexic students; in the new universities this dissatisfaction figure rose to an extremely high 93%. The most frequently cited reasons for dissatisfaction were: inconsistencies between LEAs, the time-consuming nature of DSA application, the fact that the DSA does not cover the cost of initial assessment, and the fact that various categories of students are excluded from the DSA at the present time (see Figure 8).

3.2.10 Special provision for students with dyslexia in examinations

Over two thirds of institutions reported having a general policy on provision for dyslexic students in examinations, the remainder reporting that such policy was delegated to the examination boards for different subjects. Virtually all institutions (99%) reported allowing extra time for students with dyslexia in written examinations. In approximately one third of cases, this provision was standard for all dyslexic students, whereas in the remaining cases it varied from student to student depending upon the severity of the student's problem and other factors.

Figure 8. Percentage of HEIs that view the DSA system as unsatisfactory with respect to students with dyslexia (Q32, N=155).

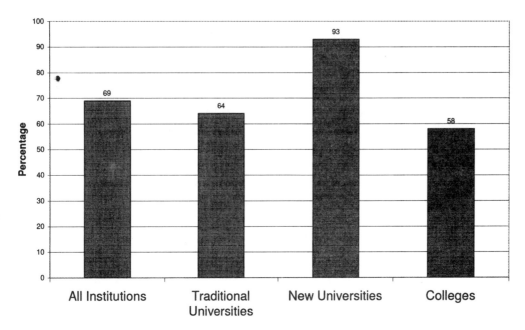

Of those institutions making *standard* provision in examinations regarding allowance for additional time, almost a half reported allowing ten minutes' additional time per hour and a similar number reported allowing fifteen minutes' extra time per hour. A very small proportion of institutions reported allowing more additional time than this, up to thirty minutes' additional time per hour. There were significant differences between the categories in this respect, with the traditional universities most commonly allowing ten minutes' additional time per hour, whereas the new universities typically preferred fifteen minutes' time per hour (see Figure 3.9).

Figure 9. Percentage of HEIs allowing various standard amounts of additional time in examinations for students with dyslexia (Q37, N=82).

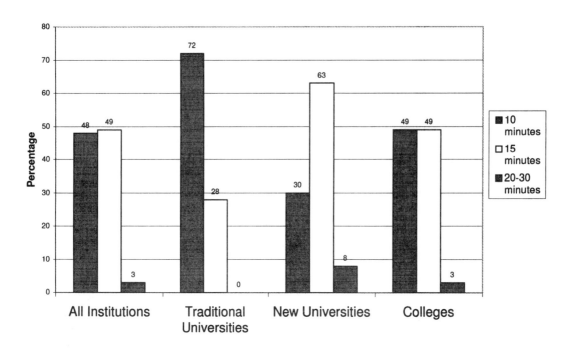

The majority of HEIs reported allowing further special arrangements in examinations for candidates with dyslexia, including use of an amanuensis, a reader or a word processor. Only two thirds of HEIs permitted dyslexic students to tape-record answers in examinations, and the new universities and colleges were somewhat more inclined to allow this than were the traditional universities. A similar finding was revealed in connection with allowing dyslexic students to have an oral examination instead of a written one, where again, the new universities and colleges were more disposed to this solution than were the traditional universities (see Figure 10). Some HEIs mentioned further special provision, including separate rooms for dyslexic candidates, enlarged question papers, use of coloured overlays, use of electronic spelling checkers, and rest breaks during examinations.

Figure 10. Percentage of HEIs that permit students with dyslexia to have an oral examination instead of a written examination (Q43, N=153).

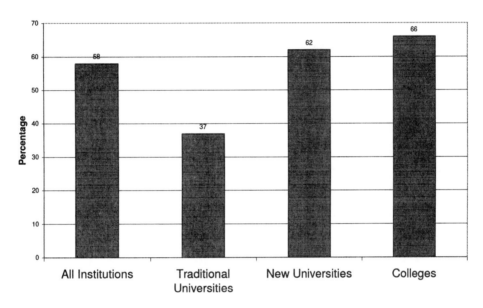

3.2.11 The biggest problem?

Finally, HEIs were asked to outline any provision made for dyslexic students not already covered in the questionnaire, and to identify the 'biggest problem' confronting the institution at the present time in relation to students with dyslexia. In response to the first question, the most frequently mentioned provision was giving support in study skills and practice in carrying out assessments. A large number of different problems were mentioned, the most frequent being:

- funding for assessments

- equipment and support

- lack of knowledge about dyslexia amongst staff and students

- lack of qualified staff to help dyslexic students

- increasing numbers of students with dyslexia in higher education and the problems of identifying them

- difficulties associated with obtaining the DSA.

3.3   Conclusions

This survey has revealed a number of disturbing findings which confirm that the higher education sector as a whole is still a long way from providing a fully satisfactory service to dyslexic students. In the vital areas of study-skills support, specialist technology services and staff development programmes, only about half of all institutions had facilities that began to address the educational needs of students with dyslexia. There were worrying disparities between institutions in relation to the procedures for identification of dyslexia and the provision of additional time in examinations, which mean that from the point of view of the dyslexic student it can be a lottery whether or not one receives effective support.

It should be remembered that these results are based on data collected during 1996. There is anecdotal evidence that since 1996 provision for students with dyslexia in higher education has improved somewhat, but there are no objective data to quantify this. The improvement in provision that has been perceived seems to have come about as a result of two main factors. First, there appears to have been steadily increasing awareness of dyslexia issues in HEIs, to which the consultative process carried out by the Working Party has doubtless contributed. Second, HEIs have been more focused on disability issues generally, partly in response to encouragement from the Higher Education Funding Councils, and partly because of the requirements of the *Disability Discrimination Act 1995* regarding the publication of Disability Statements (see Section 1.1.3).

Looking generally at these results, the question springs to mind: are students with dyslexia better off in the new universities? The evidence indicates that dyslexic students have been more likely to receive the support the needed in one of the new universities compared to the traditional universities. In the new universities, for example, students with dyslexia have been more likely to:

- be given a screening assessment prior to full psychological assessment
- have access to a specialist dyslexia support service
- have access to a trained dyslexia tutor
- be able to participate in group activities or taught modules which are beneficial to study skills development
- be taught by academic staff who have participated in staff development concerning dyslexia
- have special help in using the library
- have access to counselling services which are specially for dyslexics
- have access to special computer facilities
- have technical assistance when using such computer facilities
- be given more additional time in written examinations
- be permitted further special arrangements in examinations, especially in relation to oral examinations instead of written examinations.

What might the reasons be for these findings? In the first place it should be pointed out that this state of affairs is probably not very different to that which exists with respect to other disabilities. The new universities were initially more successful in bids for funding from the HEFCE to support special initiatives to widen access to students with disabilities, which may have helped some of them to develop facilities such as specialist support services. In addition, the incidence of dyslexia is slightly higher in the new universities compared with the traditional ones (1.31% as opposed to 0.95%) and in the new universities, students with dyslexia are more likely to be unequally distributed across different subject areas. This may have caused the new universities to focus on the needs of these students and address critical issues such as examination arrangements, staff development, etc. Perhaps because of the academic ethos in some of the traditional universities, staff may have been slower in recognising that they have some students who have dyslexia and who need special support. Nevertheless, by no means *all* the new universities have got to grips with how to make appropriate provision for students with dyslexia. Even though there is evidence for differences between the categories in this survey, what is abundantly clear is that there is considerable room for improvement across the higher education sector as a whole. It is the function of this Report to provide guidance to *all* HEIs on how to improve their facilities for students with dyslexia.

4   Results of the consultative process

4.1   Regional and national consultative meetings

4.1.1   Organisation of the consultation process

During the spring and early summer of 1996, a series of five regional meetings was held in Birmingham, Edinburgh, Bristol, Manchester and London, respectively, in order to consult interested parties from HEIs, Local Authorities and voluntary bodies. Pre-consultation documentation indicated the major issues that would be addressed and primed those attending to undertake preparatory work. In addition to the members of the Working Party, the five regional meetings were attended by a total of 121 individuals representing HEIs and Local Authorities. A further twenty-two LEA Awards Officers and seven members of the Working Party attended the national meeting of Awards Officers. Attendance at these meetings is summarised in Table 3.

Table 3. Attendance at regional and national consultative meetings.

Meeting	Date	Numbers of representatives attending	Attendance by members of Working Party
Birmingham	13th March, 1996	12	4
Edinburgh	20th March, 1996	24	4
Bristol	27th March, 1996	13	3
Manchester	17th April, 1996	24	4
London	1st May, 1996	48	9
DSA Awards Officers (London)	16th May, 1996	22	7
TOTALS		143	31

Each meeting followed a common two-part structure. In the first session, the Chair of the Working Party, or an alternate, outlined its aims and the methodology adopted to achieve these. Findings from the survey of policies, demography, practices and provision in HEIs in England, Wales, Scotland and Northern Ireland were presented. Concerns, questions and comments were elicited. The second, and major, part of each meeting was devoted to a consideration of the challenges presented and the responses to dyslexia in higher education, as seen by the participants. Discussions took place in small groups, each with at least one member of the Working Party in attendance. Notes were kept of concerns expressed and ways in which these could be addressed. Plenary sessions enabled summaries of the group discussions to be reported and discussed. Each participant at the meetings was provided with a three-page discussion paper outlining three areas of concern, and each area comprised seven issues to be discussed. Each group determined its own sequence and approach. The three areas were as follows.

1. *Identification of dyslexia at the higher education level.*

2. *Evaluation of the learning needs of students with dyslexia in higher education.*

3. *Institutional perspectives on the support for students with dyslexia in higher education.*

Members of the Working Party acted as reporters to groups at the five regional meetings and provided summaries of the issues raised and concerns expressed. Several of these were often contained in a single entry. The total number of entries collated from the five regional meetings was 440.

At subsequent meetings of the Working Party, the concerns that had been expressed were reorganised under extended headings that better summarised the concerns of those who had attended the regional meetings. The first of these was Staff Development and Awareness. There followed a sequence of six further headings representing stages in tertiary education from Admissions to Careers. In each of the seven areas, major concerns were identified. These are listed in Sections 4.1.2 The entries listed in these tables each represent a condensation of the larger number elicited during the consultations: the 440 have been reduced to 64.

Whilst our concern is with students with dyslexia wishing to enter, or in, higher education, many of the points made in the tables in this Chapter apply equally to other legally recognised forms of disability (Wolfendale and Corbett, 1996). The assumption is that, despite specific difficulties with aspects of literacy in particular, the dyslexic student has the requisite ability and motivation to complete higher education successfully, given appropriate differentiation of the curriculum and support from the institution. At the Regional and National Consultations, the focus of deliberations was on entirely appropriate special needs and equal opportunities issues: specifically, what can be done to address the problems involved in identifying and helping students with dyslexia gain entry to, and succeed, in higher education?

4.1.2 Major concerns expressed in the regional consultative meetings

4.1.2.1 Summary of concerns

There was a general concern expressed about the increase in numbers of students with dyslexia in higher education, and the resultant impact which that was having on facilities for psychological assessment, DSA applications, learning support, examination provision and HEI finances. Issues connected with staff development and awareness were perceived to underpin all other concerns about dyslexia at higher education level. Without the awareness and understanding of the academic and other staff who come into contact with students with dyslexia, no HEI can be said to be making satisfactory provision for such students (see Section 4.1.2.2). Widening access to higher education for students with dyslexia raised complex concerns about equal opportunities and academic standards (see Section 4.1.2.3). Obtaining official recognition of a student's dyslexia through a diagnostic assessment, sometimes following other screening procedures is problematic (see Section 4.1.2.4). The subsequent evaluation of the special needs of students with dyslexia and the support to which they are entitled, presents difficulties (see Section 4.1.2.5). Students identified as having dyslexia, or considered as possibly having dyslexia, face more than academic stresses (see Section 4.1.2.6). Problems of equity arise in the organisation of examination and assessment arrangements (see Section 4.1.2.7). Finally, are the legitimate interests of students and potential employers compatible? (see Section 4.1.2.8).

4.1.2.2 Staff development and awareness

1)   Making known to colleagues the experiences of students with dyslexia who have successfully completed courses of higher education is helpful in raising the awareness of academic staff concerning how they, and the institution, can more effectively understand and address the challenges to higher education presented by the entry of students with dyslexia.

2)   Despite information available from UCAS forms, suspicions exist amongst many academic staff in higher education concerning the assertion that students with dyslexia are registered each year and are capable of meeting the demands of higher education courses.

3)   An effective programme of staff development requires the support and involvement of higher education Senior Management in promoting awareness of equal opportunities policies, provision and practices in respect of all disabled students at Departmental, Faculty and University levels.

4) Raising the awareness of academic staff concerning the identification and support of students with dyslexia presents additional demands on resources already under other severe pressure, e.g. staff time and energies.

5) Lack of expertise in identifying and alleviating the difficulties of students with dyslexia is (understandably) endemic amongst academics in higher education.

6) Several contributors commented on the basis of their subjective experiences that academic-related and non-academic staff are perceived as more responsive than many academic staff in supporting students with dyslexia.

7) Better internal and external networking between all professionals responsible for students with dyslexia can increase staff awareness of promising practices.

8) Student Unions can help considerably in raising awareness about dyslexia as a recognised disability in higher education.

4.1.2.3   Admissions

1) Liaison between Admission Officers, Higher Education Disability Officers, Schools and LEA Awards Officers is unduly variable across the country.

2) Discrimination against students with dyslexia is perceived to exist in some disciplines and some professions: this is perceived as contrary to equal opportunities policies.

3) Advice concerning DSA is not sent out early enough to higher education applicants.

4) Tensions exist between academic views about 'standards' and the concern that students with dyslexia may reduce these standards.

5) Course choices by students with dyslexia are not always adequately informed by a detailed consideration of the demands of a given course.

6) Transitional planning and support between school/college and university for students with dyslexia is often inadequate.

7) Unless the applicant or referees make the existence of the disability known, higher education admission tutors will not know whether an applicant is dyslexic. This can distort their assessment concerning whether the applicant is likely to succeed if offered a place on a particular course.

4.1.2.4   Identification, including screening and diagnosis

1) Continuing legitimate problems exist concerning the conceptualisation, identification and alleviation of dyslexia.

2) Variations exist in the content of diagnostic reports, their validity, length and utility.

3) Nationally adopted higher education-related identificatory screening test batteries, given before sending students for a full assessment, could help improve the consistency of both individual and institutional decision-making in the identification of dyslexia and the award of DSA.

4) Diagnostic assessment of dyslexia at the higher education level is important in the interests of equity but professional judgements will still be required of those responsible for the formal identification of students with dyslexia.

5) Greater awareness of the nature and content of valid diagnostic reports identifying dyslexia is required by staff responsible for resource allocation decisions in higher education.

6) The British Psychological Society provides a competency-based accreditation course for non-psychologists interested in using psychological tests. If there were demand for a nationally

recognised qualification to assess, this represents one possible avenue that non-psychologists could pursue.

7)   A national register of professionals qualified to assess whether students are, or are not, dyslexic is needed. (N.B. Qualified Chartered Psychologists have a Register).

8)   When professionally aware of the complexities of dyslexia, the staff of Access Centres can be of great value in relation to evaluation of technology needs, provided their professional links with the higher education institution are well-established. However, not all Access Centres have staff who possess high levels of knowledge about dyslexia, in comparison with knowledge of other disabilities. (For details of the National Federation of Access Centres, see Section 4.2.4.)

9)   Training in assessment techniques and their interpretation is required by staff involved in the identification of dyslexia.

10)   Anomalies exist concerning who should pay for the assessment of a potentially dyslexic student.

11)   In some cases, a 'No cash; no assessment; no DSA' system operates for students who may have dyslexia.

4.1.2.5   Evaluation of needs and support provision

1)   Higher education should consider adapting and adopting the needs assessment principles concerning specific learning difficulties in general, and dyslexia in particular, explicit in the *Code of Practice on the Identification and Assessment of Special Educational Needs* used in schools (DfE, 1994).

2)   Student's support needs must be individually determined because of the various types and degrees of dyslexia and the demands of different degree subjects and courses.

3)   The diagnostic report and, if subsequently completed, a needs assessment report should be discussed with the student. The reports must be written in an accessible style.

4)   It is important to identify and value the distinctive intellectual assets of students with dyslexia in relation to particular courses of study. Profiles of a student's abilities assist in this.

5)   Faster processing by LEAs of DSA applications is required.

6)   Fears exist that a very small number of students without significant disability perceive the DSA as a means of obtaining 'free' and useful IT equipment.

7)   Counselling students with dyslexia concerning needs assessment reports and their personal and educational implications is seen as an integral part of the work of a higher education Disability Support Service.

8)   Collaboration between involved parties in LEAs and higher education is essential as Awards Officers make no claim to being experts in dyslexia.

9)   HEIs vary significantly in the expertise available and resources allocated to support students with dyslexia.

10)   Currently, provision for students with dyslexia via the DSA is 'All or nothing'.

11)   Networks are essential. Collaborations between Disability Officers, DSA Awards Officers in LEAs, specialists in dyslexia including the National Bureau for Students with Disabilities (SKILL), Adult Dyslexia Organisation, the British Dyslexia Association and the Dyslexia Institute are likely to lead to improved practices. (For further information about these organisations, see Section 4.2.4.)

12)   Each department requires a 'named person' with responsibility for supporting students with dyslexia. Currently, the support of students with dyslexia is in too few hands in higher

education.

13) Fears exist amongst some academic staff that support can lead to over-dependency, rather than academic autonomy, on the part of some students with dyslexia.

14) Differential support for full-time and part-time undergraduates and post-graduate students with dyslexia present equity problems for higher education.

15) Lack of trained Support Tutors in higher education is widespread.

16) Variations in practice exist between LEAs in paying for study support of students with dyslexia.

17) Keeping abreast of rapidly developing technological innovations that facilitate the learning of students with dyslexia is essential.

18) Electronic networking allows the rapid dissemination of promising practices between professionals involved in managing or providing support for students with dyslexia.

19) Practices for ensuring a basic level of support entitlement/provision for students with dyslexia in higher education varies across HEIs: equity indicates that greater consistency is required.

20) The effectiveness of the support given to students with dyslexia must be monitored and evaluated.

4.1.2.6   Counselling

1) The significant motivational and academic pressures on students with dyslexia underline the importance of a formally established counselling service for such students.

2) Students with dyslexia can benefit from the emotional support provided by sharing their experiences in a group, e.g. discussing approaches to organisational and study skills.

3) Staff involved in such counselling must be knowledgeable about dyslexia. They must understand its potentially adverse emotional, social and intellectual effects and how these effects can be constructively addressed by the student and by the institution.

4) The availability of counselling expertise is relevant to all of the other six areas of concern identified in this Chapter.

4.1.2.7   Examinations and assessment

1) Equal opportunity and fairness considerations in examination and assessment policy and practice must be seen to apply to all students in higher education.

2) Flexibility in both examination modes and marking of the work of students with dyslexia is important.

3) The increasing variety of methods and materials whereby the academic work of students with dyslexia can be assessed provides opportunities for differentiated examination arrangement provision consonant with the equal opportunities policies of higher education and the demands of quality assurance.

4) Accepting that course requirements and the associated assessment/examination demands across disciplines and years of a course legitimately vary, where course requirements are similar, consistency in examination arrangements should be sought within higher education.

5) The use of word processors in preparing examined course work, and also in writing unseen and/or revealed conventional examination papers, can enable students with dyslexia to demonstrate their knowledge and understanding of the field in which they are studying.

6) The examination and assessment materials submitted by students with dyslexia should ideally

be assessed as are those of all other students. Allowance for the effects of extenuating circumstances, such as a previously documented disability, should be considered subsequently by the examiners.

7) Informed consideration of the cases of students with dyslexia who fail at the end of year 1, or in their re-sit examinations, is essential.

8) Payments from the DSA could be used to meet for any additional costs involved in providing differentiated examination arrangements for students with dyslexia.

4.1.2.8   *Careers*

1) The career successes of students with dyslexia in various fields demonstrate what can be achieved by determined individuals in institutions that provide appropriate support.

2) Academic and professional concerns exist as to whether awards obtained by students with dyslexia under officially supported special provisions affect the validity of the award.

3) Some potential employers expect a degree obtained by a dyslexic student receiving official special support during a course and its examinations, to indicate explicitly the student's receipt of such support on the award.

4) When writing references to employers for a post with, for example, particular literacy requirements of the successful candidate academic staff in higher education face the issue of whether, or not, to refer to a student's dyslexia.

5) Higher education course selection and the career aspirations of students with dyslexia require explicit consideration and counselling by higher education staff of the individual student in the contexts of the demands of both course and potential career.

6) The equipment provided via the DSA to support a student's studies becomes, and remains, the property of the student after the course in higher education is completed. Alternative arrangements are possible.

4.1.3   *Major concerns expressed in the national meeting with LEA Awards Officers*

A further, national consultative meeting, specifically restricted to Local Authority Awards Officers having specific responsibilities for administration of Disabled Student Allowances, was held in London on 16 May 1996. This was attended by Awards Officers representing 22 different LEAs. In addition to the briefing notes used in the regional consultative meetings, each participant was presented with a list of questions that had been derived from the previous consultative meetings. The purpose of this list was to facilitate discussion and exchange of views between Awards Officers and members of the Working Party at the meeting. Under similar reporting arrangements to those operating at the regional meetings, a total of approximately 67 entries was counted. The major 21 points are summarised below.

1) DSA Awards Officers are not experts in dyslexia. Such Officers cannot be expected to be fully informed about the considerable variety and severity of all disabilities that exist. For Awards Officers to operate effectively, it is *administratively* essential that they are provided with the results of a diagnostic assessment carried out by a qualified professional. Normally this will be a Chartered Psychologist experienced in the assessment of adolescents and adults.

2) DSA is a lump sum not broken down into disabilities, insofar as reporting to the DfEE is concerned. If the demand for a DSA from applicants claiming to be dyslexic continues to grow at its present rate, the financial resources available will be unable to meet it.

3) The operation of the DSA in relation to dyslexia is often contentious and generates excessive and costly administrative loads.

4) Many Awards Officers would prefer not to be involved with students who may be dyslexic because, at present, the Officers have full responsibility and accountability without adequate guidelines and/or training concerning the interpretation of reports diagnosing dyslexia.

5) The DSA for students with dyslexia could be top-sliced from the rest of the DSA, ring-fenced, and managed directly by HEIs.

6) There is a case for making the whole of the DSA operate in a similar way to Access funding, i.e. the funds being administered by the HEI.

7) Some Awards Officers considered that some HEIs and some students are trying to exploit the current system insofar as it concerns DSA for dyslexia. The criteria on which such views are based, and the extent of the asserted exploitation, remain unclear.

8) Dyslexia typically has a lengthy history from earlier schooldays. Whilst it may first be identified on application for entry to higher education, it is unlikely to have recently developed suddenly. 'Would this individual have been afforded the protection of a Statement whilst a pupil in school?' is seen as an important question to ask by at least one LEA.

9) There is mistrust by some Awards Officers of students who fail re-sit examinations in their second year and only then claim to be dyslexic.

10) A small proportion of applicants for DSA appear to have levels of general ability considerably below average and below that likely to be required to complete a degree successfully.

11) Where the Awards Officers appear circumspect, this is typically because of their sensitivities to the controversies concerning the nature and identification of dyslexia, coupled with the formal accountability they have to their auditors.

12) Inconsistencies in the information reaching Awards Officers in general, and in connection with psychologists' reports in particular, cause concern.

13) Administration works most efficiently where a dyslexic individual's legally recognised special needs can be validly and unambiguously identified and the individual then reliably categorised as entitled, or not entitled, to a DSA. Such clarity in connection with dyslexia is unlikely because of *entirely legitimate* professional disagreements concerning the nature, identification and alleviation of a variable syndrome such as dyslexia.

14) DSA forms should be standardised and simplified. The Scottish Education Department provides one possible example of how this can be achieved.

15) The diagnosis of dyslexia by professionals having what might be perceived as vested interests, causes concern to Awards Officers. A register of suitably accredited and qualified assessors is required if the system is to be seen as equitable.

16) Access Centres were, in general, found to work well by virtue of their ability to upgrade equipment and to provide students with opportunities to try out various options.

17) Provision for students with dyslexia in higher education requires the appointment of a manager within each institution having formal responsibilities for the organisation of an efficient support service. Regional advisors could monitor services and encourage greater consistency of policies and provision within a region.

18) Both common concerns and promising practices concerning the identification and support of students with dyslexia exist. These can be discussed and disseminated via networks between Awards Officers, higher education Welfare Officers and representatives from higher education registries. One such recent meeting known as an 'Open Forum' was attended by about 70 professionals. Subsequent quarterly meetings have been arranged.

19) Some problems arise as LEAs provide equipment that is then owned by the student. The use of rental systems run by commercial firms was seen as holding promise. In the case of one LEA, equipment was obtained on a 18 months rental paid by direct debit by the LEA, but the contract is signed by the student. If a student defaults, it is claimed that the LEA is not

involved. The rental option is being included in DfEE guidelines.

20) The provision of IT and other equipment is not necessarily sufficient for a dyslexic student. Training in its use, technical support and maintenance are frequently required if the equipment is to be used effectively.

21) There is a danger in assuming that the provision of IT equipment for students with dyslexia is the student's prime requirement. This is not always the case.

4.1.4 Conclusions

The combination of institutional and individual concerns that prompted the setting up of the Working Party are of considerable interest and importance to various groups. Economically and socially, it is essential that our system of higher education enables, rather than discourages, *all* students to achieve. Each of the points raised in Section 4.1.3 indicates at least one, and usually more, of the salient concerns currently reported by informed and involved professionals from many institutions and disciplines. Improving the adequacy of current policies and practices affecting the identification and support of students with dyslexia in higher education requires that staff development and both basic and applied research in such fields be continued, and/or initiated to this end. Making explicit the considered concerns of a widespread sample of involved professionals is an essential step complementing the empirical findings of the national survey of the policies and practices of HEIs. The purpose of the remaining Chapters of this Report is to integrate the salient concerns of professionals working in this field into a coherent framework so that clear guidelines for policy and practice can be put forward.

4.2 Other sources of information and evidence

4.2.1 Published material

The Working Party consulted a wide range of published material relating to dyslexia in higher education. The references that have been cited in this Report are listed in full in Section 14.1 and a basic reading list which should be helpful for professionals working in this area is provided in Section 14.8.

4.2.2 Results of HEFCE Special Initiative projects on dyslexia

Since 1993 the HEFCE has funded a number of individual projects in HEIs as part of its Special Initiatives on disability. Many of these projects have addressed provision for students with dyslexia, and the findings of these projects (where available) have been extremely useful to the Working Party in its deliberations on good practice. The HEFCE Special Initiative projects on dyslexia are summarised in Table 4.

For the first Special Initiative in 1993-94, a total of £3M was allocated to support projects in 38 HEIs. Ten of these projects focused on the support of students with dyslexia and comprised a wide diversity of approaches, including:

- setting up learning support units (three institutions)

- widening access to HE for students with dyslexia undertaking Access courses

- an American assessment model for the HE sector

- a mentor training project

- appointment of specialist staff to embed dyslexia support (two institutions)

- implementation of policies for special needs

- establishment of support tutors at departmental level

- study skills support for students with dyslexia.

Table 4. HEFCE-funded projects specifically relating to dyslexia.

Institution	Project aims and activities related to dyslexia, and duration
University of Bradford	Greater awareness of dyslexia; establishment of a dyslexia self-help group. (1994–95)
University of Brighton	Establishment of a learning support unit to give support to students with dyslexia. (1993–94 and 1994–95)
City University	Development of dyslexia support. (1996–99)
University of Central Lancashire	Extending support for students with dyslexia. (1994–95)
University of Hull	Evaluation of techniques used in dyslexia screening (1996–99) Evaluation of ways in which assistive technology can benefit students with dyslexia. (1996–99)
University of Kent	Investigation of factors concerning the admission to higher education of students with dyslexia who have completed Access courses. (1993–94) Establishment of a hypertext Dyslexia Archive on the Internet. (1994–95).
Kingston University	Creation and evaluation of a test for assessing dyslexia at adult level. (1993–94 and 1994–95)
Nene College of Higher Education	Developing high quality learning and support for students with dyslexia. (1996–99)
University of Leicester	Promoting awareness and curriculum support for students with dyslexia, including staff development. (1993–94)
University of North London	Development of a mentor training programme for graduates to be able to give support for students with dyslexia. (1993–94) Matching new trends in teaching and learning in higher education to the needs of students with dyslexia. (1996–99).
University of Plymouth	Development of a whole-institution approach to supporting students with dyslexia. (1993–94)
Roehampton Institute	Appointment of a dyslexia support tutor and implementation of a staff development programme; initiation of a research programme to develop a computer-based dyslexia screening instrument. (1993–94) Screening students for dyslexia; training dyslexia counsellors; completion of the computer-based dyslexia screening instrument. (1994–95)
South Bank University	Creation of study skills support materials and training staff in support for students with dyslexia. (1993–94)
University of Surrey and St Mary's College	Establishment of a resource centre and provision of dyslexia support sessions. (1993–94)
Westhill College	Support for students with dyslexia, including instruction on study skills and establishment of a network of support tutors. (1993–94)

Most institutions have continued these initiatives but a small proportion subsequently dissolved their project activities for financial reasons. Dissemination of the good practice that had been developed in these projects has enabled the initiation of services in other institutions (HEFCE, 1995).

The second HEFCE Special Initiative during 1994–95 funded 48 projects at a total cost of £3M. Of these, projects carried out in eight HEIs focused on dyslexia, including:

- development of computer programs for self-assessment and other educational materials

- development of staff training materials

- development of a specialised learning resource area

- development of a quick screening test.

These additional projects have further enhanced the climate of acceptance and support for students with dyslexia throughout the sector. The executive summary of the HEFCE report on these projects addressed the critical factors that had been shown to be necessary for success in the development and implementation of such provision, which were: committed support by senior management; enthusiasm of project staff; centrally sited provision; strategic planning; integrated and effective monitoring of practices (HEFCE, 1996a).

Where available, the results of the dyslexia projects supported in the first two HEFCE Special Initiatives have been considered by the Working Party when drawing up recommendations and compiling proposals of good practice.

The third, and most recent, Special Initiative on disability was instigated by HEFCE in 1996, and will run over three years to 1999 (HEFCE, 1996b). A total of 31 HEIs have been supported in a wide range of projects, with some institutions carrying out more than one project. The total funding to date for this Special Initiative has been £4.92 million and a further £1 million has been set aside for subsequent development work. Although dyslexia features as a major component in the projects of only four of these HEIs, many participating institutions are working on the general enhancement of support services for all disabilities, including dyslexia. The emphasis in these projects is on building on the good practice established and disseminated by previous projects, and embedding disability provision firmly within institutions (HEFCE, 1996c). These projects are ongoing at the time of compiling this report and therefore it has not been possible to consider their findings here. However, one project (on pre-assessment screening for dyslexia) has published an interim report (Singleton, Trotter and Smart, 1998) that will be considered in Chapter 8.

4.2.3   Conferences

During the period November 1994 to September 1998 the members of the Working Party have enthusiastically participated in many conferences and other events that have had some bearing on the remit of the Working Party. At these events, members of the Working Party have frequently been called upon to give keynote addresses, deliver papers, organise workshop sessions or chair discussions. These activities have formed a very important part of the consultation process, for they have enabled members of the Working Party to gather additional information and discuss issues, as well as gaining reactions of delegates to the findings of the Working Party. During the latter stages of the Working Party's activities, while this report was being prepared for publication, such events facilitated a wide dissemination of the contents of the report and its recommendations in summary form to the higher education sector.

The principal events are listed below in chronological order.

International Conference on Dyslexia in Higher Education, organised by the University of Plymouth, held at Dartington Hall, Devon, November 1994. Eight members of the Working Party attended and six presented papers. It was at this conference that idea for the Working Party was first mooted, and its basic aims and objectives discussed. These papers were subsequently published in the proceedings of the conference.

British Educational Technology and Training Exhibition and Conference (BETT), January 1995. Two members of the Working Party presented a joint paper on computer support for students with dyslexia.

Conference on Dyslexic Adults in Work, in Study and Job-seeking, organised by the British Dyslexia Association, London, January 1995. One member of the Working Party presented a paper.

Dyslexia Matters. Conference organised by University of Southampton, March 1995. Two members of the Working Party presented papers.

British Dyslexia Association Conference on Computers and Dyslexia, University of Nottingham, April 1995. Four members of the Working Party presented papers.

Skill North-East Network Group Meeting, Bretton Hall, Wakefield, May 1995. One member of the Working Party presented a paper.

Matters of the Mind. Conference organised by Edinburgh Dyslexia Association, September 1995. Two members of the Working Party attended and one presented a paper.

Skill National Conference on Adult Disability, Leamington Spa, October 1995. Four members of the Working Party attended and one presented a paper.

Skill National Conference on Disability in Further and Higher Education, London, December 1995. Three members of the Working Party attended and one presented a paper.

British Psychological Society Conference, London , December 1995. Two members of the Working Party attended and both presented papers.

British Educational Technology and Training Exhibition and Conference (BETT), January 1996. One member of the Working Party presented a paper.

Conference on Dyslexia in Higher Education organised jointly by Skill and the University of Huddersfield, held at the University of Huddersfield, January 1996. Ten members of the Working Party attended and all presented papers. This provided a unique opportunity for the members of the Working Party to share its developing ideas with a large number of representatives from HEIs from across the country, and to gauge reactions to these. The proceedings of this event were published in *Dyslexic students in higher education: practical responses to student and institutional need.* (Edited by C. Stephens, Huddersfield: Skill and the University of Huddersfield, 1996).

Technology, Disability and Learning. Conference organised by the National Organisation for Adult Learning, Wolverhampton, February 1996. Two members of the Working Party attended and presented papers.

International Research Conference on Dyslexia in Adults held at Gregynog, Wales, organised by the University of Swansea, April 1996. One member of the Working Party presented a paper. A collection of papers from this conference was subsequently published as a special issue of the *Journal of Research in Reading* (Beaton, McDougall and Singleton, 1997). Much of the research presented at this conference addressed issues concerning psychological assessment of students with dyslexia.

100 Years of Dyslexia Conference, held in London in April 1996 and organised by the Adult Dyslexia Organisation. Three members of the Working Party attended and presented papers.

Conference on Dyslexia in Further and Higher Education, held at Roehampton College of Higher Education, June 1996. Four members of the Working Party attended and two presented papers.

British Dyslexia Association Conference on Computers and Dyslexia, University of Surrey, Sept. 1996. Four members of the Working Party attended, and one presented a paper.

Adult Dyslexia: the way forward. Conference organised by the Adult Dyslexia Organisation in Birmingham, October 1996. One member of the Working Party attended and presented a paper.

2nd International Conference on Dyslexia in Higher Education, organised by the University of Plymouth, held at Dartington Hall, Devon, November 1996. Six members of the Working Party attended and four presented papers. The results of the national survey (see Chapter 3) were presented and the reactions of representatives from many HEIs sought. These papers were subsequently published in the proceedings of the conference.

Conference on Dyslexia in Higher Education organised by Skill, and held in Manchester, November 1996. Three members of the Working Party attended and one presented a paper and chaired a discussion session.

National Network of Disability Co-ordinators (Scotland), December 1996, held at University of Dundee. One member of the Working Party presented a paper.

British Educational Technology and Training Exhibition and Conference (BETT), January 1997. One member of the Working Party presented a paper on computer support for students with dyslexia.

4th International Conference on Dyslexia, organised by the British Dyslexia Association, York, April 1997. Nine members of the Working Party attended and seven presented papers. In special forum, the results of the national survey (see Chapter 3) were presented and the reactions of professionals working in higher education nationally and internationally to the outline recommendations of the Working were sought.

4th World Congress on Dyslexia, Halkidiki, Greece, September 1997. One member presented a paper on the findings of the Working Party.

Conference on Dyslexia – Widening Participation in Education. Organised by Bilston Community College, West Midlands, October 1997. One member presented a paper on the findings of the Working Party.

Conference on Dyslexia in Higher Education held at Bangor University, October 1997. Two members of the Working Party attended and one presented a paper on the findings of the Working Party.

Annual Conference of the Education Section of the British Psychological Society, University of Warwick, November 1997. One member of the Working Party attended and presented a paper entitled 'How adequately does your institution deal with dyslexic students?'

Skill National Conference on Adult Disability, London, December 1997. Two members of the Working Party attended and one presented a paper on the findings of the Working Party.

National Conference on Continuing Education, Oslo, Norway, May 1998. Invited paper presented by a member of the Working Party on the findings of the Working Party.

Bolton College of Higher Education, June 1998. One member of the Working Party led a seminar on the findings of the Working Party and its implications for the examination of students with dyslexia.

University College, Worcester, July 1998. One member of the Working Party ran a regional seminar on the findings of the Working Party.

International Conference on Adult Disability, Israel, July 1998. One member of the Working Party attended and presented two papers, which will appear in the conference proceedings, to be published in 1999.

Annual Conference of the Education Section of the British Psychological Society, University of Exeter, September 1998. One member of the Working Party presented a paper entitled 'In or out? Dyslexic students and higher education' based on the findings of the Working Party.

4.2.4   *Organisations and institutions other than HEIs*

The Working Party also obtained information and advice from many organisations and institutions that are professionally concerned with dyslexia, particularly those organisations and institutions that have a direct involvement in the identification of dyslexia in adults or the support of dyslexic students. Information was obtained in a variety of ways, including correspondence, consultation with representatives and examination of material published by the organisations and institutions. These organisations (listed below) are referred to at various points in the text of this Report. Addresses of these organisations are given in Section 14.4.

Adult Development and Skills Centre. Based in London, this Centre provides professional assessment, counselling and training for adult dyslexics. One of the members of the Working Party is a director of this Centre.

Adult Dyslexia Organisation (ADO). The ADO is a national charitable organisation founded in 1991 and run by dyslexic people, from a base in London. It has a network of local groups and overseas branches and provides information, counselling and support for adults who have dyslexia, through a telephone helpline, website, regional groups, conferences, and a quarterly magazine *Dyslexia 2000.* Many ADO members are students in higher education and it is developing a mentoring service that will interlink dyslexic students for group support. By invitation, the ADO provided a representative on the Working Party. [*www.futurenet.co.uk/charity/ado*]

Association of Educational Psychologists (AEP). This is the professional association for practising educational psychologists. Most educational psychologists who are employed by LEAs belong to the AEP. The AEP publishes a journal, *Educational Psychology in Practice.*

British Computer Society Disability Group. This is a membership organisation that provides information and advice on technology support to adults with disabilities. It produces a quarterly journal called *Ability,* which often includes articles about new technology that can be of benefit to dyslexic students in higher education. [*www.bcs.org.uk*]

British Dyslexia Association (BDA). This is the national charity for people with dyslexia. The BDA provides support and information to adults, children and their families, to professionals working in the education and health services, and to employers. The BDA was founded in 1972 and now has over 100 affiliated local dyslexia associations. From its office in Reading, the BDA runs a national helpline telephone service and a website. The BDA publishes a magazine, *Dyslexia Contact,* which has a circulation of 15,000, an annual *Dyslexia Handbook*, and together with Wiley publishes the international research journal *Dyslexia*. The BDA accredits training courses for specialist dyslexia teachers (AMBDA) and has recently extended this to cover teaching students with dyslexia in FE and HE. The BDA produced a discussion document, *Help for Dyslexic Adults* (BDA, 1997), to help shape its support for adults with dyslexia, including those in higher education. The BDA also publishes a range of booklets on technology support for people with dyslexia, including *IT for Dyslexic Adults* (1998) and *Study Skills with ITC* (1998) The BDA nominated its Education Director for membership of the Working Party. Another member of the Working Party is a Vice-President of the BDA, a further member sits on the BDA Accreditation Board for Teacher Training, and the Chair of the Working Party is a member of the BDA Computer Committee. [*www.bda-dyslexia.org.uk*]

British Psychological Society (BPS). This is the professional association for all qualified psychologists. It has three grades of membership: Fellow (FBPsS), Associate Fellow (AFBPsS) and Member (MBPsS). It is empowered by law to maintain the *Register of Chartered Psychologists.* The BPS has an overall membership of over 27,000, including over 8,000 Chartered Psychologists. The Society operates a number of divisions, including the Division of Educational and Child Psychology (DECP) and the Scottish Division of Educational Psychology (SDEP). The BPS publishes several research journals (including the *Journal of Educational Psychology*) as well as a monthly bulletin, *The Psychologist.* Five members of the Working Party are members of the BPS (one FBPsS, three AFBPsS, and one MBPsS). Two are members of the DECP. Four of these are also Chartered Psychologists, and one is a member of the BPS Steering Committee on Test Standards. A Working Party of the DECP is currently preparing the report with recommendations for educational psychologists on assessment of dyslexia. [*www.bps.org.uk*]

Computer Centre for People with Disabilities. This is based at the University of Westminster and provides advice and support for disabled undergraduates as well as those who are employed or unemployed. As an ACCESS Centre it conducts assessments of disability needs and specialises in the use of assistive technology to support dyslexia and other disabilities. The director of this centre is a member of the Working Party. [*www.wmin.ac.uk/ccpd/*]

Dyslexia Institute (DI). This is a non-profit-making company with charitable status that was established in 1972. It offers assessments, tuition for children and adults, teacher training and support. It has a head office in Staines and 23 main centres distributed throughout the country as well as 147 teaching outposts. The Dyslexia Institute employs 217 full- and part-time staff, plus 70 consulting psychologists who carry out about 7,000 child and adult assessments per year. Some of these psychologists carry out assessments for HEIs. The Dyslexia Institute provides an Advanced Postgraduate Diploma Course for specialist dyslexia teachers; currently (1998) 135 teachers are taking this course. Teachers who have completed this Diploma are eligible to join the *Dyslexia Institute Guild*, which currently has over 1,000 members. The Dyslexia Institute publishes the journal, *Dyslexia Review*. Two members of the Working Party have been involved in the delivery of Dyslexia Institute services, including psychological assessment, teaching and teacher training. [*www.dyslexia-inst.org.uk*]

Dyslexia Unit, Bangor. This is an independent unit within the School of Psychology of the University of Bangor, that offers assessment, advice, support, tuition, and teacher training. It is one of the longest standing centres that provides facilities for assessment, counselling and support of HE students with dyslexia. The Student Tutor/Counsellor of the Bangor Dyslexia Unit is a member of the Working Party.

Helen Arkell Dyslexia Centre (HADC). This is an independent charity based in Farnham, Surrey, that provides a wide variety of educational services for people of all ages with dyslexia, including educational and psychological assessment; speech therapy assessment; specialist tuition; tuition in specialist skills (e.g. touch typing); parent support sessions. The Centre also provides information and training for schools, and runs training courses leading to professional qualifications, and conferences. Research work is being carried out into more effective methods of identifying and teaching people of all ages with dyslexia. One member of the Working Party is an Honorary Consultant to HADC, another has successfully completed the Centre's Diploma in Dyslexia in HE and FE.

Hornsby International Dyslexia Centre. This Centre is a registered charity, based in London. It is involved in all aspects of helping the child and adult with dyslexia, including assessment, counselling, tuition and a wide range of training courses. It is particularly well-known for the *Hornsby Diploma*, a qualification in teaching pupils and adults with dyslexia that is taught by correspondence as well as on a part-time basis at the Centre. One member of the Working Party has contributed to the correspondence materials of the Hornsby Diploma, and another has been involved in teacher training at the Centre.

London Language and Literacy Unit. This unit is based at Southwark College, London. As well as specialising in dyslexia, this Unit works in the areas of family literacy, bilingualism, ESOL and basic skills. It offers consultancy and training, and produces a range of specialist publications in these areas, including *Demystifying Dyslexia* (M. Krupska and C Klein, 1995). The unit runs a training course on developing learning support for students with dyslexia in FE, HE and adult learning.

Moray House Centre for Specific Learning Difficulties (Dyslexia). This Centre, based in Edinburgh, runs a post-graduate course for FE and HE staff on dyslexia. It also provides psychological assessments for students in FE and HE and gives recommendations for support. The Co-ordinator of the Centre is a member of the Working Party.

National Federation of Access Centres (NFAC). This is a national network of specialist centres in further and higher education which seeks to support and empower students with disabilities, particularly through the use of assistive technology. There are currently 28 Access Centres distributed across the country, which provide general assessment services and facilities for training in the use of assistive technology for disabilities. Not all Access Centres have dyslexia specialists at the present time, although this is an objective of the Federation. Two members of the Working Party are managers of Access Centres, one of whom is the current chair of the NFAC. [*www.wmin.ac.uk/ccpd/*]

Skill (The National Bureau for Students with Disabilities). This is a national organisation for the support of students with disabilities in further and higher education. It has a London office and regional network groups covering the country. It receives some government funding and has representation on various committees, including the HEFCE Advisory Group on Students with Learning Difficulties and Disabilities (SLDD). Skill organises conferences, workshops, exhibitions and training events on disability, and liaises with other relevant organisations. It also produces many publications to help disabled students and their institutions, including the annual guide *Higher Education and Disability*. Skill has also produced a *Disability Directory for LEA Awards Officers* (1997a), and *The Coordinator's Handbook* (1997b) which include basic information on the needs of students with dyslexia and guidance on the preparation of applications for the DSA being made by dyslexic students.

4.2.5 *Individuals and institutions*

The Working Party received letters and other documents from numerous individuals and institutions, particularly from parents of students with dyslexia and from personnel in HEIs. Some of these communications were requesting information and others were expressing their concerns about perceived inequities or adequacies in procedures or facilities available to students with dyslexia. Some submissions were stimulated by an article about the Working Party's activities and plans, which appeared in the *Times Higher Education Supplement* in March 1996. Others came as a result of presentations which members of the Working Party had made at conferences. Yet others were cases in which individuals were following up contact which had been established through the regional consultative meetings with representatives of HEIs (see Section 4.1). Several HEIs and institutions of further education submitted copies of documents that they used in their institutions (e.g. information on dyslexia provided for students and staff). Some centres involved with teacher training for dyslexia submitted information about their training courses. Much of this information has been very helpful to the Working Party, but lack of time has precluded any systematically organisation of it. Nevertheless, reference has been made in this report to this material where relevant.

5   Institutional and national policy

5.1   Issues, problems and challenges

5.1.1   Provision for disability

The report of the Dearing Committee commented that *'...higher education does not have a particularly well-focused understanding of disability'* at the present time. *In particular, it was noted that '...problems associated with disability are often seen as additional burdens by hard-pressed academic staff; as having troublesome resource consequences by prudent administrators; and as presenting intractable priority-setting dilemmas for senior management.'* Finally, it was observed that *'...universities would be wise to develop a more considered stance on disability over time'.* (Dearing, 1997, Sub-report 6, Section 4.17).

It is clear from these observations that addressing dyslexia, as a category of disability in higher education, requires the development of institutional policy that embodies strong and explicit commitment to disability provision, and acceptance of the consequences that this will inevitably have for resources, academic training and awareness within the institution as a whole.

5.1.2   Numbers of students with dyslexia

HESA statistics indicate that students with dyslexia currently constitute 0.7% of all students entering higher education and that this represents the largest individual disability category[10]. This is based on the numbers of students indicating on the UCAS form that they have a disability. In Chapter 3, figures on the overall incidence of students with dyslexia in higher education were carefully considered. The national survey carried out by the Working Party revealed an overall incidence of dyslexia in the student population of 1.35%. Incidence figures varied across the categories, from 0.95% in traditional universities, 1.31% in the new universities and 1.54% in the colleges. Rather more of these students were already known to be dyslexic on entry to higher education (57%), the remainder (43%) being identified or diagnosed as dyslexic after admission. Allowing for a margin of error and for the fact that, in all probability, a few students with dyslexia in higher education are *never* properly identified, it was concluded that the *best estimate* of the incidence of dyslexia in higher education in the UK at the present time lies somewhere between 1.2% and 1.5% of all students, i.e. about 20,400 – 25,500 students in total. Given that the accepted incidence of dyslexia in the general population is 4%, there would appear to be an under-representation of persons with dyslexia in higher education.

Based on the above calculations, we may expect that a university of average size (with about 15,000 students) will be required to provide for the special academic needs of between 180 and 225 students with dyslexia. This is not an insignificant number. Amongst those universities which have been able to provide recent figures for the Working Party, several have reported larger numbers than this.

5.1.3   Challenges to policy and procedure

Every HEI will find that it cannot abdicate responsibility for establishing proper and effective policies and procedures that address the needs of this sizeable group of disabled students. This will necessarily include raising staff awareness, ensuring equal opportunities in admissions and examinations,

---

[10] When 'unseen disabilities' (such as diabetes, epilepsy and asthma) are regarded as separate categories, rather than as one category (as is the case in HESA statistics). Higher Education Statistics Agency Data Report: *Students in Higher Education Institutions,* 1996/97.

providing full access to learning, and dealing with students' needs for advice and counselling. In trying to make provision in each of these areas, the institution will inevitably find itself confronting the practicalities of (a) ensuring that students who *claim* to have dyslexia do, in fact, have dyslexia, and (b) checking whether students who are struggling with their studies have problems that are due to unidentified dyslexia. These matters are addressed in Chapter 8.

5.1.4 *Disability Discrimination Act 1995*

The implementation of the *Disabilities Discrimination Act 1995* presents a further important challenge to HEIs. All HEIs are required to produce Disability Statements, outlining their commitment, provisions and future developments for students with disabilities. In order to produce a satisfactory Disability Statement and make appropriate provision for students with all disabilities, including dyslexia, HEIs require policy and procedural guidelines to embed dyslexia support within the institution as a whole. Subsumed within this belief is the need to raise the awareness of teaching and support staff regarding such policies and guidelines, through both formal and informal channels. The maintenance of professional and academic standards must underpin this process, for whilst being mindful of the needs of this particular student group, credibility for academic achievement and value of the award must be upheld. At the time that this report was going to press, new directives from HEFCE were expected regarding the content of Disability Statements.

5.1.5 *Quality and resources*

The current higher education climate in the UK is one in which institutions are progressively being ranked by various indices of quality. This generates a tension between, on the one hand, the rhetoric of equality of opportunity in HE (including encouragement by funding councils to increase access for students with disabilities) and, on the other, the reality that accepting students with dyslexia in the absence of considerable extra (ring-fenced) resources puts additional demands on staff already under pressure. Some HEIs have reported that the discussion paper *What are graduates? Clarifying the attributes of graduateness* (HEQC, 1996; see Section 1.1.5.1) created adverse effects because of its message that literacy disabilities were incompatible with the concept of 'graduateness', and therefore, by implication, that students with dyslexia have no place in higher education. In the past few years these debates have been rehearsed in examination boards and policy committees of HEIs all over the country. In many cases, decisions are being taken on these matters by personnel who have little, if any, real understanding of disability issues.

To meet this challenge there will be a need for trained, experienced personnel within each institution to provide leadership, co-ordination, staff training and development. This raises the issue of the lack of accredited training for staff involved in support of institutional policies for students with dyslexia. In many institutions, the lack of a named and trained co-ordinator with responsibility for students with dyslexia is a major barrier to the development and implementation of an effective policy. This concern is reflected in the results of the national survey (see Chapter 3) and of the findings from the regional and national consultative meetings (Chapter 4).

Overarching all these facets of an improved institutional provision for dyslexia is the need for resourcing. At the present time, the DSA pays for a large proportion of the individual support that students with dyslexia receive, whether this be technological support or study skills tuition. If, in future, every HEI is expected to make 'base level' provision for students with disabilities, we may see the value of the DSA reduced, and the resourcing implications for HEIs will be correspondingly increased. But even without establishment of 'base level' expectations, effective support for students with dyslexia will not happen in the absence of commitment by the institution to providing the necessary personnel and resources. For example, before students can obtain the DSA and access provision that will meet their needs, trained personnel (e.g. a disability officer or student services staff) are required to evaluate the nature and extent of the impairment caused by the disability and give advice and support in the complex and often bewildering process of applying for the DSA. Furthermore, support provision for dyslexia (or for any disability, for that matter) cannot be really effective unless tutors and lecturers are given staff development so that they have some strategies for enabling those students to gain full access to learning.

5.1.6   Opening the 'floodgates'?

Some senior managers and academics may worry that a pro-active support policy for students with dyslexia, incorporating widespread availability of information about dyslexia provision, will 'open the floodgates' and create demand that is impossible to fulfil. Although the incidence of students coming forward for advice seems to be somewhat higher in those HEIs where there is a successful staff development programme and vigorous promotion of dyslexia awareness, and although the numbers of students requesting screening assessments is reported to be rising in many HEIs,[11] there is no evidence of a 'flood' of students clamouring for identification and support. At present, the incidence of dyslexia in higher education is about one-third of the incidence of the condition in the general population. The numbers are significant but easily manageable with the implementation of considered policy and well-planned procedures. Over the next few years we may see a continuing slight rise in numbers of students with dyslexia in HEIs but this would not be undesirable. Quite the contrary, it would be entirely in keeping with the intention of the higher education funding councils to increase access for all students with disabilities.

5.1.7   Conclusions

Provision for students with dyslexia needs to be part of an institutional framework of disability support that is embedded within the academic ethos of the establishment and which is reflected in the Disability Statement. This framework should encompass the fundamental principles of widening student access, equal opportunities, and maintenance of academic quality, as well as the recognition that disability provision requires serious financial and managerial commitment.

5.2   Proposals on good practice

5.2.1   Embedding dyslexia support

All HEIs require policy and procedural guidelines to embed dyslexia support. The maintenance of professional and academic standards must underpin this process for whilst being mindful of the needs of this particular student group, credibility for academic achievement and value of the award must be upheld at all times. Each institution should have a clear general policy setting out regulations, procedures and guidelines, as appropriate, for the identification and support of students with dyslexia. Within that policy, dyslexia should be explicitly recognised both as a disability and as a special educational need. It will necessarily be realistic in terms of present financial and resource constraints, but should have future development built into it in terms of intent and regular review.

   The general policy should make reference to, but not necessarily provide detail in every respect of, all the following basic areas of concern:

- staff development and awareness

- admissions

- identification (including screening assessment and diagnostic assessment)

- evaluation of needs and provision of learning support (including technological support)

- counselling

- examinations and assessments

- careers advice.

---

[11] A subsequent survey revealed that 73% of HEIs carrying out routine pre-assessment screening for dyslexia reported that the numbers of students coming forward for screening is rising (Singleton, Trotter and Smart, 1998).

The policy on students with dyslexia should be incorporated into the institution's Disability Statement, published under the requirements of the *Disability Discrimination Act, 1995*, and should be included or referred to in the disability section of the equal opportunities policy of the institution. The policy should ideally apply across the whole institution, but any variations to that policy within particular sections of the institution should be justified and made public.

The policy should acknowledge the individual's right to confidentiality and should make explicit the procedures by which information can be relayed from one section of the institution to another (e.g. from the Disability Office to the student's department or faculty). It is good practice to make the student aware of the normal channels of communication within the institution, and of the benefits of the student's tutor or supervision having knowledge about the student's dyslexia. However, if, after such procedures have been discussed, students do not wish others within the institution to be made aware of their dyslexia, this wish should be respected.

5.2.2 *Overall co-ordination of support*

Before any HEI can address issues concerning provision for students with dyslexia and implement an effective staff development programme, it must first address the question: Who is to be in charge? The lack of overall co-ordination by a suitably qualified and experienced member of staff makes it extremely difficult for the complex issues which will arise to be resolved in an efficient, well-structured and authoritative manner. Consequently, the Working Party advocates that every HEI should appoint a member of staff with overall explicit responsibility within the institution for students with dyslexia, that person having qualifications, training and/or experience relevant to this responsibility.

In some HEIs, co-ordination of dyslexia support comes within the overall responsibility of the member of staff who manages disability provision within the institution (e.g. the Disabilities Officer, Head of Student Services, or Head of Student Support). In other institutions, it is the Dyslexia Support Tutor or the individual in charge of learning support. The title or overall post held by that person, and whether the individual has responsibilities other than those for students with dyslexia, are not especially important. What is crucial is that the person has knowledge and understanding about the nature of dyslexia, how it can be identified, how it can affect students studying in higher education, and the range of support that would be suitable. The responsibilities of the co-ordinator will extend beyond the implementation (and perhaps delivery of) staff development. The co-ordinator should spearhead the institution's approach to provision for students with dyslexia, and be responsible for initiating and following through the implementation of the recommendations contained in this Report, including establishing and maintaining the institution's general policy on dyslexia.

There should be a central database containing the names of, and other relevant details concerning, the members of staff in HEIs with overall responsibility within their institutions for students with dyslexia. The Higher Education Funding Councils would be the obvious bodies to maintain such information, via the Quality Assurance Agency (QAA).

5.2.3 *Resourcing and monitoring provision*

The policy on dyslexia and its associated practices require the backing of central management in terms of finances and resources, and of encouragement and promotion, otherwise its intentions may be frustrated and the institution's achievements in this area limited. Budgets should be set for the various components of the process, especially for identification and support provision.

Provision should also be made for monitoring the special services and facilities available to students with dyslexia. This serves two purposes: (a) quality control and (b) to provide data for future planning. Many HEIs have a Disability Committee, which may be the most appropriate body to take responsibility for monitoring provision and for making recommendations for improvement. What is important is that the body charged with monitoring dyslexia provision should be able to have its views considered at a high level within the institution, and therefore should have access to the principal governing bodies of the institution, such as a general policy committee, Senate or Council.

5.3   Recommendations on institutional and national policy

1) Dyslexia should be explicitly recognised by all HEIs both as a disability and as a special educational need.

2) Each institution should have a clear general policy setting out regulations, procedures and guidelines, as appropriate, for the identification and support of students with dyslexia. The general policy should make reference to, but not necessarily provide detail in every respect of, all the following basic areas of concern: staff development and awareness, admissions, identification, evaluation of needs, provision of learning support (including technological support), counselling, examinations and assessments, and careers advice.

3) The institution's general policy on dyslexia should:

   a) be incorporated into the institution's Disability Statement, published under the requirements of the *Disability Discrimination Act, 1995;*

   b) be referred to in the disability section of the equal opportunities policy of the institution;

   c) have the backing of central management in terms of finances and resources, and of encouragement and promotion;

   d) apply across the whole institution, with any variations to that policy within particular sections of the institution being clearly stated and justified;

   e) protect confidentiality, and procedures for relaying information should clearly be stated;

   f) cover issues which relate to potential students as well as current ones;

   g) have future development built into it in terms of intent and regular review; and

   h) make provision for monitoring of the special services and facilities available for students with dyslexia in the institution for the purposes of quality control and in order to provide data for future planning.

4) Every HEI should appoint a member of staff with overall explicit responsibility within the institution for students with dyslexia, that person having qualifications, training and/or experience relevant to this responsibility.

5) The Higher Education Funding Councils should maintain a database of the names of, and other relevant details concerning, the members of staff in each HEI with overall responsibility within the institution for students with dyslexia.

6) The Government accepts the recommendation of the Dearing Committee regarding the establishment of an Institute for Learning and Teaching in Higher Education and particularly that the learning needs of students with disabilities should be incorporated within the activities of such an Institute, including being a component of accredited teacher training courses in higher education *(Dearing Report, Recommendations 6, 13 and 14).*

6 Staff development and institutional awareness

6.1 Issues, problems and challenges

Major obstacles to the establishment of effective staff development and awareness of dyslexia within HEIs at the present time appear to be:

- lack of institutional resource and commitment to dyslexia support

- lack of policy and structure

- lack of an overall co-ordinator with appropriate qualifications and experience

- lack of experienced/qualified staff to undertake training of other staff

- lack of knowledge and information about the impact of dyslexia within the HE sector

- pressures and time constraints on members of staff.

6.1.1 Institutional and departmental structure

Students with dyslexia present challenges for academic and support staff, who find themselves having to work with students whose styles of learning may conflict with more traditional teaching methods. These students also have a need for individual support on a continuing basis, which tends to conflict with the modularisation of courses now being seen in most HEIs. The new modularised course structures, in themselves, militate against departmental staff developing and maintaining a holistic view of the student, which can frustrate the support process.

The Dearing Committee noted that at present '...*disability awareness is poorly developed in most HEIs*' (Dearing, 1997, Sub-report 6, Section 4.17). Staff development has to build an ethos of awareness and recognition of the impact of dyslexia on the individual in order to assure that equality of opportunity is integral to and maintained within the institution.

6.1.2 Attitudes of senior management, academic and support staff

Dyslexia is sufficiently complex to evade a quick understanding of the issues that face a student and a department (and staff may be quite unaware of its manifestations). If institutional policies are not in place, staff may not feel sufficiently committed to participate in training. The contrast between obvious intelligence and poor literacy skills evident in the profile of the student with dyslexia may evoke suspiciousness from staff and, in some cases, outright hostility. Senior academics and management staff may reason that an institution seeking to enhance its academic reputation should not allow students who demonstrate literacy difficulties to achieve higher qualifications. They may hesitate to support policies which they consider might undermine their institutional credibility and which run counter to their personal notions of 'graduateness' (see Section 1.1.5.1). Inevitably, senior management responses are dominated by resource and financial constraints which lead to a reluctance to build support into the institutions budgets.

Dyslexia places a burden of responsibility and personal demand for understanding, tolerance and time commitments on academic staff in a climate of increased numbers and reduced tutorial time. Staff may respond with impatience when faced with missed deadlines and badly presented assignments by students when their own deadlines have become so pressured. To develop awareness of the needs of students with dyslexia demands flexibility and understanding at a time when academic staff are under intense pressure. The situation is similar for all support staff who face financial and time constraints in service delivery.

There are still many higher education staff for whom dyslexia is not seen as a relevant issue, especially since policies may not exist to embed the notion of provision for students or to underpin the need for a staff development programme. In this context, the category 'staff' refers not only to academic and managerial staff, but also to staff working in university libraries, computer centres, counselling services, etc. Staff may be unaware of students with dyslexia within their area of responsibility, or the numbers of such students may appear so small as to be trivial. This is particularly true of those academic staff who adhere to more traditional teaching methods and who may hold entrenched views related to student learning.

6.1.3   *Implications for teaching and learning*

In order for teaching and support staff to understand the different learning styles of a student with dyslexia, they need to understand the nature of dyslexia and its impact on higher order learning skills. For example, limitations in short-term (working) memory are likely to affect the student's ability to listen and record simultaneously. Insufficiently clear directions for reading tasks, for example, may involve a student with dyslexia in hours of additional reading and produce extra stress that affects their academic performance. Without raised staff awareness, tutors may resort to non-reflective practice, lack of flexibility and rigid demands for modes of presentation. Deadlines for submission of written work may coincide with exam revision or may overlap between modules.

Issues of this nature may be reduced by awareness of the need for good practice. While staff development may focus on the needs of students with dyslexia, the good practice that is suitable for students with dyslexia will enhance the learning environment of other students as well. Where an institution or department has a clear policy on assessment, extenuating circumstances and study provision, it is more likely to ensure a commitment to staff training.

6.2   Proposals on good practice

6.2.1   *General policy*

A fundamental part of any attempt to address provision for students with dyslexia in higher education is the need to raise the awareness of teaching, support and other staff of the needs of this group of students, and of the policies and guidelines which the institution has decided to follow.

Key issues in staff awareness of dyslexia are:

* attitude of senior management, academic and support staff

* institutional and departmental structure

* the implications for teaching and learning in relation to the dyslexic student group.

Staff development for dyslexia needs to target staff who may not perceive the need for training in relation to dyslexia, as well as targeting those open to the development of their teaching and support skills. It also needs to make the best use of limited time, money and human resource. Mechanisms for ensuring good practice for these students will embrace good practice in the support and teaching of students who do not have dyslexia. To these ends, it is recommended that institutions aim to provide staff development and promotion of institutional awareness on training on three levels: 1) Formal, 2) Informal, and 3) Targeted.

6.2.2   *Formal staff development*

There should be a programme of staff development and awareness within the institution that relates explicitly to provision for students with dyslexia, which should be referred to in the institution's general policy on provision for students with dyslexia. A professional with understanding and experience of dyslexia support should be consulted about the programme of staff development and awareness.

The induction programme for new staff should include:

- general information about dyslexia

- specific information about the provision that is available for students with dyslexia

- advice on the good teaching practice that is most suited to students with dyslexia.

There should be a member of the academic staff within each faculty and/or sub-faculty unit (e.g. school or department) with explicit responsibility for students with dyslexia within that area. Attendance at the programme of staff development and awareness should be compulsory for those members of the academic staff having explicit responsibility for students with dyslexia.

Staff training will only be effective if senior management are willing to address the significance and provide the policy structure to embed and encourage widening understanding and provision for the study requirements of this group of students.

6.2.2.1   Using the faculty/school/departmental structure

This provides an opportunity to target all staff and to explore issues of dyslexia support that are particularly relevant to subject/discipline areas. It can provide a brief overview of dyslexic characteristics and support issues. The opportunity to air problems pertinent to the faculty or department can be a fruitful beginning. It also allows for the identification of staff who may be willing to take a particular role in this area, and those for whom dyslexia information is urgently required to widen their understanding. It also ensures that staff with managerial responsibilities are present. Using a centralised staff development structure, other staff may benefit personally and professionally from general awareness raising sessions open to all personnel.

6.2.2.2   Provision of accredited training

Some staff may be teaching courses or postgraduate modules within an integrated Masters programme. New staff without prior teaching experience in the higher education sector may be involved in the Teaching and Learning in Higher Education Programme. All these offer opportunities for raising awareness of the nature of dyslexia and of improving teaching skills to support students with dyslexia. They also offer opportunities for developing personal qualifications and transferable skills in the area of dyslexia. Programme organisers should be alerted to the need to integrate an understanding of dyslexia within the core structure of such programmes and to identify appropriate staff to deliver training.

The Working Party is especially pleased to note that the Dearing Committee has recommended that all teaching staff in higher education should receive training under a programme accredited by a national organisation (the Institute for Learning and Teaching in Higher Education), and that the learning needs of students with disabilities should be incorporated within the activities of such an Institute, including being a component of accredited teacher training courses in higher education (see Dearing, 1997,, Recommendations 6, 13 and 14). If accepted, these proposals would go a considerable way towards enhancing awareness of higher education teaching staff about dyslexia and enabling them to make learning more accessible for students with dyslexia.

6.2.2.3   Senior management bodies

Papers and presentations to central policy making bodies (e.g. Senate, Council, Academic Boards, Registry) will help to ensure consideration of the needs of students with dyslexia at all levels. Training will only be effective if those in senior management are willing to acknowledge its importance and provide the policy structures to embed and encourage widening understanding and provision. The Dyslexia Support Service needs to provide statistical data to raise awareness. In their applications for resources in a competitive academic environment such data should inform current levels of provision, student numbers and distribution, degree classification, and first destinations.

6.2.3   *Informal staff development*

6.2.3.1   *Networking*

In order to combat possible ambivalence or negativity towards this student group and to reduce the need for costly staff development sessions that do not always succeed in reaching the appropriate staff, it is recommended that there should be a programme of informal staff development. This should arise from the learning needs of individual students and during the establishment of individual assessment requirements. Some more experienced staff may be happy to offer mentoring to colleagues working with individual students with dyslexia.

All appropriate staff of the institution, including academic, academic-related, and administrative staff, should become aware of the institution's policy on dyslexia, of the needs of students with dyslexia, and of the support that is available within the institution. Staff bulletins, newsletters, and poster communications are all helpful ways of disseminating information and raising awareness. Short articles written by staff and students on their dyslexic difficulties may convince and motivate staff support. Liaison with the Students' Union can be extremely beneficial.

Liaison between feeder institutions is advisable as it not only raises awareness of the different support methods available in different sectors, but also improves the understanding of academic expectations in HE which FE and Access Tutors can pass on to their students.

Networking can also take place between HE institutions to inform good practice and to prevent unnecessary duplication of research and development materials. Training packages can be delivered on an inter-institutional basis, as well as by distance mode and the Internet. Skill (The National Bureau for Students with Disabilities) maintains a regional support network that enables disability staff from HEIs within a region to interact and inform one another.

6.2.3.2   *Building on personal experience*

Experience suggests that in many cases initiatives and good practice have stemmed from staff members' personal experience of dyslexia. Their positive and empathic attitude is likely to encourage and reassure their peers in offering support. Frequently these staff have an increased commitment in the delivery of support to students with dyslexia and can play a key role in fostering staff awareness within a department. These staff also provide valuable role models for the students, acknowledging their acceptance within a professional group.

6.2.4   *Targeted staff development*

It is important to establish targeted training of staff so that particular professional groups within the institution identify their key responsibilities and concerns in relation to students with dyslexia.

6.2.4.1   *Admissions staff*

Admissions staff are crucial in aiding students with dyslexia and departments to make informed decisions concerning appropriate courses and institutions. Consequently, admissions staff need to:

- understand the process of identification of dyslexia and educational psychologists' reports
- understand the implications of dyslexia on course choice, course delivery, mode of delivery and on assessment
- know what structures are in place in the institution to support the student.

These issues are addressed in more detail in Chapter 7.

6.2.4.2   *Teaching staff*

All academic staff should be encouraged to be aware of those aspects of good teaching practice that are especially helpful to students with dyslexia. To achieve this, teaching staff (including postgraduates and research staff who may be involved in teaching) need to:

- understand the learning difficulties of students with dyslexia, including awareness of the difficulties students may have with the organisation of ideas

- be aware of and use alternative methods of delivery that meet the learning styles of students with dyslexia in order to provide equal opportunities of access to the curriculum

- know about specific provision that can assist students with dyslexia to access learning, such as use of photocopied materials, copies of OHPs, early booklists, guidance on issues of presentation and help with organisation of ideas and work

- be given guidance on the marking of work submitted by students with dyslexia and helpful feedback that should be given to such students.

These issues are addressed in more detail in Chapter 9.

6.2.4.3 *Library staff*

Many students with dyslexia find using libraries difficult and stressful, and for these reasons may avoid use of a library, which will hinder their studies. Consequently, library staff need to:

- establish practices which allow students with dyslexia easy access to library facilities

- be aware that students with dyslexia may be under high levels of anxiety and stress when accessing library facilities, and so be instructed in techniques for dealing with this

- consider setting up systems whereby students with dyslexia may identify themselves if they wish (e.g. using different coloured library cards) to obtain additional support

- consider extended loan periods for books and other library materials that may be borrowed for students with dyslexia

- consider providing a range of books on tape

- consider cheaper photocopying costs for students with dyslexia

- consider implementing a system that will enable students with dyslexia to locate books more easily (e.g. floor/section/aisle/shelf referencing by colour – although this should supplement, rather than replace, traditional methods, otherwise it may work to the disadvantage of students who are colour-blind).

6.2.4.4 *Administrative staff*

When preparing and making available administrative information for students and prospective students, all staff should try to be mindful of the needs of students with dyslexia. They should endeavour at all times to make information accessible, particularly where entry procedures, examination arrangements, deadlines for submission of work and access to library resources are concerned.

6.2.4.5 *Student services, welfare and support staff*

Students with dyslexia are likely to need the services of personnel traditionally sited within Student Services. These staff will need to be aware of all of the above but also need to pay particular regard to:

- welfare issues including accommodation and social difficulties

- financial hardship issues, e.g. money management

- organisation issues

- the possibility of stress-related illness

- the need for counselling support

- study skills.

These issues are discussed in more detail in Chapters 9 and 10. In the present climate of special funding from HEFCE for some institutions, these issues may be the remit of a Dyslexia Support Service. If this service is separated by internal structures from those staff offering generic student services support, a culture of awareness, dialogue and referral (with student consent) needs to be fostered to offer an effective overall service to students with dyslexia.

6.2.4.6   *Examinations staff*

Staff in the examinations office and examination invigilators should be aware of the difficulties and needs of students with dyslexia in relation to examinations, and should be involved in staff development on dyslexia. For further coverage of the issues concerned, see Chapter 11.

6.2.4.7   *Careers staff*

Careers staff will need to give appropriate advice on courses and careers, highlighting particular skills required and relating these to the dyslexic student's profile of strengths and deficits. It is essential they understand the complexities of dyslexia. For further discussion and recommendations on this topic, see Chapter 12.

6.3   Recommendations on staff development and institutional awareness

1. All appropriate staff of each HEI, including academic, academic-related, and administrative staff, should become aware of the institution's policy on dyslexia, of the needs of students with dyslexia, and of the support that is available within the institution.

2. There should be a member of the academic staff within each faculty and/or sub-faculty unit (e.g. school or department) with explicit responsibility for students with dyslexia within that area.

3. There should be a member of the administrative staff within each of the relevant sections of academic services (i.e. administration, library, examinations, careers) with explicit responsibility for students with dyslexia within that area.

4. There should be a programme of staff development and awareness within the institution that:

    a)   relates explicitly to provision for students with dyslexia;

    b)   should be referred to in the institution's general policy on provision for students with dyslexia;

    c)   has been constructed with the advice of a professional with understanding and experience of dyslexia support.

5. Attendance at the programme of staff development and awareness for dyslexia should be compulsory for those members of the academic and administrative staff who have explicit responsibility for students with dyslexia.

6. The induction programme for new staff should include information about the provision that is available for students with dyslexia.

7. All academic staff should be encouraged to be aware of those aspects of good teaching practice that are especially helpful to students with dyslexia.

8. When preparing and making administrative available information for students and prospective students, all appropriate staff of the institution should try to be mindful of the needs of students with dyslexia. They should endeavour at all times to make such information accessible, particularly where entry procedures, examination arrangements, deadlines for submission of work and access to library resources are concerned.

7 Admission to higher education

7.1 Issues, problems and challenges

7.1.1 *Admissions policy and disclosure of dyslexia*

The Government, the funding councils, and the Dearing Committee all wish to see increased access to higher education for people with disabilities. This has implications for resources, for staff training, for the DSA, and for admissions policies of HEIs. The Disability Statement produced by each HEI should state the admissions policy with respect to students with disabilities.[12] The national survey revealed that only twelve of the 195 responding institutions (6%) said that they *did not* admit students with dyslexia to *all* courses (see Section 3.2.1). Ten of these twelve institutions offered an explanation of this policy. In seven cases this was in respect of teaching courses, and in three cases in respect of medically-related courses (including pharmacy). There are obviously many more courses of a teaching-related or medically-related nature than are represented in this group of 12 HEIs, and many of them responded to the questionnaire. This raises a number of important questions. What admissions policy is *actually* being operated by the others? Do they admit students with dyslexia? If so, why are some teaching and medical courses prepared to accept students with dyslexia and others not? Do some, in fact, operate a covert ban?

For prospective students with dyslexia there are important decisions to be made as to whether there should be a declaration of dyslexia in the UCAS form. The Dearing Report observed that *'Some applicants fear that disclosure may prejudice the likelihood of being offered a place.'* (Dearing, 1997, Sub-report 6, Section 4.8). There is no compulsion to disclose. If it turns out that students with dyslexia are not welcome on certain courses at some institutions (either explicitly or implicitly) then students with dyslexia who would like to gain entry to those courses might be advised *not* to declare that they have dyslexia. If they then subsequently gain admission, what are the implications of a 'discovery' of dyslexia at a later date? Might they even be denied a degree?

7.1.2 *National implications*

The issues in this matter are highly complex and cannot be resolved by this Working Party. Nor are they matters which HEIs can necessarily resolve on an individual institutional basis. They impinge on the responsibilities of various national bodies for these professions, including those which oversee medicine, nursing, pharmacy, and teacher education and which have a role in the accreditation of training for those professions. There is a potential conflict here between (a) the spirit of the *Disability Discrimination Act*, which seeks to promote equality of opportunity in employment, (b) the desire of the Higher Education Funding Councils to widen access to higher education for students with disabilities, and (c) the responsibilities of various professional bodies to the public to ensure that their members have competencies which are deemed appropriate to their professions.

We can perhaps distinguish the situation in the teaching profession from that in the medically-related professions. In the teaching profession, the problem seems to centre on the general desire for all teachers to have good literacy skills in order to be able to deliver the curriculum. There also appear to be some concerns that teachers with dyslexia might be unable to find employment after qualifying. On the other hand, the presence in the teaching profession of individuals who have dyslexia could be argued to be desirable on the grounds that could promote a greater awareness and understanding of pupils who have dyslexia, as well as models of achievement for such pupils. These issues have been discussed in greater depth by Morgan and Rooney (1997).

---

[12] HEFCE Circular 8/96 – Specifications for Disability Statements required from Institutions.

In the medically-related professions the concerns in this regard appear to be about the possibility of errors being made by persons with dyslexia when prescribing medication or carrying out treatment. Such errors might arise from problems in reading and writing, transposition of digits in numbers, and failures of working memory, especially in situations of emergency when decisions have to be made quickly. Even if a student with dyslexia progresses satisfactorily through a course of professional medical training, a particular official may still bear the responsibility for certifying that the student is 'competent to practice'. This is the situation in nurse training, for example. To what extent might the official (or their employers) be held legally liable for any subsequent professional mistake of the person who has been accredited if a court holds that the mistake was probably 'due to' the person's dyslexia and that it was known by the official that this person had dyslexia? Contemplation of such a scenario might incline those in charge of medically-related training to decline admission for students with dyslexia. On the other hand, it is unlikely that there aren't individuals with dyslexia already successfully employed in various branches of the medical professions, which may indicate that there are strategies which these individuals have developed which have enabled them to function efficiently in their employment despite having dyslexia. If such individuals were studied, we might be in a better position to help other students with dyslexia who wish to enter these professions.

It is regrettable that some students with dyslexia believe that they have to be covert about their dyslexia because of the detrimental effect that it may have on their chances of being accepted for a higher education course or of subsequently being offered employment in the profession for which they have trained. It would appear that the national bodies concerned with teacher education and medically-related education have barely begun to address these very important issues. There may well be other professions to which this issue applies but which are not yet fully aware of the matter nor of its wider social and political implications. Sooner or later, this is something that all professions will have to address, and it is preferable that this is done before the stimulus is litigation either based on the Disability Discrimination Act, or arising from action in professional negligence.

7.1.3   *Information regarding support provision*

Different HEIs offer different levels of support for students with dyslexia. The majority cannot offer cohesive support and provision throughout the institution, because of the absence of funding or policy structures. Others may have greater numbers of students with dyslexia because of their greater overall size or their reputation for having support mechanisms in place. Potential students need to be able to make informed choices about:

- whether they want to attend an establishment that offers support

- their eligibility for that support

- the nature of the support offered within specific departments

- whether they want to go to a particular university because of the course/location irrespective of the support

- whether they wish to decline support in the first instance and try to 'go it alone' and whether they would be eligible to re-enter the support network should they chose or need to.

The extent to which HEIs specify the nature and amount of support provided for students with dyslexia on the Disability Statement is a matter of debate. On the one hand, HEIs that have good provision may feel inclined to broadcast this in the expectation of enhancing recruitment of students. On the other hand, there may be worries regarding the institution's ability to maintain such facilities in the face of future financial uncertainties and reliance on a small number of specially qualified staff. What would be the outcome if a student with dyslexia enrols at a particular university because of support facilities that have been declared on the institution's Disability Statement and such facilities are subsequently unavailable? What right of action would that student have against the university? If HEIs respond to these worries by producing Disability Statements that are vague and unhelpful to students with disabilities who are deciding where to apply, then one of the principal purposes of that part of the *Disability Discrimination Act* will have been frustrated and HEIs may be less motivated to improve facilities.

7.1.4   *The admissions process*

Admission officers or tutors may be making choices to invite or reject students with dyslexia without the mechanisms in place to inform that decision. Whilst they may seek further evidence to support the application of a student with dyslexia – e.g. a psychologist's report – they may lack the experience to interpret the information that is available to them. It is also unlikely that the report will be related to a particular course of study, the mode of assessment used, the availability of support mechanisms, and the competency required of the student on entry. A further issue is that of the discrepancy that can occur between predicted and achieved 'A' level grades, which often has particular relevance for late admission during the clearing process, with the consequences of less preparation for entry on the part of the student. This can disadvantage *any* student entering via the clearing process, but the reduction of time and opportunities for information sharing prior to entry may have more serious implications for the student with dyslexia. Under these circumstances, mistakes regarding suitability of courses and misunderstandings about support available are more likely.

If the 'traditional' student with dyslexia (i.e. 18 year old having completed 'A' level study) has experienced recognition, support and examination provision as a standard response to their dyslexia throughout their schooling, their self esteem, coping strategies and modes of learning may be sufficient to sustain them through transition to higher education, providing they are met with a similar degree of acceptance and value. Other students may have received less favourable responses to their difficulties in the field of study. This is often true of those students who have recently been diagnosed as dyslexic. They may carry additional burdens of guilt, anger and low self-esteem resulting from failed opportunities, poor peer relationships, unsupportive education and familial dismissal of their abilities. For mature dyslexic students, pressure of family responsibilities during studying, may add to the problems (Riddick, Farmer and Sterling, 1997).

7.2   Proposals on good practice

7.2.1   *Equal opportunities*

The provisions of the *Disability Discrimination Act 1995* imply that only where there is good justification should any individual with dyslexia be excluded from admission to a course of education or training or, having successfully completed such training, be excluded from employment within any profession. All HEIs should maintain and publish an admissions policy that does not discriminate against students with dyslexia, except in those subjects and areas of study for which a clear, explicit and published justification is given by the institution. The admissions policy should be referred to in the institution's general policy on provision for students with dyslexia, and should be incorporated into the institution's Disability Statement, published under the requirements of the *Disability Discrimination Act, 1995*.

In some professions there may be a reluctance to employ individuals with dyslexia – a matter that requires debate on a national level.[13] The national survey carried out by the Working Party noted that this was sometimes the case in teaching, medicine and medically-related professions such as nursing, pharmacy, and dentistry. HEIs provide courses of education and training for these professions but they do not control them. It would clearly not be acceptable for students with dyslexia to be admitted to higher education and then obtain qualifications which they find they cannot use in gaining employment because of their dyslexia. Where this is likely, the admissions officers and tutors need to understand the situation.

The Working Party does not believe that dyslexia should be a barrier to entry to any profession, nor a reason for denying any student admission to a course of professional training. There are ways of compensating for the effects of dyslexia that can enable dyslexic individuals with ability to obtain professional qualifications and to achieve the necessary standards when working within those

---

[13] Skill has produced a useful publication *('Into Teaching')* that encourages disabled people (including those with dyslexia) to become teachers, and staff in colleges to accept disabled people as potential teachers.

professions: see Morgan and Rooney (1997) and Pumfrey (1998), for further discussion of these issues. Where there are perceived barriers to entry to any given profession, the national bodies with responsibility for accrediting training, maintaining entry standards and monitoring continuing competence in that profession need to give careful consideration to their position with regard to individuals with dyslexia training for or entering the profession. HEIs, which have a responsibility to individual students and to the nation for the delivery of high-level education and training, should take a prominent role in such discussions – and may, in some cases, even need to initiate them. In such consideration, every effort should be made to consult with experts on dyslexia, with institutions providing professional training and with persons who have dyslexia already practising within that profession, in order to obtain a realistic picture of the issues involved, of the risks and potential dangers to the public, and of the possibilities of managing the dyslexia through appropriate coping strategies. *If, after careful consideration, any professional body decides that it is not desirable for individuals with dyslexia to train for or enter a given profession, this decision should be published together with a full justification.*

7.2.2   *Guidance on support*

Like all students applying for higher education, students with dyslexia want to maximise their opportunity to be accepted on to their chosen course, and to optimise final degree grades. Institutions also want to maximise the likelihood that students who have been admitted will complete their studies successfully. To achieve these objectives, dyslexic students require realistic guidance and information, pre-admission advice, and knowledge of the nature of support and provision they can expect from an institution. In order to facilitate this, admissions officers and tutors should endeavour to understand in general terms the educational problems and needs of students with dyslexia. Information that will be relevant to prospective students who have dyslexia, especially the nature and extent of support that will be available (both centrally and departmentally), should be provided to such students.

Over and above the general requirements of the dyslexic student, it is important that the admission process also takes account of individual student differences, their patterns of strengths and weaknesses, their support needs and their coping mechanisms. The admissions tutor should ensure that the student understands what will be expected of him or her on the course(s) that have been applied for – i.e. the type, level and quantity of work required and the skills demanded of the student. Admissions tutors should also endeavour to ascertain, as far as possible, that a student with dyslexia will be able to complete the chosen course with the support that is available and with the provisions allowed.

Every student with dyslexia who has been admitted to the institution should be known to the member of staff who has overall responsibility in the institution for students with dyslexia, and to members of the academic staff within their department(s) who have responsibility for students with dyslexia.

7.2.3   *Liaison within the institution*

Where admission of students with dyslexia is concerned, admissions personnel should liaise as closely as possible with members of the academic and support staff who have explicit responsibility for students with dyslexia. Documentary evidence (such as a copy of a psychologist's report) should be obtained wherever possible, in order to ascertain the nature and extent of the students' difficulties. When examining such documentary evidence, admissions tutors should consult with the dyslexia tutor or other member of staff with responsibility for students with dyslexia and, where necessary, take professional advice regarding the adequacy of the evidence and its implications for the student's education. (For further information about reports of diagnostic assessments, see Chapter 8.) Any documentary evidence obtained by admissions staff should be passed as soon as possible to the relevant academic support staff. It is imperative that all students with dyslexia are followed up by the relevant academic and support staff. If this does not happen, there is a danger that that these students will fail to receive the support they need. Furthermore, because evidence of dyslexia was submitted at the time of admission, the student may erroneously assume that special examination arrangements will automatically follow.

7.2.4 Admission routes

When we consider the admission process for students with dyslexia, it is imperative that we hold the differing needs of these students clearly in mind. They may enter higher education through different routes. For the post 'A' level entrant, who has already been identified as having dyslexia and has been supported prior to entry, early advice, identification of support mechanisms and information on the process of gaining such support may be all that is required to maintain their personal and intellectual development during higher education.

For students entering higher education from further education colleges and from foundation year courses in FE, it is important for those involved in advising and admitting such students to understand the different funding methodologies which support students in the two sectors. Unless both institutions and the student take this into account, unrealistic expectations of future levels of individual and institutional support may result in poor progression advice or learning needs which cannot easily be met if support services for this student group are in their infancy.

Admissions tutors should be aware of the special problems which can be experienced by students with dyslexia entering higher education via Access courses. Mature students frequently enter via this route. On Access courses, although there is the intention to prepare students for further and more advanced study, students with dyslexia may have been heavily supported and directed in their learning, and emphasis will have been on assessment through course work assignments and projects. Such students may have greater-than-average difficulties in adjusting to study at higher education level, where there is an emphasis on independent learning and assessment is largely by unseen written examinations.

7.3 Recommendations on admissions

1.   Each HEI should maintain and publish an admissions policy that does not discriminate against students with dyslexia, except in those subjects and areas of study for which a clear, explicit and published justification is given by the institution. (See also Recommendation 6 of this sub-section).

2.   The admissions policy on dyslexia should:

   a)   be incorporated into the institution's Disability Statement, published under the requirements of the *Disability Discrimination Act, 1995;*

   b)   be referred to in the institution's general policy on provision for students with dyslexia; and

   c)   be declared in the institution's prospectus, on ECCTIS and all UCAS documentation.

3.   When dealing with the admission of students with dyslexia, admissions tutors or officers should endeavour to:

   a)   understand the educational problems and needs of students with dyslexia;

   b)   ascertain, as far as possible, that a student with dyslexia will be able to complete the chosen course with the support that is available and with the provisions allowed.

   c)   liaise as closely as possible with members of the academic staff who have explicit responsibility for students with dyslexia;

   d)   obtain documentary evidence (such as a copy of a psychologist's report) in order to ascertain the nature and extent of the students' difficulties;

   e)   consult with the dyslexia tutor or other member of staff with overall responsibility within the institution for students with dyslexia and, where necessary, take professional advice from elsewhere within or without the institution regarding the adequacy of any documentary evidence provided by the student and its implications for the student's education;

f) ensure that the student is made aware of the nature and extent of support that will be available in the institution; and

g) be aware of the special problems which can be experienced by students with dyslexia entering higher education via access courses.

4. Every student with dyslexia who has been admitted to the institution should, with that student's permission, be known to the member of staff who has overall explicit responsibility in the institution for students with dyslexia, and to members of the academic staff within faculties or sub-faculty units who have explicit responsibility for students with dyslexia in their area.

5. Before entry, students with dyslexia should be encouraged to find out what skills will be required on any courses which they are required to take or which they opt to take, and to discuss the courses and their suitability with an appropriate person, such as the admissions tutor or the dyslexia tutor.

6. The Working Party does not believe that dyslexia should be a barrier to entry to any profession, nor a reason for denying any student admission to a course of professional training. In any profession in which there is a perceived barrier or reluctance to accept persons with dyslexia, those national bodies which have responsibility for the profession should give careful consideration to their position with regard to individuals with dyslexia who are training for or entering their profession. If, after careful consideration, any such body has decided that it is not desirable for individuals with dyslexia to train for or enter that profession, this decision should be published together with a full justification.

8 Identification of students with dyslexia

8.1 Issues, problems and challenges

8.1.1 The need for institutional policy

Before any HEI can make proper provision for any students with dyslexia, it must have a realistic policy and effective procedures for identifying such students.[14] In addressing this task, all institutions will inevitably find themselves confronted with certain critical issues, including:

- ensuring that students who *claim* to have dyslexia do, in fact, have dyslexia

- checking whether students who are struggling with their studies have problems that are due to *unidentified* dyslexia

- deciding what *personnel* are to have responsibility for identification of dyslexia

- deciding on the *contents* of identification procedures

- arranging a *funding* mechanism for covering the costs of identification.

All HEIs need appropriate policy on such matters. The validity of the disability label 'dyslexia' has important implications for DSA application, for learning support, and for special examination arrangements. HEIs are under a public duty to ensure (insofar as they are able) that requests for public funds made with their authority (e.g. DSA applications) are both genuine and justified. Ethically, as well as on grounds of academic quality and standards, it is essential that students are not able to gain an unfair advantage in examinations (e.g. by obtaining additional time) by fraudulent means, such as claiming to have dyslexia when this is not, in fact, the case. It is equally important that students with dyslexia are not unfairly handicapped in examinations by the institution's *failure* to recognise their disability and make appropriate provision.

The policy that the institution adopts in relation to identification of students with dyslexia should recognise the numbers of students that are likely to be involved and create a mechanism by which the process can be funded appropriately. If Disability Support staff are trying to secure a budget for dyslexia assessments, senior managers will want to know the level of finance that will be necessary to cover the costs each year, and this will to some extent be a function of the numbers of students who are likely to require assessment. The national survey carried out by the Working Party found that the overall incidence of dyslexia in higher education is currently in the region of 1.2% – 1.5% (compared with about 4% in the general population), with 43% of this group being identified as dyslexic *after* admission (see Section 3.2.3). These figures are broadly consistent with HESA statistics (see Section 1.1.5.1). Consequently, it may be anticipated that a university of average size (with about 5,000 new students entering annually) will have about 35–50 students entering who declare dyslexia on their UCAS form, plus approximately another 25–40 students with dyslexia who are unidentified on entry.

---

[14] The term 'identification' is used here to refer generically to those processes which are necessary to ascertain whether or not a student has dyslexia. These processes may include a 'screening assessment' and a 'diagnostic assessment' (the latter will usually be a 'psychological assessment'). The term 'diagnosis' by itself will be avoided as far as possible because of 'disease' connotations. Note also that 'screening assessment' and 'diagnostic assessment' are distinct from what should be referred to as 'evaluation of needs' (sometimes called 'needs assessment') where investigations are made to determine what technological support and other provision will be necessary to enable dyslexic students to pursue their studies and fulfil the requirements of their courses. Evaluation of needs is addressed in Chapter 9.

Some HEIs (e.g. those specialising in or having a preponderance of courses on art and design) are likely to have a much higher incidence.

A proportion of those who declare dyslexia on their UCAS form will have had a formal diagnostic assessment carried out at some time prior to entry, although re-assessment may be required before application for the DSA can be made – especially if the assessment is discovered to have been inadequate in some way or was carried out some years previously.

To these figures should be added those students with dyslexia entering in the current year (or who have entered in previous years) but who have yet to be identified or properly assessed. Some of these students have no idea that they could have dyslexia, while others may already have suspicions. It is almost certain that a few students with dyslexia are *never* formally identified by the HEI either before or during their degree course. We have no way of knowing how many fall into this category. Some may have developed good compensatory strategies (perhaps without being explicitly aware of this) and some may know they have dyslexia but choose to keep this to themselves (possibly because they are frightened that disclosure will prejudice their prospects in some way).

Taking all the above factors into account, an average HEI can expect somewhere between 60 and 100 *new* students each year who come forward for some type of consideration because of dyslexia. In most cases, this consideration will involve a formal process of identification. Issues concerning the costs of these assessments are discussed further in Section 8.3.4.6.

8.1.2   The aims of the identification procedure

All students who show, or claim to have, a literacy or study problem which could feasibly be caused by dyslexia will generally require a diagnostic assessment. If they have already been diagnostically assessed prior to entering higher education, various factors need to be taken into account in order to decide whether a re-assessment is necessary. Diagnostic assessment should be carried out as early as possible. From the institution's point of view valid, reliable and up-to-date assessment is necessary because it is important to establish not only whether the student is dyslexic, but also because it is essential to have as much information as possible about:

- the severity of the student's current difficulties

- how those difficulties are likely to affect their particular studies

- what support would therefore be appropriate

- what examination arrangements would be fair.

All this information is necessary for the *student* as well as for the *institution*. If the student is proposing to make an application for the DSA, up-to-date evidence of the student's dyslexia will be required (see Chapter 9). Feedback to the student in the form of counselling (see Chapter 10) is an essential and often neglected part of the diagnostic assessment procedure. Note that these matters will also be the concern of the person who will be responsible for evaluating the student's needs – in general, the diagnostic assessment will give only a broad indication of such matters, whereas the needs assessment will give much finer detail (see Chapter 9). It should be apparent that what is required from a diagnostic assessment is not only a valid and hence reliable diagnosis of the student's problems, but also an assessment of the *degree of current impairment* created (or which is likely to be created) by those problems in studying a particular type of course at higher education level.[15]

---

[15] An alternative view is that people with dyslexia do not have 'current impairments' (in the sense intended here) but rather that the effects of their dyslexia are highly specific to the task which is being undertaken, e.g. one book may be easy to read and another difficult. Arguably, it might be desirable to take account of this in diagnostic assessment; unfortunately, no objective (or even systematic clinical) methods exist for measuring such task-specific impairments. Such matters can be explored in interview as part of screening or diagnostic assessment, and should be discussed with the student as part of an evaluation of needs and in study skills support. See also Section 8.3.3 for further discussion of these issues.

8.1.3 Students who declare themselves to have dyslexia on entry

The national survey showed that a little more than half of students with dyslexia declare that they have dyslexia on the UCAS form. The remainder are identified as having dyslexia at some point during their course. It would be easy to assume that those who declare that they have dyslexia on the UCAS form do not require any 'identification' as such, since they have already identified themselves before admission. This assumption is unwarranted for a number of reasons.

- A student may *believe* they have dyslexia or have been told this by someone (perhaps a teacher or a GP) but the validity of this belief is uncertain until a proper diagnostic assessment has been carried out. A tick in the 'dyslexic' category on the UCAS form does not, by itself, provide *sufficient evidence of dyslexia*.

- The student may have had a diagnostic assessment carried out, but this may have been inadequate, e.g. because inappropriate tests were used, or because it was carried out by a person not thoroughly qualified for the job. An inadequate diagnostic assessment would not furnish *satisfactory evidence* of dyslexia.

- The student may have had a diagnostic assessment carried out, but may be *unable to supply satisfactory evidence* of this, e.g. because the report has been lost or is otherwise unobtainable.

- The student may have had a diagnostic assessment carried out, and may be able to supply documentation, but the report refers *solely to examination provision* and contains no evidence of the diagnostic assessment.

There could be serious consequences of admitting students with previous assessments for dyslexia where those assessments were inadequate or where satisfactory documentary evidence is not provided. In further education, for example, such students may have secured considerable concessions in examinations, which can have implications for the student's capacity to cope with the demands of higher education. If the original assessment turns out to have been inadequate and the student does not actually have dyslexia (but may have limited ability and/or poor literacy skills) the situation is highly unsatisfactory for both the student and the HEI. The student will probably have to struggle to survive in an educational environment to which they are intellectually unsuited or cope with the emotional and economic problems of withdrawing from university. The institution will be faced with the decision either to try to support a weak student, or to encourage withdrawal in the best interests of the student, or to abandon the student to face the inevitable consequences of examination failure.

Of those students with dyslexia who enter higher education having already had a diagnostic assessment, it will often be the case that the diagnostic assessment was carried out over two years before entry; in several instances it will have been over six years earlier, when the student was still in primary education. Such outdated diagnostic assessments may be quite useful to an assessor at an HEI in demonstrating the history of the problem, but will still not provide evidence of the *degree of current difficulty*.

Even if a student with dyslexia enters higher education having already had a diagnostic assessment which was fairly up-to-date (say, within two years of entry) and conducted by a professional who was properly qualified and experienced and who used appropriate tests, such diagnostic assessments will usually fail to provide evidence of difficulties which are *specific to that student's educational circumstances*. The significance of any difficulty is relative to the nature of the course which the student is studying. Since this has implications for admission and course selection, the earlier information of this nature is obtained, the better for all concerned.

Two examples may suffice. A very creative dyslexic student who has good visual skills but severe difficulties in written expression might be expected to fare better in a subject that placed particular emphasis on visual creativity (e.g. architecture, graphic design, art) rather than one in which written expression was at a premium (e.g. English, history), although the former may still require students to produce pieces of writing (e.g. a project or dissertation) as part of their degree studies. A dyslexic student who has a severe problem with numbers (e.g. habitually reversing order of digits, misreading digits) would not be expected to be seriously impaired on a course in which numbers are not of central significance (e.g. drama, English). On the other hand, if the course is one in which the use of numbers is an integral part of the subject (e.g. mathematics, physics, engineering, economics, statistics, psychology) then number-related difficulties will have much more serious consequences for the student, although these can often be managed through appropriate coping strategies.[16] In each of these cases, it is impossible to gauge the impact of the dyslexia on the student's studies without relating their individual difficulties to the particular demands of their chosen subject.

Ideally, diagnostic assessments should address the nature and extent of *all* difficulties that the student is likely to encounter on the particular course that is being studied. In practice, this is problematic. Few personnel carrying out diagnostic assessments are thoroughly familiar with the requirements of the wide variety of courses that a given institution may offer, and it is probably unrealistic to expect them to be. *Furthermore, not all difficulties can be foreseen.* Changes of course, selection of optional course modules at a later stage during higher education, may all defeat attempts to give a definitive description of a given student's capabilities and needs in higher education at the outset.

To resolve this matter requires the intervention of a professional who both understands dyslexia at higher education level and knows about the nature of the studying requirements of different courses (or who knows how to obtain this information). This process is properly part of the evaluation of needs, and the ideal person for the job will generally be the dyslexia tutor or the disability officer (see Chapter 9). Evaluation of needs is a procedure that can (and should) be updated in relation to changes which affect the student's studies, such as a change of course.

8.1.4   *Students with dyslexia who are identified after entry*

Most of the students with dyslexia who are identified after entry come to the attention of HEI staff for one or more of the following reasons:

- tutors have noticed an unusual incidence of problems in the student's written work

- the student has failed (or performed poorly in) examinations or other assessed work

- the student has recognised that he or she is experiencing studying difficulties

- another student with dyslexia has noted the student's problems and recognised that dyslexia may been the cause.

It should be obvious that the earlier the student with dyslexia is identified the better. Where the true nature of the student's problem is not recognised until the later stages of his or her course, it typically creates a deeply unsatisfactory state of affairs for both the student and for academic staff concerned. Nevertheless, some students with dyslexia manage to struggle through one or two years of a degree course, perhaps failing some examinations and/or assessments and then passing by a narrow margin on re-sit, only to be identified as having dyslexia in the final stages of the course. Or, in some types of courses (e.g. art and design), where there may not be a particularly strong focus on writing in the early part of the course, the student with unidentified dyslexia might cope reasonably well until they are faced with the task of writing a lengthy dissertation in the final year. Not only is the student with a late identification of dyslexia less likely to be able to obtain a DSA, but also the opportunities to acquire study strategies which will help to compensate for the student's dyslexic difficulties will be much restricted. Examination Boards are sometimes confronted with mitigation that students with dyslexia could have performed better in examinations had their difficulties been diagnosed and addressed earlier in the course.

---

[16] It has been estimated that approximately 60% of people with dyslexia experience some problems in dealing with numbers (Miles and Miles, 1992) but the incidence of number-related difficulties among students with dyslexia in higher education is unknown. Unfortunately, diagnostic assessments do not routinely provide information about a student's number skills, unless the student or the institution has raised this as a particular problem. 'Ruth' (the vignette described in Section 2.6.1.5) is a case where difficulties with numbers impinged directly on her course.

Students' awareness that the problems which they are experiencing might be due to dyslexia may have been raised by posters or literature in the institution or elsewhere. Students may also realise that, if they do have dyslexia, they could be entitled to financial support in the form of a DSA which could help them purchase a computer or other technology to help address their difficulties. They also probably know that if they have dyslexia they are likely to be accorded special arrangements for examinations, including extra time. These are understandable attractions for some students, and although there is no evidence of significant fraud, it would be unrealistic to ignore the possibility that some students may be motivated to claim or attempt to fake dyslexia in order to obtain the 'benefits' which they judge are likely to accrue. It is thus incumbent upon all HEIs to establish the veracity of the student's claim to have dyslexia. It is also essential that all HEIs ensure, as far as possible, that students who present with studying difficulties are assessed for dyslexia in a satisfactory manner, and that students with dyslexia are accorded provision which is reasonable, fair and appropriate to their needs. Furthermore, such intentions need to be *embodied within the disabilities policy of the institution* and implemented at an institutional level in order to maintain academic standards and to prevent inequities (or perceived inequities) arising within the institution.

The scenario of late identification of dyslexia is a powerful rationale not only for the establishment of effective procedures for identification but also for encouraging awareness about dyslexia within all HEIs.[17] The findings of the national survey suggest that awareness raising and staff development are, as yet, a relatively undeveloped area of dyslexia provision in higher education. But if academic staff have some knowledge about dyslexia, they are more likely at an early stage to refer for identification those students who seem to be having particular difficulties. If students have access to information about dyslexia from the beginning of their higher education course, it is likely that they will come forward for advice if they find themselves struggling.

Furthermore, when students who ask for advice and help regarding their studies are given psychological assessments and *not* found to be dyslexic, it is usually the case that they are still experiencing a 'problem' of some sort on their course and which consequently needs addressing, whether at an individual, departmental or institutional level.

Discovering that one has dyslexia can have a very emotional impact on a student, which can have all manner of repercussions on studying and life in general. Therefore, establishment of identification procedures also requires attention to counselling needs of such students. Counselling issues are addressed in Chapter 10.

8.1.5   *The need for guidelines on identification procedure*

Other than specifications (now superseded) from an earlier draft of this report, which were published by Skill in its *Disability Directory for LEA Awards Officers* (1997a), there have not previously been any guidelines specifying what a diagnostic assessment of a student in higher education should comprise, nor *who* is qualified to identify a student in higher education as having dyslexia.

Diagnostic assessment is traditionally carried out by a psychologist (usually an educational psychologist) and many LEAs, when considering the award of a DSA, are reluctant to accept assessments from other professionals. In the absence of guidelines, each LEA has tended to set its own criteria about what constitutes acceptable evidence of dyslexia and (understandably) there are reported discrepancies between LEAs in such criteria (see Sections 3.2.9, 4.1.2.5 and 9.1.2.2).

One of the main reasons why the Working Party came into being was to explore the issues surrounding identification of dyslexia and produce independent guidelines that would (a) resolve the current difficulties and anxieties expressed in the national survey and consultation process, and (b) help to make identification of students with dyslexia more efficient and consistent across the sector. By and large, professional work on the identification of dyslexia is linked to research that is outside the realm of those who manage disability in higher education. Consequently, 'good practice' in this matter cannot be established by reference to what is currently happening in those HEIs with a good track record on disability and then extending this practice to other institutions. Instead, the Working

---

[17] There are other excellent rationales for awareness raising – see Chapter 6.

Party first had to look closely at what those working in disability support in HEIs say is *required*, and then examine the research evidence and the views of relevant professionals on the matter. Paramount has been the Working Party's aim to produce guidelines that will be workable, efficient, cost-effective and equitable as well as maintaining both academic standards and professional integrity.

In the national survey it was found that in about 80% of cases, dyslexia assessments were obtained from psychologists (see Section 3.2.2). However, since anyone may call themselves 'a psychologist' regardless of whether they have qualifications in psychology, it is important that any HEI using a psychologist should satisfy itself regarding the person's qualifications and professional competence for the job. Even if the person does possess a psychology qualification (e.g. the person has a degree in psychology or is a lecturer in psychology in an HEI) this does not necessarily equip them either to carry out assessment using psychometric tests or other psychological assessment methods, or to undertake the complex (and often controversial) task of diagnosing dyslexia.

Any professional in this field will recognise that psychological assessment of adults with dyslexia is a complicated technical activity. As individuals get older they discover ways of hiding their problems and often acquire compensatory strategies. The true extent of their difficulties is usually masked (for discussion of this issue see McLoughlin, Fitzgibbon and Young, 1994; Rack, 1997; Stacey, 1997; Turner, 1997). There is a shortage of psychologists who are qualified to carry out such assessments and there is a lack of appropriate tests for assessment at higher education level. In some instances, tests which are designed for assessing children have been misapplied to adults (Singleton, 1995).[18] By ensuring that personnel who undertake diagnostic assessments have proper qualifications and experience, it should follow that the assessments carried out adhere to professional standards. Because of the unacceptable variation in methods and standards that has existed until now, it is also necessary to give guidance on procedure and content of dyslexia assessments.

There is an urgent need for more psychological research into the characteristics of dyslexia in otherwise literate adults and into criteria which might be employed for diagnostic purposes (Beaton, McDougall and Singleton, 1997b). Regardless of any scientific contentions between psychologists, the fact remains that students regularly come forward asking if they 'might have dyslexia', or are referred by their tutors because of problems with literacy and/or study skills. It would be hopelessly unrealistic to put the job of dyslexia identification 'on hold' until all the various scientific issues are resolved. Whilst recognising that improvements in methods and materials for the purposes of assessing adults for dyslexia are long overdue, we must in the meantime try to ensure that as far as possible the techniques which are applied *now* are of an acceptable standard. There *are* valid scientific methods which can and should be followed, even if the tools which are currently available to do the job are not perfect, and the personnel with the skills to carry out such assessments are in short supply.

The Working Party strongly recommends that individuals and HEIs, when engaging or recommending the services of personnel who will carry out diagnostic assessments:

- ensure that such personnel belong to one or more of the professional categories specified in Section 8.3.1 of this report as being competent to assess dyslexia in higher education, and

- request that such professionals adhere to the guidelines on the conduct of dyslexia assessments presented in Sections 8.3.2, 8.3.3 and 8.3.4 of this report.

8.1.6   Dyslexia screening

8.1.6.1   Purpose of screening

In this context, term 'screening' usually refers to a form of assessment which precedes diagnostic assessment. It is sometimes referred to as 'pre-assessment screening' or 'screening assessment'. The sense in which the term 'screening' is being used here is somewhat different from what might be termed 'population screening' – i.e. the administration of a selection or classification process to *all*

---

[18] A similar situation has been observed in the US: see McGuire et al (1996).

members of the group (i.e. all students). Dyslexia screening is not generally applied to all students entering an institution, only to those whose difficulties seem to warrant such procedures. In the consultative meetings held by the Working Party, several representatives of HEIs suggested that universal screening for dyslexia on entry to higher education might be desirable (see Section 4.1.2.4). Cost would clearly be a major factor here, but the validity and reliability of screening methods will also be important matters to consider before implementing such procedures.

The purpose is of screening for dyslexia is generally to ascertain whether a full psychological or diagnostic assessment would be warranted (because psychological assessment is quite expensive and time consuming) but screening may serve other valuable functions as well. Screening can save the cost of full assessment in those cases where the outcome of screening suggests that full assessment would be unwarranted. It can also help to establish a point of contact and trust between the student with difficulties and the agencies of support within the institution. In the national survey, 70% of HEIs reported using some form of screening or preliminary assessment before referral for a full psychological or diagnostic assessment.

8.1.6.2   *Accuracy of screening*

The meaning of 'screening' as it is used within education is the identification of a sub-group from within a larger group or population. The *original* meaning of the term 'screening' was to sieve materials such as coal through a coarse mesh (or 'screen') in order to eliminate unwanted matter such as stones or dust. Such a method, although by no means perfect, had the advantage of being speedy and much more economical than having the materials sorted by hand. Screening, therefore, was an acceptable but essentially *rough-and-ready* approach, and the term has partly (but not entirely) retained this nuance. More recently, the idea of screening being a rough-and-ready solution to identification has steadily given way to expectations that screening will have much higher degrees of reliability and validity (the former being a necessary but not sufficient condition of the latter). In education, this trend has been a significant one, although somewhat less pronounced than in the field of medical screening (Singleton, 1997a).

The effectiveness of any screening procedure largely depends on the percentage of misclassifications that it generates. There are two categories of screening error: 'false negatives' and 'false positives'. Any screening procedure should satisfy criteria regarding the incidence of false negative and false positives before it can be regarded as acceptable.[19]

If a student *who has dyslexia* is shown by a screening procedure to be 'not at risk' (false negative) is it unlikely that the student will be referred for diagnostic assessment and probably will not receive the help which is needed. Moreover, the academic staff may quite understandably believe that the student's poor attainment and other problems are due to lack of effort rather than the symptoms of a disability. Under these circumstances, the student may well become discouraged and lose motivation and confidence. On the other hand, if a student who *does not have dyslexia* is shown by a screening procedure to be 'at risk' ('false positive') is it likely that the student will then be referred for diagnostic assessment, which will have major financial implications for either the institution or the student. Hence the student's problems can become compounded by the outcome of an inaccurate screening process.

8.1.6.3   *Issues in screening*

The first problem confronting any HEI developing or selecting a screening method for dyslexia is to decide which personnel are going to carry out the screening. Dyslexia screening is a delicate task. Students often come to the situation in a state of low morale having performed poorly in their course. Although they may suspect that they have dyslexia, they will generally have little appreciation of what this might mean. They often have deep seated anxieties about their abilities and are worried about what the assessment may reveal. The task of the screener is to investigate the nature and extent of the

---

[19] Screening procedures which generate more than 25% of false negatives or false positives (expressed as percentages of those predicted to be 'dyslexic' or 'not dyslexic' in each case) are not likely to prove very useful (Kingslake, 1982; Potton, 1983; Singleton, 1997a).

student's difficulties, using appropriate techniques. The process should neither be unduly lengthy nor threatening, but must yield information which is as valid and reliable as could reasonably be expected under the circumstances and which will have the confidence of the student and any other individuals for whom this information is necessary, such as the student's academic supervisor or the institution's disability officer.

The second problem is to decide on the method(s) to be used for screening. The choice of what methods to adopt for pre-assessment screening for dyslexia is not particularly straightforward, as there are no 'standard' procedures for this. It has been left to the staff of each individual institution to decide on a method which appears to them to be suitable, although in some HEIs the psychologist(s) carrying out diagnostic assessments may advise on screening methods. There is a trade-off between the two fundamental requirements of (a) ease of administration, and (b) accuracy of results. Thus a compromise is necessary. Relatively coarse procedures for screening are not, in general, very accurate, and rarely are accurate procedures simple, cheap or easy to administer (Singleton, 1997a). Finding a satisfactory compromise between practicality and accuracy is by no means an easy task.

A recent survey showed that in those HEIs carrying out dyslexia screening, there were quite wide variations in techniques adopted (Singleton, Trotter and Smart, 1998). For example, although almost all used a dyslexia check list and gave the student an interview of some kind, about half also used various standardised tests of reading and spelling while the other half did not. Often, the screening process is more of an informal exploration of students' problems than an 'assessment'. Some institutions are fortunate to have very experienced personnel carrying out this work while others had to rely on staff who were relatively inexperienced and who felt that much of the time they were 'working in the dark'. Consequently, there is a need for a proper evaluation of various screening methods, including several new computer-based methods of dyslexia screening. The HEFCE has funded such an evaluation, which is currently being carried out by the University of Hull, and this is due to report during 1999 (see Sections 8.2.3 and 8.2.4).

8.1.6.4   *Criteria for referral from screening to diagnostic assessment*

After students have been screened, upon what basis is the decision going to be made whether or not they will be referred for full assessment? At present, clearly stated criteria are rarely employed; instead, the decision to refer or not to refer for diagnostic assessment is usually made on the *implicit expertise* of the screener, who generally weighs up the various pieces of evidence gained in the screening in an *ad hoc* manner. Although there are experienced personnel within higher education currently carrying out dyslexia screening who, we must presume, are making sound and reliable judgements, there is no empirical evidence on this. Reliance on unspecified skills developed by individuals through experience will not help the higher education sector *as a whole* tackle the problem, because there are insufficient 'experts' of this type available. HEIs with 'experts' are also vulnerable if those persons leave the institution and new, inexperienced personnel have to take over. Consequently, it is recommended that each HEI should establish *explicit criteria* according to which students who have been screened will – or will not – be referred for diagnostic assessment. The existence of clear criteria, as well as promoting accountability, will help to maintain continuity in the event that the person(s) carrying out screening have to hand over the job to new personnel.

8.1.7   *Cost of diagnostic assessments*

When establishing or approving procedures for diagnostic assessments, HEIs should have regard to the issue of how the costs of diagnostic assessments are to be met. The national survey carried out by the Working Party showed that about half of all HEIs administer their own internal assessments for dyslexia, and the remainder refer or leave the student to seek assessment outside the institution (see Section 3.2.2). In about three-fifths of cases institutions bear the cost of diagnostic assessment. Current rates for independent psychologists carrying out such assessments are in the region of £200 per student, although many institutions have negotiated lower rates with psychologists who carry out such assessments on a regular basis. The questionnaire study carried out by Singleton, Trotter and Smart (1998) found that the average cost of dyslexia assessments reported by the 75 HEIs responding was £150, with a range from £60 to £350.

In those cases where students have to bear the cost of assessments, the financial burden can be heavy. Although there are no statistics on this, some professionals in the field report instances of students with suspected dyslexia being unable to afford the cost of the assessment, and so having to remain unassessed (and hence undiagnosed and, usually, unsupported). The vignette of 'Laura', given in Section 2.6.1.3, is an example of a student in this dilemma.

In an age of widening access to higher education coupled with diminishing state support for individual students, situations of gross inequity exist where one student with suspected and then confirmed dyslexia is able to secure a DSA, specialist support for their difficulties, and additional time in examinations, and another student with suspected dyslexia has none of these things simply because funds were not available to pay for the assessment. Such scenarios are unlikely to square either with an institution's policy for equal opportunities, or with that for disability. Indeed, it could be argued to go completely against the spirit of the *Disability Discrimination Act, 1995*.

8.1.8   Creating a framework for provision

There are a substantial number of issues that every HEI needs to consider before policies can be decided upon and an effective procedure for identification of dyslexia can be implemented. Staff involved in various stages of the process (both academic and administrative) need to know the policies and the procedures that have been put in place. All students and staff should also be aware that there are such policies and procedures and have access to information about the details if they require it.

The principal issues which should be considered in this context (and the appropriate sections of this report that deal with them) are listed below. Many of the issues can be seen to be interrelated. By addressing these issues in an integrative – rather than piecemeal – manner, the institution will be able to develop a coherent framework for provision for students with dyslexia in which the identification process can be firmly embedded. This helps to ensure that systems are as cost-effective as possible, that identification procedures yield information that is efficacious in applications for the DSA, and that academic standards are not only maintained but also *seen to be* maintained.

1. Who should carry out diagnostic assessments? What qualifications and/or experience should they be required to have? (see Section 8.3.1).

2. Which tests and procedures are appropriate? To what extent should the HEI stipulate the information which it expects from a diagnostic assessment? (see Sections 8.3.2, 8.3.3 and 8.3.4).

3. What procedures are to be operative for students who declare themselves to be dyslexic on entry and/or have been previously assessed for dyslexia? (see Section 8.3.4.5).

4. By what manner, and by whom, are the results of screening and diagnostic assessments to be conveyed to the student? (see Section 8.3.4.3).

5. What procedures should be in place to ensure confidentiality of screening and diagnostic assessment? (see Section 8.3.4.4)

6. How are the costs of screening and diagnostic assessments to be met? (see Sections 8.2.6 and 8.3.4.6).

7. Should a screening assessment be carried out before referring for diagnostic assessment? If so, who should carry out screening assessments and what procedures should be followed? (see Section 8.2).

8. What are the criteria by which students who have been screened are subsequently referred for diagnostic assessment? (see Section 8.2.5).

9. How are the student's individual needs to be evaluated and what support provision should be offered to students found to be dyslexic? (see Chapter 9).

10. What counselling services should be available to help newly identified students deal with the revelation that they have, or do not have, dyslexia? (see Chapter 10).

11. What procedures should be put in place to provide for the special examination requirements of students with dyslexia after diagnosis? (see Chapter 11).

12. What special careers advice should be available for students with dyslexia after diagnosis? (see Chapter 12).

8.2   Provisional proposals on dyslexia screening

It should be noted that screening for dyslexia in higher education is the subject of an HEFCE-funded investigation currently being carried out by the University of Hull. That project arose largely as a result of findings from the national survey (Chapter 3) and the consultative process (Chapter 4), which indicated that many HEIs had recently instigated, or intended to embark on, screening for dyslexia but needed guidance on how to go about this task efficiently and effectively.

An interim report on the screening study has been published (Singleton Trotter and Smart, 1998) and a final report is due in 1999. Some of the findings published in the interim report have been included in this Section. The proposals on good practice outlined here, however, should be regarded as provisional pending the final report of the investigation on screening.

8.2.1   *Personnel administering screening assessments*

Dyslexia screening is not a purely administrative job, but rather a role requiring considerable knowledge as well as a complex range of professional and interpersonal skills, including:

- counselling skills

- interview skills

- assessment skills

- knowledge of dyslexia and how it affects study at higher education level

- experience of working with students with dyslexia

- knowledge of the courses which students are undertaking (since difficulties reported by the students will have to be considered in relation to the demands of their courses)

- understanding of the difficulties in studying experienced by students who do not have dyslexia (especially those for whom English is not their first language) as it is important to distinguish between these students and students with dyslexia (whilst being aware that students from non-English language backgrounds may also have dyslexia)

- knowledge of the procedures and provision within the institution for supporting students with dyslexia and/or study difficulties.

The demands placed on the screener are therefore considerable, and at the present time there appears to be a shortage of personnel with such skills (Singleton, Trotter and Smart, 1998). It would be unrealistic to expect – in the short-term, at least – that all HEIs should have personnel who are highly trained for this job. At the present time, in many institutions screening is carried out by the disability officer, or a manager or administrator with responsibility for disability matters. Few have received any training for this task. There is consequently a need for short but highly practical certificated courses to enable suitable personnel to obtain an appropriate standard of training for this responsibility. There are in existence a small number of specialist diploma and advanced diploma courses for dyslexia teaching at adult level, and these could include within their programmes training for dyslexia screening.[20] The British Psychological Society also has plans for a certificate in educational assessment, following the lines of its highly successful certificate in occupational assessment, but it is not known when this will be in operation.

---

[20] A list of some of these courses is given in Section 14.7. The British Dyslexia Association has an accreditation procedure for such courses (see Section 14.6).

8.2.2   Screening referral procedure

Most HEIs allow for a variety of channels by which students can be referred for screening, including self-referrals. It should be the *student* who decides whether or not they wish to be screened for dyslexia, but it is recommended that tutors should be aware of the availability of screening and be encouraged to suggest to students with literacy and/or study difficulties that they consider attending for screening. Most HEIs bear the cost of screening themselves, but some ask the student to make a small contribution towards the cost, more as a gesture of 'good faith' and to discourage flippant applications. The outcome of screening should be confidential to the student and to the service carrying out the screening, unless the student wishes that information to go further. Finding out the results of a screening assessment can be emotionally upsetting for some students, and so should be conveyed in sensitive manner.

8.2.3   Current methods of screening

There are a number of methods of screening for dyslexia in higher education that may be styled 'conventional' in the sense that they have been fairly widely applied for quite a few years, although by no means all HEIs use such techniques. The figures given in brackets refer to the percentage of HEIs that reported using the method (out of 93 HEIs that all administer routine pre-assessment screening and that responded to a questionnaire on screening methods; Singleton, Trotter and Smart, 1998).

Interview. [94%] The main purpose of this is to obtain information from the student about how they perceive their difficulties, how long those difficulties have persisted (e.g. were difficulties encountered at school or have they arisen only in higher education?) and what strategies (if any) they use to try to overcome those difficulties.

Questionnaire. [39%] This serves a similar function to an interview, except that answers are written.

Adult Dyslexia Checklist. [72%] Checklists are not a particularly reliable technique of obtaining information because they are crude, highly subjective instruments which can be misleading and which may easily be falsified. But they can be useful in a screening procedure because they are easy to administer. They can provide a rapid way for an assessor to get a rough idea of the range of a student's problems, as apparently portrayed by that student, and this can be used as a basis for further discussion between the student and the assessor, e.g. on compensatory strategies. There are several types of adult dyslexia checklists but all have similar questions, which relate to the individual's self-perceptions of difficulties in activities such as reading, spelling, writing and remembering (e.g. see Vinegrad, 1994).

Standardised assessment of literacy skills. [40%] This may be accomplished by means of standardised tests of reading and spelling. For example, the Wide Range Achievement Tests (WRAT-3; Wilkinson, 1993) comprise measures of reading accuracy, spelling and mathematics and have norms extending from 5 to 75 years of age. WRAT-3 has been widely recommended (e.g. Beech and Singleton, 1997a; McLoughlin, Fitzgibbon and Young, 1994; Rack, 1997; Turner, 1997). Unfortunately there are few good standardised tests to use with this population, especially tests of reading comprehension and writing ability (see also Section 14.5 for a list of educational and psychological tests.)

Informal assessment of literacy and study skills [58%] This refers to non-standardised tests, including miscue analysis of reading ability (e.g. Klein, 1993) and qualitative assessment of writing. The value of informal methods of literacy assessment is heavily dependent on the skills and experience of the assessor.

Bangor Dyslexia Test (Miles, 1982/1997, 1993). [56%] This is a screening test designed for use with individuals 7 – 18 years of age. It comprises 10 subtests, including repeating polysyllabic words, saying the months of the year forwards and in reverse order, and recitation of multiplication tables. It is not fully standardised and is not particularly discriminating when used with adults. Nevertheless, many assessors report finding the subtests useful for investigating students' difficulties in a range of non-literacy skills that are often associated with dyslexia and also for counselling purposes (see also Section 14.5).

Cognitive and intellectual measures. These are used less frequently, perhaps partly because such tests are restricted to use by psychologists. 17% reported using the *Standard Progressive Matrices* (Raven, 1958), a group intelligence test. 24% reported using cognitive tests of memory, language and visual processing.

There is insufficient space here to go into details about these methods. They are explored in some depth by McLoughlin, Fitzgibbon and Young (1994) and by Krupska and Klein (1997). It is not within the remit or capacity of the Working Party to evaluate these various methods nor to make specific recommendations in the absence of evidence of their relative validities. It is anticipated that the HEFCE project on screening methods being carried out by the University of Hull will provide such an evaluation in its report, which is due to be published in 1999.

8.2.4   Recent developments in screening

More recently, three alternative approaches to adult dyslexia screening have been under development.

Dyslexia Adult Screening Test (DAST; Nicolson and Fawcett, 1997). This comprises 11 sub-tests, including reading, spelling and cognitive tasks that are generally believed to be sensitive to dyslexia (e.g. backwards digit span, phonemic segmentation, rapid naming). DAST is a standardised assessment which takes about 30 minutes to administer, and is currently being trialled in a number of HEIs. The authors reported on a small-scale pilot study of the accuracy of this instrument, which produced encouraging results (see also Section 14.5).[21]

The Dyslexia Test (McLean, 1997). This is a standardised self-administered computer program that takes about half-an-hour, and is confidential to the user. It covers a range of activities including spelling, proof-reading, digit span and knowledge of phonology. Feedback given to the students indicates whether they would benefit from further assessment or support with tasks involving reading and writing. The predictive validity and reliability of this instrument has yet to be established.[22]

Quick Scan (Zdzienski, 1997). This is part of a larger self-administered computerised diagnostic system, called *Study Scan*. The latter takes several hours to administer, but *Quick Scan*, which is a questionnaire-based program, takes only about 10–15 minutes. *Quick Scan* aims to estimate risk of dyslexia as well as giving practical recommendations to students based on their perceived learning styles. Details of the predictive validity and reliability of this instrument have yet to be published.[23]

While it is too early to say how valuable these new methods will prove to be, they appear to have some potential. The HEFCE project on screening methods being carried out by the University of Hull also includes independent evaluation of these new techniques. It is interesting that the last two of these three new approaches are computerised methods, both of which originated in HEFCE-funded disability projects. The advantages of computer-based assessment of dyslexia can be considerable. Not only are there savings in cost and time, but also in the case of adults, assessment can be self-administered and therefore confidential (Singleton, 1997b).

8.2.5   Procedures for referring from screening to diagnostic assessment

The establishment of standard procedures for carrying out screening, and explicit criteria by which students who have been screened are subsequently referred for diagnostic assessment, helps to ensure professional continuity and protect the institution. This will be particularly important where the HEI

---

[21] For further details contact the Psychological Corporation (address in Section 14.4).

[22] For further details contact the Helen Arkell Dyslexia Centre (address in Section 14.4).

[23] For further details contact Interactive Services Ltd., Corporate Education Centre, Phibsboro Place, Phibsboro Road, Dublin 7, Tel. +353 1860 0277. Fax: +353 1860 0276. E-mail: sales@isl.ie Internet: http://www.isl.ie

has (quite rightly) referred to dyslexia screening in its *Disability Statement*. An example of such criteria might be: a student whose interview indicates difficulties consistent with dyslexia, who has significant literacy and/or study problems (revealed in both qualitative and standardised assessment of reading, writing and spelling), and who scores more than a critical threshold on an Adult Dyslexia Checklist.

The HEFCE project on screening methods currently being carried out by the University of Hull includes consideration of the criteria whereby institutions refer students from screening to psychological assessment.

8.2.6   Cost of screening

The Interim Report of the HEFCE project on screening methods currently being carried out by the University of Hull (Singleton, Trotter and Smart, 1998) found that the average time taken for a screening assessment was 1 hour 23 minutes, although it is not altogether clear whether respondents were referring to test administration time only, or whether preparation and report-writing time were also included. The mean number of students screened per year was 43 (range 3 to 160). HEIs were also asked about the realistic cost to the institution of carrying out screening. The figures given ranged from £10 to £175 per student (mean £56). Some institutions ask students to make a small contribution towards the cost of screening (usually in the region of £10 – £20), partly to defray costs and partly try to ensure that self-referrals are *bona fide*.

The following hypothetical calculation provides a useful check on the figures reported by Singleton, Trotter and Smart (1998). Assuming that personnel carrying out screening will be paid on university academic-related or administrative scales in the region of £20,000 per annum, and allowing for national insurance, pension costs and holidays (but not office or materials costs), the effective hourly cost of such personnel to the institution is about £15 per hour.[24] Furthermore, assuming that it is difficult to carry out a reasonable screening of an individual student in less than one hour (whether this be by means of interview and/or administration of tests) and that at least a further hour is required to examine the findings and compile a brief report, the *minimum cost* for each student screened is therefore about £30. If other costs, such as secretary, office, materials, etc., are added, a figure of about £50 per student screened would not be an unreasonable estimate. At the average rate of 43 students screened per annum the total cost to the institution would be £2,150, less any charge made to students. This is not a particularly substantial sum for an HEI to find, but it should be remembered that many institutions will be faced with screening much larger numbers of students.

It may be concluded that those institutions which carry out screening are doing so without incurring inordinate costs at the present time and that the benefits of screening probably justify the expenditure. However, Singleton, Trotter and Smart (1998) found that a substantial majority of HEIs responding to the survey on screening reported that the number of students requesting screening was rising, and consequently costs must be expected to increase. In the long term, therefore, the financial advantages of briefer, but perhaps more objective, screening procedures, as well as self-administered or computer-delivered screening systems, are likely to make these increasingly attractive alternatives for HEIs to consider.

8.3   Guidelines for diagnostic assessment of dyslexia

8.3.1   Personnel administering diagnostic assessments

Diagnostic assessment of dyslexia in higher education requires a high degree of professional competence and experience, and ideally requires use of sophisticated psychometric techniques that are only available to psychologists with appropriate training. Rarely can it be carried out to the proper professional standard by personnel other than psychologists who have been trained for this

---

[24] Calculated by approximation on the basis of 25% salary on-costs, 230 working days per year and 7.5 hours per day = £14.49 per hour.

responsibility. Consequently, other persons – e.g. learning support staff, disability officers, and lecturing staff in psychology or education – will generally not be suitable unless such persons also have the required qualifications and experience. It is also highly desirable for assessors to have a good understanding of the demands placed on students in higher education today. HEIs and LEA Awards Officers should be thoroughly satisfied that those undertaking diagnostic assessments are appropriately qualified and possess sufficient experience for the job.

Taking all the above factors into account, the Working Party strongly recommends that diagnostic assessment of dyslexia in higher education should normally be carried out *only* by professionals in the five categories listed below and *provided they have appropriate training in, and experience of, adult assessment.*[25]

1. Chartered Psychologists with a current Practising Certificate.

2. Educational Psychologists employed by an LEA or who are members of the Association of Educational Psychologists.

3. Qualified Clinical or Occupational Psychologists.

4. Experienced teachers with a qualification from a professional training course involving assessment of adults for dyslexia, and who have demonstrated competencies in psychometric testing.

5. Psychologists or persons in related professions who have substantial experience in the assessment of dyslexia in adults and who have demonstrated competencies in psychometric testing.

In general, it is recommended that the task of dyslexia assessment be undertaken by properly qualified psychologists, because not only will they have had the training and experience in psychometric testing, but they also have access to a wide range of test materials to which non-psychologists do not have access. When conducting diagnostic assessments, it is necessary to collect evidence of neurological and/or cognitive impairment, which is very difficult to do satisfactorily without the right tools. However, having considered the matter very carefully, the Working Party can see no reason to reserve diagnostic assessment of dyslexia to psychologists, for what is of paramount importance are the *content* of the assessment and the *competence* with which it is conducted. The provisos are that, regardless of the category to which they belong, persons carrying out diagnostic assessments must have (a) had appropriate advanced professional training and supervised experience, so that they know what to do and understand why they are doing it, (b) employ the appropriate techniques for assessment (these are set down in the guidelines in Section 8.3.2), and (c) observe the other recommendations contained in this chapter (e.g. on the ethics of assessment). Further explanation of the categories outlined above is given in the next five subsections.

8.3.1.1   Chartered psychologists

The British Psychological Society (BPS) is empowered by law to register appropriately qualified and experienced psychologists as *Chartered Psychologists.*[26] It is illegal for anyone who is not so registered by the BPS to call themselves a Chartered Psychologist. All Chartered Psychologists are listed in *The Register of Chartered Psychologists*, which is published annually by the BPS. Chartered Psychologists are deemed to possess adequately developed professional skills, and expected to know the limitations of those skills. Chartered Psychologists must observe a strict *Code of Conduct* including, in particular, refraining from claiming competence in any area of psychology in which they

---

[25] It should be noted that the provisional guidelines on personnel that should be permitted to carry out dyslexia assessments, which were published in 1997 by Skill in its *Disability Directory for LEA Awards Officers* were based on an earlier and unratified draft of this report. These guidelines have now been modified, particularly with respect to assessment by experienced and appropriately qualified teachers.

[26] For information about the British Psychological Society, see Section 4.2.4. Chartered Psychologists may, if they so desire and if they have appropriate qualifications and experience, be classified as having a specialism within psychology such as clinical psychology, educational psychology, occupational psychology, forensic psychology, or counselling psychology, and hence may style themselves 'Chartered Clinical Psychologist', etc. Many Chartered Psychologists have professional expertise which cuts across such boundaries and prefer to be known simply as 'Chartered Psychologist'.

do not possess appropriate qualifications and have not established their competence. Chartered Psychologists who wish to offer their services to the public must hold a valid *Practising Certificate* which must be renewed each year. Any Chartered Psychologist who is found guilty of misconduct can have his or her Practising Certificate withdrawn, or may be removed altogether from the Register. Where an assessment is required from a psychologist, using a Chartered Psychologist rather than any other type thus provides some safeguards regarding the quality of professional expertise.

8.3.1.2   *Educational, clinical and occupational psychologists*

Although less experienced members of these professions (particularly recently qualified Educational Psychologists employed by LEAs) may not yet have achieved Chartered status, most experienced psychologists in these categories are Chartered. Most Educational Psychologists employed by LEAs are members of the Association of Educational Psychologists. In the majority of cases, it is Educational Psychologists who are called upon to carry out diagnostic assessments, but such persons may not always able to provide a thoroughly satisfactory diagnostic assessment of an adult. This is because most Educational Psychologists (especially those employed by LEAs) work mainly in the school system with children up to the age of 16, and relatively few have much experience of assessing adults. In the independent sector there are a number of Educational Psychologists who will provide assessments for dyslexia, and many work in conjunction with the Dyslexia Institute.[27]

Some Occupational Psychologists or Clinical Psychologists will carry out diagnostic assessments for dyslexia, but again such persons are not always able to provide a thoroughly satisfactory diagnostic assessment, because their experience is typically with a completely different type of client. Although they will probably have appropriate assessment skills, they may not have a clear understanding of the various difficulties which dyslexics can encounter in higher education. In view of the BPS Code of Conduct, Chartered Psychologists who do not have sufficient expertise in this field should refrain from carrying out assessments of students in higher education. What constitutes 'sufficient expertise' is a matter of professional opinion which would have to be considered carefully by the Disciplinary Board of the BPS before any action could be taken against a Chartered Psychologist in this respect.

8.3.1.3   *Experienced and appropriately qualified teachers*

Qualified and experienced teachers who possess an additional qualification from an advanced professional training course involving assessment of adults for dyslexia may be suitable to carry out diagnostic assessments provided they have demonstrated competencies in psychometric assessment and have had supervised experience of such work. *It should not be assumed that all persons who have obtained qualifications in specialist dyslexia teaching will automatically be qualified to administer dyslexia assessments at higher education level.* Examples of professional training courses at HE/FE level are given in Section 14.7. The British Dyslexia Association (BDA) accredits courses that meet its published criteria for dyslexia teachers working at FE and HE levels.[28] The Working Party recommends that a required component of such qualifications be the demonstration of competencies in psychometric testing to BPS standards.[29] It is notable that a comparable move is being made by the Joint Forum for GCSE and GCE, which from 1999 will accept assessments by suitably qualified

---

[27] For information about the Dyslexia Institute, see Section 4.2.4.

[28] A copy of the British Dyslexia Association Accreditation Criteria is given in Section 14.6. For further information about the BDA, see Section 4.2.4.

[29] See *Psychological Testing – a user's guide* (a general introduction available from the BPS). The BPS operates a national system for assessing competencies in psychometric testing, which is widely used within occupational and careers settings. The BPS is currently considering how this can be extended to cover testing in educational settings. For further information about the BPS, see Section 4.2.4.

personnel other than psychologists when considering special arrangements in GCSE and 'A' level examinations.[30]

8.3.1.4   *Other professionals*

Some other psychologists or persons working in related professions may be suitable for dyslexia assessment, *provided they have appropriate competence and experience*. These will be professionals who have experience in the assessment of dyslexia in adults and who have demonstrated competencies in psychometric testing. These include some psychologists working in a research capacity in some HEIs, and usually such personnel will be working under the supervision of a Chartered Psychologist.

8.3.2   *Content of diagnostic assessments*

8.3.2.1   *Rationale for having guidelines*

There are four main reasons for producing guidelines on the *content* of diagnostic assessments for dyslexia in higher education.

First, because it is necessary to provide *objective and professionally acceptable evidence* that the poor literacy skills or poor studying skills displayed by the individual being assessed are due to a disability. If not, application for the DSA would be fraudulent and the allocation of special provision such as additional time in examinations would be grossly unjust. It is the objectivity of psychometric assessment, together with the professional observation of qualitative differences in the student's performance, which enables the assessor to provide valid and reliable evidence of a disability.

Second, because of increasing concerns about variability in methods of diagnostic assessment currently being applied in the higher education sector, which resulted in a widespread dissatisfaction on the part of disability officers and LEA Awards Officers (see Sections 1.2.1, 4.1.2.4 and 4.1.3). These concerns were major stimuli in the establishment of the Working Party.

Third, to establish comparability with other sectors of education that operate within national guidelines. In primary and secondary education, guidelines regarding the type of evidence that is necessary in cases of dyslexia are set down in the *Code of Practice on the Identification and Assessment of Special Educational Needs* (DfE, 1994). The Division of Educational and Child Psychology of the British Psychological Society is currently engaged in preparing recommendations for educational psychologists when carrying out assessments for dyslexia with children (British Psychological Society, 1998). The Joint Forum for GCSE and GCE produces regulations and guidelines regarding the nature of the evidence required in making special arrangements for students with dyslexia in GCSE and 'A' level examinations (Joint Forum for GCSE and GCE, 1997).

Fourth, because informal methods of dyslexia assessment, which have become popular in some sections of further education (e.g. Krupska and Klein, 1995), are inadequate for the purpose. Such informal methods, which rely mainly on inspection of students' literacy skills without detailed examination of the cognitive aspects of dyslexia, inevitably generate unacceptably high numbers of false positives (i.e. students who have weak literacy skills but do not have dyslexia) and of false negatives (i.e. students who have dyslexia but who have compensated quite well for this in their reading and writing). For these reasons, the Working Party does not consider that it is appropriate to rely on these informal methods in higher education, where identification of dyslexia will have a direct bearing on whether or not the student will be entitled to a substantial grant (the DSA) and to additional time and possibly other special arrangements in degree examinations. These consequences place particularly heavy responsibilities on assessors, for there is a need not only to safeguard public funds but also to ensure academic quality and overall fairness of examination procedures.

---

[30] A circular from the Joint Forum for GCSE and GCE, October 1998, specified that holders of a RSA Diploma for Teachers of Specific Learning Difficulties can provide appropriate evidence of need instead of a psychologist. Acceptability of other qualifications for this purpose are under consideration.

8.3.2.2   Summary of the evidence required in diagnostic assessments

The Working Party recommends that any assessment of a higher education student for dyslexia should provide the following evidence.

1. Evidence of any significant difficulties in reading, writing, spelling (and mathematics or number work, if appropriate) relevant to the standards in these skills required in higher education, and using, wherever possible, up-to-date standardised tests and professionally established procedures (see Section 8.3.2.3).

2. Evidence of a significant discrepancy between the abilities assessed in (1) and the level of those abilities that would reasonably be expected of the student, based on the student's general intellectual ability and other relevant factors, using, wherever possible, up-to-date standardised tests and professionally established procedures and having due regard to regression effects (see Section 8.3.2.4).

3. Evidence of any cognitive disabilities or neurological anomalies (e.g. in memory, visual perception, phonological processing or motor co-ordination) which are likely to have adverse effects on learning (see Section 8.3.2.5).

4. Evidence that the manner and extent to which the difficulties or disabilities that have been identified are likely to affect learning in the higher education setting (see Section 8.3.2.6).

5. Other relevant evidence, including (where this can be obtained) that of any family history of language and/or literacy difficulties, of birth difficulties and/or early developmental difficulties (e.g. in speech or motor development), and educational history (see Section 8.3.2.7).

6. Evidence that the difficulties or disabilities that have been identified are not due *primarily* to (a) limitations in experience of written and/or spoken English, (b) lack of motivation, application or educational opportunity, (c) emotional causes, or (d) poor general health or a medical condition (see Section 8.3.2.8).

In the remainder of this Chapter, these guidelines on the content of diagnostic assessments are explained in greater detail. However, it is not the function of this report to provide an instruction manual for the diagnosis of dyslexia in adults. Professionals who are suitably qualified and have appropriate experience to carry out the task of diagnostic assessment and who fall within the categories defined in Section 8.3.1 should not have any undue difficulty in understanding and acting on the guidelines in this report. For an overview of the scientific debate in this area, see Beaton, McDougall and Singleton (1997b). For descriptions of the materials and procedures involved in assessment of dyslexia in adults, see McLoughlin (1997), McLoughlin, Fitzgibbon and Young (1994), Rack (1997) and Turner (1997).

8.3.2.3   Assessment of literacy skills

Without first having satisfactory evidence on the nature and extent of the student's difficulties in reading and writing and other basic aspects of studying, the assessor cannot begin to make an objective or convincing diagnosis. The first point in the guidelines requires that, wherever possible, evidence of significant difficulties in literacy (and numeracy skills[31]) should be established by use of *up-to-date standardised tests and professionally established procedures*.

Some of those working professionally in this field (e.g. Klein, 1993) have suggested that dyslexia may be identified purely on *subjective methods* – such as informal analysis of the student's reading and writing – and that standardised tests of literacy and measures of intelligence are unnecessary. This approach is insufficient. Informal methods may well be able identify some students with poor literacy skills – although they will not tell us *how* poor they are because there is no yardstick for comparison. The extent of the difficulty will then be purely a matter of the assessor's subjective judgement, which is quite unsatisfactory. There is no evidence that informal methods (however elaborate) can distinguish between dyslexics and other individuals who may have poor

---

[31] For information on assessment of arithmetic skills, see Section 14.5.

literacy skills for a variety of reasons. As yet, we have no evidence that there are *unique* features of the reading or writing of the person with dyslexia that are distinguishable from the reading or writing of the rest of the population. Dyslexics are liable to make a greater number of errors and more severe errors in most, if not all, kinds in reading and/or spelling and writing. Furthermore, reliance on informal methods may well fail to identify the well-compensated students with dyslexia whose reading and writing is satisfactory but who may have major problems of recall in examinations.

In order to establish the nature and extent of any significant difficulties in reading, writing and spelling, the assessor will therefore need to employ at least some standardised tests. When using standardised tests, a direct comparison can be made between the performance of the student in question, and that of the population on which the test was standardised. This facilitates an objective estimate of significant difficulties. It should always be borne in mind that it is necessary to relate the student's performance to the level of attainment required in higher education generally, and in the student's subject area in particular. Informal procedures may help the diagnosis, and may be essential in those areas where there are no suitable standardised tests available.

An annotated list of some of the currently available tests is provided in Section 14.5. Unfortunately, there are few standardised tests that are appropriate to this age and ability group that can be strongly recommended at the present time and there is an urgent need for research and test development in this area.

Although dyslexia is often recognised to be a problem with word decoding and phonological processing (rather than reading comprehension), an evaluation of the student's reading comprehension will be necessary *as well as* assessment of single word reading out-of-context (decoding). Comprehending difficult reading material is one of the principal challenges of studying at higher education level. Furthermore, as texts become increasingly complex and technical, so are decoding problems increasingly likely to affect comprehension of the material. Age-appropriate tests for assessing reading comprehension are also quite limited in number. Because of their availability and familiarity to educational psychologists and other professionals in this field, many assessors resort to using tests designed for measuring reading comprehension in *children*, but this practice is to be deprecated as most students in higher education, even if they have dyslexia, will be performing at or near the ceiling on such tests.

An alternative to standardised assessment of reading comprehension is to attempt an informal analysis with the student using text material connected with his or her course. A comparison between listening comprehension and reading comprehension may also prove instructive. Since pressure of time is typically a feature of student life, where students often feel that there is 'too much to read and too little time to do it in', reading comprehension under time pressure may also give insights into a student's difficulties. Students with dyslexia frequently complain of being unable to get through the required reading, and of having to re-read material many times before understanding it.

Poor spelling can interfere with the quality of written expression in children and in adults (Brown and Ellis, 1994; Moseley, 1997). Spelling is a learned skill and many adults make spelling errors in free writing; by no means all of these individuals have dyslexia. In free writing, students with dyslexia may not necessarily make qualitatively different spelling errors to those of other students, but their spelling errors will almost invariably be more numerous unless they adopt the strategy of choosing only those words which they are reasonably confident they can spell correctly. In standardised tests, students with dyslexia usually perform significantly poorer than other students.

Students with dyslexia tend to be slow at writing. There is a dearth of information about handwriting speeds generally (Moseley, 1997), and in the higher education population in particular. McLoughlin, Fitzgibbon and Young (1994) suggest that about 20 words per minute is a reasonable estimate for undergraduates. Much depends on the conceptual and technical difficulty of the ideas that the student is trying to convey. Since there are no standardised tests of writing ability and handwriting speed for this population, the assessor cannot obtain objective measures of these. It is worth pointing out that the assessment of handwriting speed is regarded as problematic even for the purposes of applying for special arrangements in GCSE and 'A' level examinations (Sawyer, Francis and Knight, 1992), and the need for a valid, reliable and well-normed test of handwriting speed for these purposes has been signalled by Sawyer, Gray and Champness (1996).

One solution is to ask students to write for 20–30 minutes about the subject which they are studying – e.g. to explain what it involves, why they chose this subject, what they think of it, and what their objectives are. The student should also be asked to bring some examples of their written work on their higher education course (or before entry to higher education, if the assessment is prior to or at the point of entry). In this way it is possible for the assessor to get a reasonable idea of the student's competence in handling subject-related technical vocabulary and communicating complex ideas within his or her subject domain, as well as obtaining a fair estimate of writing speed. However, in a free writing task such as this, some dyslexic students will avoid using terminology that they cannot spell, and this may give a misleading impression of writing speed. To circumvent this problem some assessors, as well as looking at speed of free writing, also measure writing speed for dictated or copied passages of text that involve more advanced vocabulary.

8.3.2.4   *Evidence of discrepancy*

The second point in the guidelines calls for evidence of a *significant discrepancy* between the student's abilities reading, writing, spelling (and mathematics or number work, if appropriate) and the level of those abilities that would reasonably be expected of the student, based on the student's general intellectual ability and other relevant factors, using, wherever possible, up-to-date standardised tests and professionally established procedures and having due regard to regression effects.

By 'significant' we mean 'so much poorer than the level which would be expected on the basis of the person's age and intelligence that the discrepancy is unlikely to be due to normal variation within the population of students in higher education or to chance'. What is important is not the *absolute* level of the student's performance but the *degree of discrepancy* between their observed literacy skills and the level of literacy ability that we would reasonably *expect* such students to have. The conventional way in which psychologists make valid comparisons between performance on different tests or measures is by reference to standardised scores (such as centiles or standard deviation units), which have a clear rationale in psychometric test theory and practice. This method is to be preferred because of its objectivity and fairness.[32]

Traditionally, the concept and diagnosis of dyslexia has been based on the notion of *discrepancy* between what the student *is* achieving in literacy and what they can reasonably be *expected* to achieve on the basis of age and intellectual ability. It is assumed that the student has experienced normal education and that the problems are not primarily due to any emotional or medical cause (Pumfrey, 1996; Pumfrey and Reason, 1991; Thomson, 1993). This discrepancy accounts for the fact that dyslexia is typically characterised by serious and unremitting literacy problems in children who otherwise would be expected to make reasonable progress in the acquisition of literacy (Singleton, 1988). The term 'specific learning difficulty' (which for a generation or more has been preferred by many educational psychologists to the term 'dyslexia') means little more than a discrepancy between ability and attainment. The principal difference between 'dyslexia' and 'specific learning difficulty' is that dyslexia presupposes the existence of certain cognitive deficits which are believed to underpin the condition. Such cognitive deficits (e.g. in phonological processing, memory, visual processing, or motor co-ordination) are believed to be either inherited or due to neurological anomalies which have arisen before (or during) birth or in early childhood.

Sometimes the discrepancy model is applied rather crudely in terms of a difference between intellectual ability (e.g. as measured by an intelligence test) and literacy attainment (e.g. as measured by standardised tests of reading and spelling). However, this is misleading, for the following reasons. The discrepancy model relies on the statistical correlation between the two variables. It is true that, in general, people with higher intellectual ability have better literacy skills, and *vice versa*. In other

---

[32]   A difference of at least one standard deviation (or 15 standard scores where the distribution has a mean of 100 and standard deviation of 15) can for practical purposes be taken as the *minimum* indication of a significant discrepancy (i.e. one that is unlikely to be attributable to normal or chance variation). The larger the difference in terms of standard deviation units (e.g. 1.5, 2 or greater), the correspondingly greater can our confidence be regarding the statistical and educational significance of the observed discrepancy. See also Section 8.3.3.1.

words, the two variables (intelligence and literacy ability) are said to be *positively correlated*. The higher this correlation, the more accurately can it be predicted that a student with a known IQ would be expected to have literacy skills within a given range. In turn, the more confident one can be that if they fall *below* this range there is a real discrepancy and not just a chance variation. In fact, the correlation between intelligence and literacy skills is not perfect.[33] This statistical fact results in a phenomenon known as 'regression to the mean', which, in simple terms, implies that there will always be a margin of error. Individuals with scores on one measure (e.g. IQ) will tend to have scores on the other measure (e.g. reading) that are somewhat closer to the mean (or average). For example, a person with an IQ of 130 (which would be at about centile 98, i.e. within the top 2–3% of the population and so very high), would not necessarily have reading skills that were also within that range, but more probably in the region of centile 85–90, which is still fairly high, but not exceptionally so.

Ideally, the discrepancy model should be applied using 'regression discrepancy', i.e. in a form that takes account of regression to the mean (McNab, 1994). This involves using the student's IQ to predict his or her expected scores on literacy measures, and then calculating the difference between expected scores and actual scores. This requires use of tests that have been standardised on the same population, and such tests are not always available. In practice, the assessor should regard the existence of a discrepancy as a *necessary* but *not sufficient* condition for a diagnosis, and should seek corroborating evidence of dyslexia (e.g. from quantitative and qualitative assessment of cognitive abilities) to counterbalance any diagnostic doubt that might arise as a result of statistical regression.

In higher education most students will be of at least average intelligence.[34] Poor literacy and/or study skills in higher education students who have met academic admission criteria cannot generally be attributed to lack of overall intellectual ability. If students in higher education have dyslexia, they will usually show a marked *discrepancy* between intellectual ability and some (but not necessarily all) aspects of literacy skills (Rack, 1997), even allowing for a margin of error that is necessary because of statistical regression effects. The use of an intelligence measure (such as the Wechsler Adult Intelligence Scale, Revised – WAIS-R; Wechsler, 1981) is generally advocated because it so often gives a clear indication of that discrepancy.[35]

On the other hand, poor literacy and/or study skills *may* also be the result of inadequate teaching or insufficient learning and/or experience and *do not necessarily* imply that the student has dyslexia. Establishing a discrepancy, as well as seeking evidence of neurological anomalies or cognitive impairments, helps the assessor to rule out these environmental factors as primary causes of the student's problems. However, the discrepancy model of identification should not be used blindly: it should be part of a more extensive process by which the assessor seeks to build up an understanding of the individual's difficulties based on quantitative and qualitative evidence.

There is an ongoing scientific debate about the role of intelligence in dyslexia (e.g. Ashton, 1996; Frederickson and Reason, 1995; Nicolson, 1996; Siegel, 1989a, 1989b, 1992; Solity, 1996; Stanovich, 1991; Turner, 1997)[36] and ways in which the condition should be diagnosed in adulthood

---

[33] Correlation statistics range from +1.0 (perfect positive correlation) through zero to −1.0 (perfect negative correlation). (Negative correlation implies that as one variable increases the correlated variable is found to *decrease*.) The correlation between reading and intelligence is frequently reported to be between +0.6 and +0.7 (Rayner and Pollatsek, 1989).

[34] The average IQ range is usually taken as either (a) 90 – 110 (which will account for 50% of the population, with 25% scoring above 110 and 25% below 90), or (b) 85 – 115 (which will account for 66% of the population, with 17% scoring above 115 and 17% below 85). The latter is a statistical convention that corresponds to + and − one standard deviation from the mean, and hence tends to be employed more in research studies. In practice, when making diagnostic assessments, psychologists more commonly use IQ 90 as the chosen cut-off point for 'below average'.

[35] The WAIS-R can only be administered by appropriately-qualified psychologists. Measures of general intellectual ability which non-psychologists can use include the *Standard Progressive Matrices* (Raven, 1958). See Section 14.5 for further details.

[36] A special issue of the journal *Dyslexia* (Vol. 2, No. 3, Nov 1996) contains a symposium on dyslexia and intelligence.

(Beaton, McDougall and Singleton, 1997). Some researchers argue that other types of discrepancy have better diagnostic value (e.g. between *oral* language abilities and *written* language abilities, or between *listening* comprehension and *reading* comprehension), although these could be problematic in cases of dyslexic individuals who have developed effective strategies for compensating for reading and writing difficulties. Others suggest that identifying those with chronic difficulty in phonological processing would be the most efficient way of diagnosing dyslexia in adulthood (Snowling et al, 1997), although by no means all adult dyslexics seem to have phonological difficulties (Rack, 1997). At the present time, however, such academic disputes are not particularly helpful to those trying to diagnose dyslexia in students in higher education. We do not yet have tests nor well-developed procedures derived from these theories that have been thoroughly researched and validated and which are suitable for the higher education population.

It should be noted that conventional measures of overall intelligence (usually based on an aggregate of scores from different sub-tests) are not necessarily the best or most reliable indicators of the intellectual or academic potential of students with dyslexia, or of their ability to follow a degree course successfully. Individuals with dyslexia (adults and children) typically have a very uneven intellectual profile, with strengths as well as limitations. This pattern often shows itself in the form of a significant discrepancy between skills involved in verbal reasoning, oral comprehension and non-verbal problem-solving on the one hand, and skills which depend heavily on working memory, on the other. If the overall IQ measure aggregates scores across those different areas, including the memory-dependent sub-tests, the outcome may be to depress the IQ measure significantly, which could give a misleading picture of the person's overall ability, especially when interpreted by non-psychologists. Some specialists in this field (e.g. McLoughlin, Fitzgibbon and Young, 1994) advocate evaluating intellectual strengths and limitations *independently*, rather than *aggregating* intellectual strengths and weaknesses to produce an overall IQ measure. Nevertheless, an overall IQ measure can be useful as a general guide.

In cases in which a student has compensated for their dyslexia extremely well (or where the dyslexia is mild) there may be no major difficulties in reading, writing, spelling or mathematics which can be detected. It may well be that this student has dyslexia (because there are further criteria, such as evidence of neurological disabilities, which have been satisfied) but unless it can be shown that there are other significant impairments which will affect the student's studies and examination performance (e.g. in memory), or that the *discrepancy* between observed and predicted literacy skills is significant (even though the former may be in the average range), then it would be improper to try to make a case for DSA or other special provision.

8.3.2.5 Evidence of cognitive disabilities or neurological anomalies

The third point in the guidelines calls for evidence of any cognitive disabilities or neurological anomalies that are likely to have an adverse effect on learning. This is most important. Dyslexia is a neurological condition which is characterised by a variety of cognitive impairments or neurological anomalies (see Section 2.3). Individuals with dyslexia typically manifest problems in areas such as phonological processing, memory (especially short-term or working memory), visual perception (e.g. visual discomfort) and motor co-ordination (dyspraxia). Difficulties in these areas will not necessarily all be seen in the same individual with dyslexia, but if *no difficulty in any of these areas* can be detected then a diagnosis of dyslexia must be regarded with suspicion. There is a range of established psychological procedures for assessing these difficulties but unfortunately not many psychometric tests.

Research evidence points strongly to the two most important cognitive areas being phonological processing and memory. Difficulties with phonological processing have been well-documented in many studies of children with dyslexia, using techniques such as ability to detect rhyme and alliteration (e.g. see Frith, 1997; Snowling, 1995; Snowling and Nation, 1997). Researchers are now turning their attention to studies of phonological processing by adults with dyslexia (e.g. see Beaton, McDougall and Singleton; 1997a). At the present time there are no properly validated tests of phonological processing for use with adults, although there are tasks which can give some indication of difficulties in this area (e.g. Snowling et al, 1997) and the *Dyslexia Adult Screening Test* (DAST, Nicolson and Fawcett, 1997) contains a phonemic segmentation test. However, dyslexia is not simply a phonological processing difficulty: some adults with dyslexia do not show phonological processing problems or may display difficulties in other cognitive areas, such as visual-motor coordination (Hanley, 1997; Rack, 1997). In order to identify adults with dyslexia, tests or tasks of phonological processing are useful clinical indicators, but they cannot be relied on, nor can they replace all the other diagnostic evidence that is necessary. Whether there are distinct subtypes of dyslexia is a thorny issue that remains unresolved, even in the literature on dyslexia in children (see Nicolson and Fawcett, 1995; Stanovich, Siegel and Gottardo, 1997; Tonnesson, 1997). At the present time, the most prudent interpretation of the conflicting data on this topic is that there are dimensions of individual differences manifested in dyslexia rather than discrete subtypes (Ellis, McDougall and Monk, 1996a, 1996b).

Some of the sub-tests of *WAIS-R* (Wechsler, 1981) will give the psychologist good indications of deficits or relative weaknesses in memory (see McLoughlin, Fitzgibbon and Young, 1994; Turner, 1997). There are other clinical measures that psychologists can employ, including the *Wechsler Memory Scales* (Wechsler, 1987). Sub-tests from the *British Ability Scales* (Elliott, Murray and Pearson, 1979; Elliott, Smith and McCulloch, 1996) can be used to assess aspects of visual memory.[37] The *Bangor Dyslexia Test* (Miles, 1982/97, 1993) and the *Dyslexia Adult Screening Test* (DAST; Nicolson and Fawcett, 1997) also include memory items (see Section 14.5 for further details of tests).

The other main areas of concern – visual perception and motor skills – should not be overlooked, even though problems here are seen less frequently than with memory and phonological abilities. For further information on assessment of visual discomfort see Section 9.2.3.2. A variety of tasks can be used to investigate motor coordination and to detect dyspraxia, including pegboards, mazes and timed handwriting activities. At the present time, there is little by way of norms or established criteria against which to compare the performance of students in higher education, so persons carrying out assessments have to use their own judgement based on clinical experience. Further research is needed in this area.

8.3.2.6   Evidence of effects on learning

The fourth point in the guidelines calls for evidence of the manner and extent to which the difficulties or disabilities that have been identified are likely to affect learning in the higher education setting. Assessment by personnel who are unaware of the learning requirements in higher education are unlikely to be able to give a very clear picture of the problems which the student may encounter, or fully understand the problems which they are currently facing.

Higher education places special demands on the learner. Some of these demands are generic to higher education (e.g. use of higher education libraries, word processing, research techniques) and others are specific to particular subject areas (e.g. use of particular computer applications in learning, particular critical approaches in methods of study). Some demands are like those encountered in learning at school or at further education level (e.g. use of textbooks, writing essays, taking written examinations, and involvement in group projects).

For most students, certain demands are likely to be encountered for the first time in higher education, such as writing a substantial dissertation or giving a seminar presentation. However, the main differences between higher education study and other forms of learning are:

- the greater depth and breadth of study
- the increased volume of work
- the increased technical and conceptual difficulty of the material
- the switch to independent learning and self-reliance in the organisation of study.

---

[37] E.g. Visual Recall, Recall of Designs. The norms for these tests only extend to the age of 17 years 5 months, but until age-appropriate norms are established, this is sufficiently close to the adult range to be satisfactory for use in higher education assessment.

The last point is especially important. For example, in higher education there is no one to tell you when to stop reading, to check that you have understood what you have read, and not always someone who will tell you *what* to read at any given time.

For students who do *not* have dyslexia and who have not been properly prepared for higher education, the transition to study at this level can be hard. For students with dyslexia, however, it can present extreme difficulties. Those students with dyslexia who have received substantial support before reaching university may be quite unprepared for independent learning. Those who enter university without realising that they have dyslexia may assume that the strategies which they have consciously or sub-consciously evolved to circumvent their difficulties will work in this new educational environment; if this assumption turns out to be false, they may find their confidence dashed.

The memory difficulties of people with dyslexia do not only affect the ability to *retain* information: they impede the processes of *organisation* of information, too. The latter has repercussions on the general organisation of everyday living as well as the organisation of studying. Students with dyslexia typically have greater problems in adjusting to independent learning than do other students because, in addition to lacking the relevant experience, the necessary organisational capacity is also weak. This is something that is very difficult to assess directly, but it can be inferred from performance on tests of working memory. Talking to the student about organisation of life and study can provide additional clues.

8.3.2.7   Other relevant evidence

The fifth point in the guidelines covers other relevant evidence, including (where this can be obtained) that of any family history of language and/or literacy difficulties, of birth difficulties and/or early developmental difficulties (e.g. in speech or motor development), and educational history. The significance of these factors to the identification of dyslexia should be apparent from the outline *What is dyslexia?* provided in Chapter 2. Dyslexia is a constitutional condition and, even if the condition has not been formally recognised in a particular individual prior to the present assessment, there will often be some indications of the disorder during childhood or schooling. Such evidence can provide valuable confirmation of conclusions drawn from other aspects of the assessment.

When assessing adults, however, it can be very difficult to obtain reliable information about such matters. The individual will usually be able to recall recent educational history, but may not be able to remember much which is useful to the assessor regarding their primary schooling. They will rarely be able to relay information about birth or early development unless they have recently been told about this by a parent. Occasionally, relevant information is found to have been documented by a disinterested professional involved with the child and his or her family. Fortunately, such information is not crucial to a diagnosis of dyslexia in adults, although it is obviously helpful as it can corroborate other evidence and provide support for a diagnosis. It is sometimes useful to contact the student's parents about such matters, having obtained the student's permission.

Some LEAs, in considering DSA applications from students with dyslexia, stipulate that there should be evidence that the dyslexia has been identified when the student was at school, and that special arrangements were made at GCSE/'A' level. Other stipulations include product of evidence that specific literacy difficulties were evident in discrepancies at GCSE/'A' level between results of different subjects (e.g. between English and Maths or practical subjects). There seems to be an assumption that if dyslexia has not been diagnosed nor shown up clearly while the student was at school, then it is unlikely that they really have dyslexia, and so the claim for DSA may be rejected.

While evidence that dyslexia was identified when the student was at school would obviously support a case for DSA support, the lack of such evidence should not prejudice a student's claim, and the imposition of such criteria is quite unjustifiable. The national survey (see Section 3.2.3) found that 43% of students with dyslexia were only identified as having dyslexia *after* entry to higher education. In the past, some LEAs have operated an explicit or implicit policy of non-recognition of dyslexia. In such circumstances, it is unsurprising that a dyslexic student will not have had their condition diagnosed, nor special examination arrangements made, when they were at school. In less serious cases of dyslexia (see Section 8.3.3.1), the student may have been able to cope with the level of work at school, but be unable to manage without support in higher education, because of the much greater pressures on literacy skills, learning and recall. In other words, there are good reasons why many students with dyslexia are not identified until after they enter higher education.

LEAs are under a duty to scrutinise all DSA applications carefully, to ensure that as far as possible, any bogus or unjustified claim is rejected. At the present time, the incidence of dyslexia in higher education is in the region of 1.5% or less compared with about 4% in the general population (see Section 3.2.3). That difference in incidence does not suggest that the label 'dyslexic' is being over-applied to students in higher education, nor does it lead one to imagine that unwarranted claims for DSA support are widespread. The Working Party believes that if HEIs, dyslexia assessors and LEAs all observed these *Guidelines on diagnostic assessment of dyslexia*, then the evidence supplied in support of applications for DSAs would be of an appropriate content and satisfactory standard to enable LEA Awards Officers to make a clear decision without the imposition of unacceptable criteria such as evidence of diagnosis while at school.

8.3.2.8   *Evidence that the difficulties are not due to other factors*

The sixth and final point in the guidelines calls for evidence that the difficulties or disabilities that have been identified are not due *primarily* to (a) limitations in experience of written and/or spoken English, (b) lack of motivation, application or educational opportunity, (c) emotional causes, or (d) poor general or mental health or a medical condition.

With widening access to higher education generally, and increased admission of foreign students in particular, the number of students with limited experience of written and/or spoken English is likely to increase. Students whose first language is not English may show poor grammar and vocabulary in spoken and written English. Students with hearing impairments may also show these symptoms, as well as scoring low on test or tasks of phonological processing because of a relative lack or distorted experience of spoken language. If purely informal methods of diagnosis are employed, it will be difficult to distinguish within these groups of students those whose limitations in literacy are due solely to such lack or distortion of experience, and those who may have additional problems caused by dyslexia. The importance of including assessment of cognitive factors such as memory, which can help to untangle these problems, should be apparent.

Students in higher education have usually had to demonstrate fairly good academic capabilities in order to enter higher education.[38] It is unlikely that any *serious* difficulties which they display in literacy have been due to lack of opportunity, although less serious ones – e.g. in spelling – may well be because they were not taught that particular skill when at school. The assessor should try to obtain information that will enable lack of educational opportunity to be ruled out as a *direct cause* of the student's difficulties. Even so, it may be an *indirect cause*, in that failure to identify dyslexia while at school may have resulted in loss of some educational opportunities and even resulted in dropping out of school altogether. Academic attainment at higher education level probably depends as much on interest in the subject, motivation and hard work as on intellectual ability. Thus it is important for the assessor to try, as far as possible, to ensure that these factors are unlikely to be the *direct cause* of the student's studying difficulties, even though they may manifest as *secondary effects* of dyslexia (e.g. depression and associated poor concentration, or loss of motivation due to anxiety about poor performance).

Poor general and mental health, as well as many medical conditions, can have deleterious effects on learning capacity of any student, both directly and indirectly (e.g. because of the side effects of medication, or the emotional and motivational consequences of ill-health). If the student has dyslexia, then this should be revealed in the types of evidence referred to in points 1 to 5 and 6 (a) and (b) of the guidelines given in Section 8.3.2.2. But health problems and medical conditions, as well as affecting learning ability generally, can affect the results of psychological and educational tests, producing misleading results. Although persons carrying out diagnostic assessment for dyslexia are not expected to have medical expertise, they should nevertheless try to ascertain (as far as is ethically and professionally appropriate to do so) that medical or health problems are not a significant factor in

---

[38] A notable exception is the Open University, which admits all students who wish to attempt its courses.

the case. This information can be gained by asking the student concerned, but to ensure the student's right to privacy this should be prefaced with a suitable caveat. For example, 'You are not obliged to supply me with any information regarding your state of health, but it would be very helpful if you could tell me whether...' (your current health is satisfactory; whether you have any history of ill-health; whether you know of any significant medical or health problems that you have had that are likely to have affected your studies). Where there are suspicions of significant medical or health problems, it may be necessary to ask the student's permission to contact the student's General Practitioner and request a report. If the student has not yet consulted his or her G.P., then this should be recommended.

8.3.3 *Assessment of individual variation in dyslexia*

8.3.3.1 *Degrees of severity of dyslexia and its effects*

Dyslexia is a condition in which there are considerable individual differences (see Section 8.3.2.5) and which can vary in severity from one individual to another (Turner, 1997). Individuals with dyslexia also show varying degrees of compensation for their difficulties (see Section 8.3.3.2). When considering provision for students with dyslexia (including DSA and examination provision) it is therefore entirely appropriate that individual variation and the severity of the student's problems should be taken into account. The national survey revealed that some HEIs already attempt to allow for the severity of a student's difficulties, giving higher levels of support and more additional time for the more severe cases. LEA Awards Officers also attempt to do this, trying to make a judgement about whether the amount of DSA provision that is being requested for the student is appropriate in relation to the difficulties that have been documented. In attempting this, the Awards Officer may enlist the assistance of an Educational Psychologist of the LEA (for further discussion of this see Section 9.2.7).

It is doubtful whether it is possible, in practical terms, to assess severity of dyslexia *per se*. In standardised tests (e.g. of reading or spelling) students with dyslexia will be found to differ in the degree of difficulty which they display. But to rely on this information alone to classify the severity of their problems is problematic. In part, this is because dyslexia is a heterogeneous condition which can manifest itself in different ways in different individuals, and also because we do not have entirely satisfactory ways of measuring 'severity'. If there are two different dyslexic students, one of which is very poor at reading but who still manages to produce reasonable written work, and the other who is poor at writing but can manage to read satisfactorily, should their dyslexia be regarded as being of 'equal severity' or should one student be regarded as being more severely affected than the other? Alternatively, one could look at the degree of difficulty which they show in underlying cognitive skills, such as working memory. A student with limited working memory capacity might be assumed to encounter greater difficulties than one whose working memory was only a little below average. However, if the first student has received intensive specialist support at school, they will probably have developed fairly good literacy skills (although revision and recall for examinations may still be a major problem). If the second student has not had the benefit of specialist support then their literacy skills may, in fact, be less well developed than those of the first student, even though their working memory is not as poor. Which is the more severely affected?

Turner (1997) describes a prototype system for assessing severity of dyslexia that provides a possible solution to the problem described above by computing the *average discrepancy* manifested by the person. This discrepancy, measured in standard deviation units, is calculated (a) between the individual's intellectual ability (abstract thinking) and his or her performance on diagnostic tests of information processing (e.g. memory), and (b) between that individual's observed and expected attainment in reading, spelling and written number work. A score of 0.5 − 0.9 is rated as 'mild dyslexia', 1.0 − 1.4 as 'moderate dyslexia', 1.5 − 1.9 as 'severe dyslexia' and above 2.0 as 'very severe dyslexia'. To carry out this calculation requires the use of psychometric tests that yield scores in standard form (e.g. mean of 100 and standard deviation of 15).

Although Turner's system represents an encouraging step forwards, and is worthy of further research, it is unclear at the present time how effective it might be in the higher education setting. It cannot always be assumed that a measured discrepancy shown in cognitive or literacy test results will reliably predict that student's performance or problems in his or her studies. In the first place, all students differ in intellectual ability and motivation, and secondly, students with dyslexia differ in the extent to which they have come to terms with their difficulties (see Section 8.3.3.2). In order to assess severity, the emphasis should be on the known or likely *effects* of the dyslexia in given situations (such as reading, writing essays, making lecture notes or taking examinations), taking into account that student's individual profile of difficulties. This process should encompass both *quantitative* factors (i.e. based on standardised test scores) as well as *qualitative* factors (e.g. compensatory strategies, or difficulties for which there are no standardised measurements). Additionally, it should be recognised that diagnostic assessment and evaluation of needs cannot be expected to anticipate *every problem* which students with dyslexia could encounter during their studies.

8.3.3.2   *The compensated dyslexic*

There can be varying degrees of awareness and compensation shown by adults with dyslexia. The 'compensated dyslexic' is the individual who shows some awareness of the nature and extent of their problems and has made efforts to compensate for them by developing appropriate strategies. They may or may not know that their condition has a label ('dyslexia'). Their level of awareness will to some extent determine the degree to which they can experiment with new strategies and variations of those they have already mastered (McLoughlin, Fitzgibbon and Young, 1994). Compensatory strategies may be quite simple (e.g. always making sure that appointments are written in a diary otherwise they are liable to be forgotten, or asking another person to check one's work for spelling and grammatical errors) or more complicated (e.g. colour-coding files or work in accordance with an individual organisational scheme). Such strategies are by no means the prerogative of people with dyslexia, but for the dyslexic person, they can often make the difference between coping and failing in many situations.[39]

In order to gain entry to higher education, most individuals with dyslexia have developed some compensatory strategies. Although these strategies may have been adequate for coping in their previous environment, they may be inadequate for dealing with the demands placed upon them in higher education. Sometimes, well-compensated students are denied DSA on the grounds that their difficulties do not appear to be sufficiently severe to justify the award (see, for example, the vignette 'Ruth' in Section 2.6.1.5). Because of acquired compensatory strategies, such students may be functioning at an average rate in some areas of literacy but still have significant difficulties in memory and the organisation of information. In such cases, the assessor needs to provide evidence that even though the student has been able to compensate to some extent, there is still a *significant discrepancy* between the student's predicted attainment and actual attainment. Such evidence shows that the effects of dyslexia are clearly still of sufficient magnitude to impair the student's learning and studying, and that consequently provision (including the DSA) would be justified. The issue of allowing for compensation is further addressed in the next section.

It should also be borne in mind that the compensated dyslexic will usually have to put in a great deal more time and effort than other students in order to complete the same academic work. As they progress through their course, the quantity and difficulty of the work generally increases, and they often reach the point at which they can no longer cope. Rather than allowing such a situation to develop, appropriate support provision (including DSA) should be in place to enable the dyslexic student to sustain a satisfactory level of academic work throughout the course.

8.3.3.3   *An outline classification of severity*

In due course, the development of a better range of psychometric tests suitable for use with adults, coupled with further research on quantitative systems for assessing severity of dyslexia – such as that presented by Turner (1997) and outlined in Section 8.3.3.1 – may lead to the widespread adoption of an agreed index for classifying severity of dyslexia in higher education. However, the Working Party believes that a qualitative approach would be more pragmatic for the time being. The following is a broad qualitative classification of severity, which may assist assessors in this task. This classification

---

[39] For many practical suggestions regarding compensatory strategies, see Gilroy and Miles (1996).

has been in use in two universities for approximately three years and seems to work fairly well in practice, although research on the subject is continuing.[40]

'**Mild**': the student who meets the criteria for a diagnosis of dyslexia and who

- has a high level of compensation, and
- has mild difficulties in a *range* of learning skills, or moderate difficulties in *one* learning skill area.

'**Moderate**': the student who meets the criteria for a diagnosis of dyslexia and who

- does *not* have a high level of compensation, and
- has moderate difficulties in a *range* of learning skills, or severe difficulties in *one* skill area.

'**Severe**': the student who meets the criteria for a diagnosis of dyslexia and who

- has little or no compensation, and
- has severe difficulties in a *range* of learning skills.

There are a number of important observations that must be made about this scheme, of which those who adopt it ought to be fully aware.

First, the magnitude of dyslexic problems encountered by students with dyslexia does not neatly fit into the same categories. For example, the scheme does not mean that students classified as having with 'mild dyslexia' will encounter only 'mild' problems: they can experience more serious problems as well. In general, however, they should encounter the serious problems less frequently than students with either 'moderate dyslexia' or 'severe dyslexia'. The recommendations made for that student (e.g. DSA, study skills support) will depend as much on the particular nature of the problems as on the overall category into which the student falls.

Second, the degree of severity is not expected to be a fixed rating. With suitable support and sufficient time to develop alternative strategies to overcome learning problems, the level of compensation shown by the student should steadily increase. Hence some students are likely to require a high level of support (e.g. tuition in study skills) in the early stages of their course, but may require less support in the later stages, particularly if they have acquired an effective use of assistive technology which can compensate for their disability to some extent. It is therefore recommended that when assessors provide a statement on the severity of the effects of dyslexia, this should be as an initial guide to the likely level of support needed by the student, which may have to be modified in due course.

Third, not all cases will necessarily fit within this scheme, e.g. the student who exhibits severe difficulties in a range of learning skills (such as very slow and inaccurate reading, very poor spelling, slow and disorganised writing, very poor memory and recall in examinations) but who has developed reasonably successful compensatory strategies for some of them. In such cases, assessors will need to weigh up all the information and make judgements which they consider to be most equitable. Each case must be considered individually and, ultimately, the categorisation of the severity of the student's problems must be the decision of a qualified assessor.

Those assessors who prefer to make use of a quantitative approach may still use this scheme, but base their judgements of 'mild', 'moderate' and 'severe' difficulties *in learning skills* on measured discrepancies between observed versus expected attainments in literacy, and between intellectual ability and specific cognitive skills such as memory. Use of standard deviation (SD) units is usually the most satisfactory way to do this. In view of the fact that Turner's (1997) index is based on the *average discrepancies* shown by an individual, where *particular discrepancies* are being evaluated

---

[40] Horne and Singleton (1997) reported on a study of 72 university students with dyslexia. Students falling into the three categories of severity were found to be significantly different on an adult dyslexia checklist and also on measures of reading, spelling and memorisation.

the thresholds should be somewhat higher that reported by Turner, e.g. above 2.0 SD units for 'severe', 1.5 – 1.9 for 'moderate' and 1.0 – 1.4 for 'mild'.

Some disability officers and dyslexia tutors working in HEIs have anxieties about the adoption of a classification of severity, because of concerns that LEAs will misuse this to reject DSA applications in 'mild' cases. Since such action on the part of an LEA – if carried out routinely – would be quite improper (and legally challengeable), this should not be a reason to repudiate the classification scheme, which has scientific justification as well as pragmatic benefits. Many students with dyslexia falling into the 'mild' category will still require DSA support in order to gain access to the assistive technology and/or study skills tuition that will be necessary to cope with their studies in higher education. Each case must still be considered on its merits by both sides of the DSA application procedure (i.e. the dyslexia tutor/disability officer and the LEA Awards Officer). For further discussion on this issue, see Section 9.2.7.

8.3.3.4   *Day-to-day variation*

Persons with dyslexia frequently report that they have 'good days' and 'bad days', in the sense that the severity of the effects of their dyslexia varies from one day to another (Gilroy and Miles, 1996; Miles and Varma, 1995; Stacey, 1997, 1998). This is a contentious issue, for various reasons. Many people who do not have dyslexia would *also* contend that they have 'good days' and 'bad days', which might be associated with all manner of factors, such as general health; sleeping patterns; diet and nutrition; hormone cycles; personal relationships and experiences; climate and weather; employment circumstances; local, national and international events. Unfortunately, as yet we do not have very much information on this phenomenon; ideally, one would wish to see evidence of variable performance on standardised tasks or diary studies comparing dyslexic people with non-dyslexic people on a day-to-day basis.

There are several hypotheses that might account for day-to-day variation in dyslexia. One is the differential effect which dyslexia has on *different* tasks which the person is attempting from day to day. Another cause could be interaction effects of one activity following another – there is often a different 'mix' of activities from one day to another, which could generate the experience of 'good days' and 'bad days' when the person with dyslexia has to switch tasks. Another possible explanation is the variation in overall information load (or 'cognitive stress') from activity to activity, with which working memory has to cope. Because of working memory deficiencies in dyslexia, this could affect the individual with dyslexia more than other individuals. This hypothesis would be consistent with the observation by many parents of dyslexic children that when their children arrive home after school, they show great variability in behaviour according to the cognitive demands of the tasks which they have had to deal with at school as well as other factors in the environment (Miles and Varma, 1995).

Whatever the cause of the experience of day-to-day variation in the effects of dyslexia, to try to obtain a valid measure of this in a diagnostic assessment at the present time is out of the question, and to try to make allowances for it in support provision or examinations is unlikely to be fair to individuals who do not have dyslexia. There is one further issue – if severity of dyslexia does vary from one day to another, how are we to know whether the day on which the assessment has been carried out is a 'good day' or a 'bad day'? Either way, the outcome may be an overestimate or an underestimate of the degree of impairment the student is likely to experience and we will not know which. At the present time, at least, we have to accept that our methods for assessing dyslexia and our understanding of the condition are far from perfect. To attempt to accommodate highly complex factors, such as daily variability, in the assessment equation on the basis of our present state of knowledge is unlikely to improve on this state of affairs and may well make matters worse. What we can do, however, is *acknowledge* that some students with dyslexia will probably experience variation in their capacity to manage their dyslexia. Compensatory strategies which students with dyslexia have developed may not be maintained all the time or to the same degree (perhaps because of fatigue, emotional state, or factors to do with the nature of the task, such as the quality and degree of organisation found in a text that is being read).

8.3.4   *Other issues*

8.3.4.1   *Content of reports*

Reports of diagnostic assessments should be intelligible to the student and to any others who need to read it, e.g. disability officer, study skills tutor, LEA Awards Officer. Terminology should be clear. Scores should be explained in as straightforward a manner as possible and presented in a form that is appropriate for this client group. Score forms such as 'reading age' and 'spelling age' are often misunderstood, although many psychologists would affirm their value. During the national consultation process carried out by the Working Party, many dyslexia tutors and disabilities officers commented that they and their clients found the use of reading ages and spelling ages in psychological reports offensive and that these created unnecessary problems in explaining the assessment results to students. By contrast, use of centiles or other standard scores, as well as avoiding unpleasant connotations that reading ages and spelling ages obviously have for some clients, have the added advantage of allowing greater comparability across different tests.

The assessment evidence obtained in accordance with the guidelines given in Section 8.3.2 should be set out clearly and succinctly. A clear conclusion regarding whether or not the student has dyslexia should be drawn. A statement on the *severity* of the effects of dyslexia in the case should be provided as an initial guide to the likely level of support required, recognising that this may have to be modified in the light of subsequent evaluations of needs (see Chapter 9).

Recommendations for action should be stated, which refer in outline form to each of the following:

- DSA application for appropriate technology and other support

- study skills provision

- support from course tutors or within the student's department

- special examination provisions

- any other recommendations (e.g. for ophthamalogical assessment).

These recommendations do not need to be in great detail. They should state that in the professional opinion of the assessor, because the student has dyslexia, he or she should be entitled to the particular support or provision in order to compensate for their disability and to enable them to pursue their studies properly. Filling in the necessary details (e.g. exactly what technology to apply for within the DSA, or what extent of study skills support or examination provision is required), is a job that is best left to the person carrying out an evaluation of needs (see Chapter 9). In cases where psychologists or other assessors are not particularly familiar with the institution or with the latest developments in technology, too much detail on these matters in the report of the diagnostic assessment can be counterproductive. It can result in delays or difficulties in obtaining DSA, because the LEA Awards Officer may be confronted with one recommendation from the psychologist or diagnostic assessor and a different one in the report of the person carrying out the evaluation of needs. If in doubt, assessors should ask the disability officer of the HEI for guidance on how much detail should be included in their recommendations.

Finally, reports should include the name and qualifications of the assessor, date(s) of testing, and the age of student at the time the assessment was carried out.

8.3.4.2   *Conduct of assessments*

Anecdotally, some students with dyslexia have reported that the process of being assessed by a psychologist was rather unpleasant. They felt apprehensive, or even frightened beforehand, as they did not know what to expect, and the anticipation brought back vivid memories of failure and humiliation in school. During the assessment, they felt as though they were 'back at school' and were treated more like a child than an adult. In such cases, they were not given any rationale or explanation for the tasks that they were required to do, nor any feedback afterwards. When the report of the assessment was supplied, they had difficulty in interpreting it, and were not given any real opportunity to discuss it with someone who did understand the terminology of such reports. In some cases this provoked a personal crisis for the student, because they had acquired a label for a condition which had been diagnosed (dyslexia) but did not realise the implications of this.

Of course, none of this should happen. Not only is it unprofessional and unethical to treat clients in this way, but the creation of additional stress on the client may also invalidate test results. Assessments should always be carried out in a proper professional manner, mindful of the fact that clients are adults who have a right to know (as do all clients) what they are being subjected to and why, and to be informed of the outcome of the assessment in a clear and understandable manner. Students should be prepared for a diagnostic assessment by the person who refers them (e.g. from a screening assessment), to reassure them about the process and give them an opportunity to ask any questions, and again before the diagnostic assessment itself. It is also good practice for the assessor to chat informally with the student beforehand, in order to put him or her at ease, then to explain what the assessment will comprise, what the purpose of each part of the assessment is for (unless this might compromise the assessment process), and to point out that if the student wishes to ask questions, or request a break, they may do so.

8.3.4.3   Feedback to the student

It is not always possible for the assessor to give immediate feedback to the student. Psychological, cognitive and educational tests typically take some time to score and interpret, and the assessor will need to consider the test results and other evidence as a whole. Students should always have the opportunity to discuss their assessment report with either the assessor or some other person (e.g. disability officer, study skills tutor) who has the expertise to explain the findings and answer any questions.

It can be extremely valuable for disability officers, study skills tutors and other personnel involved in making provision for students with dyslexia to have a staff development session, delivered by the psychologist or other professional who carries out diagnostic assessments, in order to gain a better understanding of the tests and procedures used in such assessments, and the interpretations made. This understanding not only facilitates giving informative feedback to students, but is also beneficial during the next step in the process, which is evaluation of the student's needs.

Useful advice to students on understanding their assessment reports is given in Gilroy and Miles, 1996). If students are upset by their assessment findings, they may find it helpful to consult the student counselling service (see Chapter 10).

8.3.4.4   Confidentiality

The fact of having had a dyslexia screening or diagnostic assessment carried out and the findings of dyslexia assessments should be treated as confidential at all times. Where it is proposed that the information should be revealed to a third party (e.g. the student's tutor or supervisor, or the examinations officer), the reasons for this should be explained to the student and the student's permission obtained before going ahead. Even if the disability officer or another officer of the institution believes it would be in the student's interest to reveal the findings of an assessment, it would be improper to do so if the student declines to give permission.

8.3.4.5   Assessment of students already believed to be dyslexic

In Section 8.1.3, the issue was raised of students who declare themselves to have dyslexia on the UCAS form or have been previously had a psychological assessment for dyslexia. It was argued that it will usually still be necessary to carry out an assessment of such students in order to evaluate their *current* difficulties. In cases where the student has already been assessed for dyslexia a copy of the assessment report should always be obtained and scrutinised. Because of delays inherent in the system of diagnostic assessment (psychologist's waiting lists and time lapse before the report is received) it may be necessary to accept such evidence provisionally. If a copy of a previous report is obtained and the HEI is *satisfied* regarding the credentials of the person who carried out the assessment and the adequacy of the information which is contained in the report, a full psychological assessment will not usually be necessary as the diagnosis will not be in question. An assessment of the extent of the student's *current difficulties* in literacy and other studying difficulties (and, where appropriate mathematics and number skills) will still be required. Where appropriately skilled personnel are available in the institution to do this it will not be necessary to refer such a student to a psychologist, for this process can be part of the evaluation of the student's needs (see Chapter 9).

8.3.4.6   Cost of diagnostic assessments

The issues concerning the costs of diagnostic assessment were considered in Section 8.1.7. HEIs should consider carefully their position on this issue and its implications for their equal opportunities and disability policies. The Working Party recommends that, wherever possible, HEIs bear some or all of the costs of assessments rather than expecting students to pay themselves. Many HEIs already use Access Funds for this purpose. It should be noted that substantial savings of up to 50% can often be made by negotiating special institutional rates for diagnostic assessment. Use of a screening assessment can help to keep costs down by ensuring, as far as possible, that only *bona fide* cases are referred for diagnostic assessment. Alternatively, adoption of a staged response to special learning needs in higher education (whether due to disability or not) on a 'Code of Practice' model, could reduce the numbers of students who require costly psychological assessment (see Chapter 13).

8.3.4.7   Comparison with recommended guidelines in the US

McGuire et al (1996) examined documentation provided over a 5-year period by 415 US students who were applying for special examination arrangements and support (in the US: 'accommodations') because of dyslexia.[41]   These authors observed that the US Government Regulations offer no guidelines as to the quality or content of documentation in such cases. In a very large proportion of cases, documentation was found to be inadequate. Assessment reports were rarely comprehensive enough, recommendations were frequently based on insufficient and/or inappropriate information, and the tests used were often found to be unsuitable for use with this population. Consequently, McGuire et al make the following recommendations:

- testing must be *comprehensive*

- testing must be *current* (i.e. within the last 3 years)

- there must be clear and specific evidence of a learning *disability*

- *test scores* and other relevant data should be included

- tests used should be *appropriate* (i.e. valid and reliable) for an adult population

- reports should be clear and understandable

- reports should include the name and qualifications of the assessor, date(s) of testing, and the age of student at the time.

It can be seen that there is substantial concurrence in these recommendations and those presented in this Chapter.

8.4   Recommendations on identification

1.   All HEIs should formulate a clear policy on identification of dyslexia which embodies the National Working Party's *Guidelines on diagnostic assessment of dyslexia*.

2.   The policy on identification should specify:

    a)   the qualifications of personnel authorised to carry out screening and diagnostic assessment, the content and the conduct of those assessments;

---

[41] Referred to as 'learning disabilities' by these authors, as is usually the case in US studies.

b)   the institution's requirements regarding assessment of students who are admitted to the institution having already declared on the UCAS form that they have dyslexia and/or who have previously been assessed for dyslexia;

c)   the requirements regarding confidentiality of information derived from and pertaining to any screening or diagnostic assessment; and

d)   the extent to which the institution is prepared to bear the cost of any screening or diagnostic assessment.

3.   All HEIs should:

a)   enquire whether personnel carrying out diagnostic assessments conform to the National Working Party's *Guidelines on diagnostic assessment of dyslexia*, and if the answer to this enquiry is in the negative, should seek a satisfactory explanation for this;

b)   bear as much of the cost of diagnostic assessment that can reasonably be afforded;

c)   implement a satisfactory screening procedure for dyslexia; and

d)   make its policy and procedures for dyslexia screening and diagnostic assessment known to present students, to applicants and to staff.

4.   Psychologists, other professionals and organisations offering psychological or psychometric assessment to students from HEIs should:

a)   conform to the National Working Party's *Guidelines on diagnostic assessment of dyslexia*;

b)   have demonstrated competencies in psychometric testing to BPS standard;

c)   be prepared to enter into discounting arrangements with HEIs regarding the fees paid for assessment services.

5.   When considering applications for Disabled Students' Allowances from students with dyslexia, all LEAs should expect such applications to be accompanied by reports of diagnostic assessment that conforms to the *Guidelines on diagnostic assessment of dyslexia* given in this report.

6.   The British Psychological Society (BPS) should bring into operation with all speed its plans for assessing competencies in educational testing for psychologists and non-psychologists.

7.   Training courses offering specialist qualifications in the teaching of adults with dyslexia in higher education (whether accredited by the British Dyslexia Association or by a university) that purport to cover the skills of dyslexia assessment, should teach the relevant competencies in assessment prescribed in the National Working Party's *Guidelines on diagnostic assessment of dyslexia*.

9 Evaluation of needs and provision of support

9.1 Issues, problems and challenges

9.1.1 Policy requirements

Students with dyslexia often (but not invariably) require additional facilities to support their learning. Making appropriate provision for any student with dyslexia is a complicated and multi-stage process, that will usually involve consideration of whether an application for Disabled Students Allowances (DSA) would be appropriate to help meet the student's needs. A diagnostic assessment will confirm the presence of dyslexia and should establish the student's profile of strengths and weaknesses (see Chapter 8). The next stage in the process is to evaluate individual learning needs in relation to this profile and to the demands on the student in the particular course that is being studied, as far as this is possible at this stage. Arrangements for comprehensive support can then be implemented which should assist the student to study at the same level as his/her peers. Part of this should be a technology assessment, which can recommend useful items of equipment, but it should be stressed that support needs are usually much wider than just provision of technology.

Before an HEI can implement an effective provision for students with dyslexia, there is a need for policy which will clearly specify:

- the personnel who will carry out evaluation of needs

- the procedures for this evaluation

- how this process is to be paid for

- what support facilities are (or should be) available within the institution in order to meet those needs and how the costs of such support are to be met.

The last point has a direct bearing on the application for the DSA.

9.1.2 Disabled Students Allowances (DSA)

9.1.2.1 Outline of the DSA system

Full-time higher education students with a disability can apply to their LEA for special allowances (DSA) to enable them to pay for equipment and support which they need for their studies. These have enabled many students with dyslexia to study more effectively and to alleviate some of the difficulties of being an adult with dyslexia in higher education.

There are three categories of DSA, which are outlined below.

Special equipment allowance. Students with dyslexia can ask for this to purchase a computer or other technology (such as a tape recorder or electronic spelling checker) if there is good evidence that these items are required to compensate for the effects which the disability has on the student's studies. The claim should include software (programs) and consumables (e.g. printer cartridges and paper) and maintenance. The 1998/9 maximum rate is £3,995. This is a once-only grant to last for the whole course.

Non-medical helpers allowance. Students with dyslexia can ask for this to pay for personal support such as study skills tuition, training in literacy and learning skills, training to use a computer provided under the special equipment allowance, for someone to proof-read their course work, or for an amanuensis (scribe) in examinations. It is not available for additional tuition in the subject(s) that the student is studying. The 1998/9 maximum rate is £10,000 per year.

General disabled students allowance. This is for essential items that are not covered by the other two allowances. The 1998/9 maximum rate is £1,315 per year.

The LEA should supply the student with information on request about how to apply for these allowances. Most HEIs also provide advice and assistance to students in applying for a DSA (see Section 3.2.9). This role may be played by a Disability Officer of the institution, a dyslexia support tutor, or members of student services staff.

To make an application, the student will need the following:

- documentary evidence that dyslexia has been properly identified and is likely to affect the student's studies significantly (this should be in a diagnostic assessment report)

- documentary evidence that the items and financial help being requested are reasonable, justified and appropriate in addressing the student's disability needs (this should be in an assessment of needs and/or letter from the institution)

- quotations from suppliers of equipment (normally two quotations are expected).

9.1.2.2   Perceived problems with the DSA system

Although the DSA system is administered at the present time by LEAs, the financial resources are provided by the Government and the procedures and criteria are laid down in guidelines issued by the DfEE. There are many contentious issues associated with the DSA system as it currently stands. These issues were not only raised in the consultation process with HEIs (see Sections 4.1.2.5 and 4.1.3), but also figured prominently in the results of the national survey, in which 69% of HEIs responding to the questionnaire reported that the DSA was 'unsatisfactory' (see Section 3.2.9). These issues have yet to be resolved, although it should be noted that the recommendations of the Dearing Committee addresses some of them (see Section 1.1.4). There has been a call from LEA Awards Officers, from staff of HEIs assisting students with dyslexia in applying for DSAs, from *Skill* (the National Bureau for Students with Disabilities; see Section 4.2.4) and from the Dearing Committee (Dearing, 1997) for standardisation of procedures and administration by a central body, which should help to rectify many of the problems outlined below. Such changes are unlikely to come into effect before the 1999/2000 academic year.

- Although many students with disabilities find it easier to study part-time, at present they are not eligible for DSAs.

- Post-graduate students and foreign students are not eligible for the DSAs.

- There has been a substantial rise in claims for DSAs in recent years, especially from students with dyslexia, which has lead to questions about the sustainability of the DSA system in the long-term (see Section 1.1.2).

- There have complaints from LEA Awards Officers that guidelines from the DfEE regarding DSA applications have sometimes been unclear or contradictory (see Section 4.1.3).

- LEA Awards Officers argue that they do not have the expertise to evaluate DSA applications, nor the ability to rationalise between claims (see Section 4.1.3). LEAs may use 'experts' for guidance, but rarely have access to professionals who have knowledge and experience of dyslexia in the higher education context.

- There are considerable disparities in the ways in which different LEAs respond to claims from students with dyslexia (see Sections 3.2.9 and 4.1.2.5). In particular, HEIs report that many LEAs have misinterpreted specialist dyslexia support (which would be eligible for a DSA) as being no more than additional tuition for the student's subject of study (which would not). The need for specialist dyslexia support arises directly from the effects of dyslexia, and is essential to improving the study efficiency of the student with dyslexia. In this way it is entirely different from course tuition.

When considering DSA applications from students with dyslexia, LEA Awards Officers often rely to a large extent on the opinions of educational psychologists within their authority, who may have experience predominantly with children under 16. Since the problems encountered by children with dyslexia are usually rather different to those experienced by students with dyslexia studying in higher education, this may make it difficult for these educational psychologists to provide an informed opinion regarding the suitability of various provision which is being requested. Some LEAs have a policy of referring students who have applied for a DSA to Access Centres, which, although they may be specialised in evaluating needs in cases involving other disabilities, may not have any staff with a recognised qualification in dyslexia support or assessment, nor with expertise of supporting students with dyslexia in higher education.[42]

9.1.3 *Variation between individuals with dyslexia*

The evaluation of the needs of students with dyslexia involves careful consideration of many variables. Each adult presents a somewhat different profile of strengths and difficulties, and the effects of their dyslexia can vary in severity (see Section 8.3.3). Dyslexic characteristics may be more-or-less evident, depending on such factors as:

- the age of the person when dyslexia was first identified

- the levels of appropriate support that has been received

- the compensatory strategies that have been developed

- the relevance of previous study and strategies to the person's current course of study.

This means that there is no standard formula for assessing needs: each student's needs have to be considered individually. Differences in the type and extent of support required are to be expected, both in terms of recommended technology and in one-to-one support. Students' needs should always be evaluated in relation to their courses of study, current strategies, and their individual learning styles and preferences. This means that some students may need extensive support and others none at all. *Dyslexia, in itself, should not automatically entitle a person to any particular kind of support.*

It is important to recognise that the levels of technical competence in writing, reading and numeracy skills (i.e. basic study skills) vary greatly from one student with dyslexia to another. Students with dyslexia may also exhibit a range of related cognitive difficulties that may be more significant in affecting their studies than their reading and writing skills *per se*. Such difficulties can include: poor organisational skills; poor memory; excessive light or sound sensitivity; poor motor co-ordination; a weak sense of time or direction; pronunciation and other oral difficulties.

It can be particularly difficult to assess the needs of well-compensated students, and it is not always easy to judge the extent to which dyslexic difficulties will affect a particular student in their studies. Apparently 'mild' cases (e.g. as determined by the type and frequency of errors on literacy tests or by scores on 'critical' sub-scales of an adult intelligence test) do not necessarily correlate to reported difficulties with study itself. Sometimes this is because the students' compensatory strategies have involved focusing all their energies into study; difficulties may be more manifest in areas where their attention has not been focused, such as in organisational skills. The strategies required to cope with the teaching style and other demands of pre-degree courses may be inappropriate for higher level courses, resulting in previously successful students requiring assistance once they commence a university course.

There has been little research into the specific needs of students for whom English is not a first language, where English is the required language for the curriculum. Similarly, the numeracy competencies of students with dyslexia on different courses have received very little attention compared to language-based needs. At this stage, the Working Party can only make recommendations that research into these areas be encouraged and financed. In such cases, the requirements of students will need to be calculated by the needs evaluators through considering the types of difficulties

---

[42] For information on the *National Federation of Access Centres,* see Section 4.2.4.

decribed by students and how these relate to what else in known about their dyslexia, and by liaison with departmental staff.

9.2   Proposals on good practice

9.2.1   Fundamental principles in evaluating support needs

An early evaluation of learning and support needs may be vital if a student with dyslexia is to be successful in higher education. Nevertheless, some students with dyslexia may prefer to try to complete their degree without any additional help and may succeed without additional assistance. This suggests that an evaluation of needs may not always be essential until it is clear whether that student can succeed without additional technology or personal help. Students' needs may change over the duration of their course, requiring updated evaluations.

The evaluation of support needs should always be related to the particular course of study which the student is following and to the resources provided in the department, rather than on global notions of what students with dyslexia require. Wherever possible, the departmental staff should be consulted about the requirements for their course. For reasons of confidentiality, this may need to be in general terms as it may not be possible to liaise directly over individual named students (see Section 8.3.4.4). LEAs should bear in mind that students may not wish to reveal their dyslexia to departmental staff, and requests for information from departmental staff may place unnecessary emotional burdens on the student.

Although it is ideal to have a support programme in place at the start of the course, it is not always easy to ascertain how the student will cope until the demands of the course become clear and it becomes possible to tell how effective the student's coping strategies are. The identification of dyslexia and the evaluation of different types of needs should be conducted in as few stages as is possible, but may need to be re-evaluated at some point. Unnecessary repetition should be avoided, as this is wasteful of resources and can be distressing for the student.

Currently, there are anxieties that students may be given expensive support, both in the form of equipment and regular tutorials, on the basis of having dyslexia *per se* rather than on the basis of individual study needs. It is therefore important that diagnostic assessments and evaluations of needs tie down as accurately as possible what these needs are, that recommended provision is justified and is seen to be fair and consistent.

Not all students will necessarily have access to the support recommended, despite the provisions of a DSA. Some LEAs will not support claims for certain items of equipment or aspects of support that have been recommended. Whilst it is recognised that LEAs are under a public duty to vet applications for DSA very closely to ensure that the financial help requested is fully justified, reports of significant variation in responses from different LEAs to similar cases (see Sections 3.2.9 and 4.1.2.5) is extremely disquieting and suggest that some students with dyslexia may have been treated unfairly.

Where the DSA is not considered appropriate, students may not have the finance to purchase equipment, or may struggle to pay for recommended equipment. Consequently, some universities now provide (for shared use) special equipment for students with disabilities that would be rather expensive for students to purchase – e.g. text-scanning facilities to assist reading.

Many adults find assessment or evaluation of their learning needs raises a range of emotions. They are confronted – in perhaps a more obvious way than ever before – by the things that they can't do, or those with which they have extreme difficulty. Identifying support needs may conflict with the individual's feelings about their self-efficacy as an independent adult. Some individuals may react to this situation with anger about not being helped previously, some may be overcome with self-doubt about whether they can complete their course, and others may experience depression or generalised fear and anxiety. All these experiences can have a detrimental effect upon the student's studies. There can be an acute need for specialist dyslexia counselling. Students need to be aware of what counselling is provided either by the institution or in the locality. For further consideration of these issues, see Chapter 10.

When provision of learning support for students with dyslexia is under discussion in HEIs, the following questions are often raised: 'Why should students with dyslexia get extra help and support?' and 'What about help for students with problems in studying who don't happen to have dyslexia?' Other students, who are struggling in their studies, may well need guidance on study skills and access to technology support. A good case can be made for providing appropriate support to all students on the basis of *need*, rather than on the basis of labels such as dyslexia. The implementation of such a policy would have major financial implications. However, dyslexia is a registered disability and there is a public duty on HEIs to ensure (insofar as it is reasonable to do so) that students with disabilities have equal access to the teaching and learning that the institution provides and equal opportunities to benefit from higher education. This requirement does not mean that the needs of non-disabled students should be neglected, but they were not within the remit of the Working Party, nor of this report.

9.2.2   Who should evaluate needs?

Evaluation of the learning and support needs of a students with dyslexia is a skilled and complex process which requires understanding of:

- the nature of the student's problems of literacy and learning

- the nature and strengths of the student's learning style

- the demands of the student's higher education course

- the type of technology and other support available

- the procedures for DSA application.

Personnel with extensive experience in the evaluation of the support needs of students with dyslexia are in short supply. Some HEIs are fortunate in having suitable personnel who can carry out this task, e.g. a disability officer or dyslexia support tutor. At the present time there are few courses which provide training in the evaluation of learning needs of students with disabilities in higher education. This is a problem which was highlighted in the results of the national survey (see Chapter 3) and in the consultations with HEIs and LEA Awards Officers (see Chapter 4). It is clearly an area of training which needs to be addressed.

There are many models across the HE sector which work well. In some cases psychologists trained to work with adults in HE provide recommendations as part of their diagnostic assessment. Some Access Centres may include learning support guidelines as well as technology recommendations. In some HEIs, dyslexia co-ordinators or learning support workers, or trained subject area staff evaluate the student's needs. There is an argument in favour of support needs being evaluated by staff trained in adult dyslexia at a higher education level, and who are familiar with the particular institution. This will facilitate liaison with academic staff and obtaining relevant information about the demands of the student's course.

For students who have not been previously identified as having dyslexia, there are advantages in combining the identification with an evaluation of needs. It is usually more convenient for the student if this is conducted on campus or locally.

The evaluation of support needs of students with dyslexia requires co-ordination. There are two aspects to this process: one is the initial evaluation of the student's needs, the other is the interpretation and implementation of those needs. In cases where an application is being made for the DSA, the second part of the process will involve an LEA Awards Officer and possibly other professionals who are called upon by the LEA to provide an opinion about the needs of the student and how these might best be met. To this end it is recommended that each HEI and each LEA should identify a suitable member of their staff who can act as dyslexia co-ordinator. This person should have recognised training or expertise in working with adults with dyslexia at HE level. This would go some way towards ensuring parity across departments institutionally, and between institutions and LEAs nationally.

9.2.3   Procedures for evaluation of needs

The needs of the student should be evaluated against the requirements of the course, and the individual's pattern of difficulties and current strategies. These may be explored through support sessions over several weeks, or through a combination of interview and tests, which include reading, writing, listening and organisational tasks presented under different conditions. Standardised tests of spelling accuracy, or reading or writing speed or comprehension should not be necessary as these should have been carried out in the earlier diagnostic assessment (see Chapter 8).

When carrying out an assessment of learning needs it is essential that there is a realistic consideration of the following matters.

- The demands and delivery methods of the chosen course of study should be evaluated in terms of the student's individual strengths and weaknesses. This may involve gathering information from, and liaison with, academic staff delivering the components of the student's course.

- The student's cognitive strengths, learning styles, attitudes and preferences should be taken into account – students with dyslexia are often very inflexible in the ways in which they are able to learn.

- How the support will be financed.

These considerations will now be examined in greater detail.

9.2.3.1   Course requirements and the student's profile

Both the requirements of a course and the methods of delivery must be considered in order to evaluate the following factors:

- the mode of course delivery, such as emphasis on lectures or practical work

- lecturing style (e.g. with or without handouts and/or OHP)

- the amount and type of written work required and the length of time permitted

- the balance of coursework, end-of-module tests and formal examinations

- the level of technical writing accuracy required (e.g. spelling, grammar and punctuation)

- the amount and type of reading required and the time available to undertake it

- whether oral presentations are required

- the extent to which any learning strengths of the student can be brought into play.

As the student's profile of strengths and weaknesses is considered in the light of course demands, it should become evident where the problem areas lie. Particular areas of mismatch between the student's learning styles and the teaching approach of the tutor should be highlighted and addressed. In each individual case, several of the areas outlined below are likely to present difficulties.

- **General organisation**: disorganisation and poor time management has a devastating effect on all aspects of student life.

- **Attention / concentration**: difficulties in these areas affect both lectures and private study.

- **Anxiety level / stress / panic**: when these levels are high, the student can become immobilised.

- **Aural processing**: listening while note-taking, 'penny-dropping' delay, ability to play a full part in discussions.

- **Reading**: accuracy, speed, comprehension while reading, ability to skim through text, visual processing/perceptual problems (including visual discomfort – see Sections 2.3 and 9.2.3.2).

- **Oral skills**: word retrieval, pronunciation, maintaining a logical structure when speaking in formal situations.

- **Writing**: legibility of handwriting, speed of writing, omission of words.

- **Assignment writing**: (in addition to the skills in the last bullet point) research skills, determining relevant content, structuring written material, correct interpretation of task.

- **Spelling**: accurate copying; proof reading, types of spelling error..

The varied characteristics listed here are all associated with the profile of the adult with dyslexia (see Chapter 2). A summary of the degree to which the student's pattern of difficulties is affecting study and the efficacy of the student's study-related coping strategies should be contained in the assessment. Strategies can then be recommended that will assist the student in managing his/her difficulties (see Section 9.2.5). Recommendations for appropriate examination arrangements are vital and must be negotiated in good time; these may entail the employment of helpers to tape or read exam papers, scribes or extra invigilators for students requiring separate rooms (see Chapter 11).

9.2.3.2   Visual discomfort

Visual discomfort is a perceptual condition caused by hypersensitivity to the irritating effect of strong visual contrast (e.g. where parallel lines of text create the appearance of a black-and-white grating). Movement and colour illusions can be perceived, or the text may appear unstable or obscured. Reading for any length of time may causes headaches and eye strain, and so has to be carried out in short bursts, which can disrupt the comprehension process (Evans, 1997; Evans and Drasdo, 1990; Wilkins et al, 1994). This condition is also known under various other names, including 'Irlen syndrome', 'Meares-Irlen syndrome', 'scotopic sensitivity syndrome' (Irlen, 1991) and 'pattern glare' (Wilkins, 1995). Computer monitors and reading in fluorescent lighting can cause similar effects.

Visual discomfort is fairly common amongst students with dyslexia, but is not always picked up in routine sight tests (see Section 2.3). Students who have been identified as having dyslexia should always be asked if they regularly experience some or all of the symptoms described above, in which case it is likely that they suffer from this condition. In a significant proportion of case, use of a coloured overlay or tined lenses seems to alleviate the difficulty. This treatment that was pioneered by Irlen during the 1980s and continues to be available from the Irlen Institutes (for address, see Section 14.4). Testing kits of overlays are also commercially available, allowing personnel who are carrying out evaluation of needs the opportunity to explore this problem with the student and see if it can be helped by use of an overlay.[43] In a significant proportion of cases, tinted lenses are beneficial. In such cases, an optometric assessment involving use of an Intuitive Colorimeter is recommended to establish the individual's requirements. Not all opticians have this equipment, so it will be necessary to make enquiries to locate a suitable practitioner in the region.

Specialist opticians should be able to assess for certain types of visual dysfunction now known to be correlates of dyslexia; these include binocular instability, poor accommodation and convergence insufficiency (Evans, 1997; Evans, Drasdo and Richards, 1996). Unfortunately, these conditions are not generally picked up by routine eye tests. In order to claim the cost of optometric assessment and prescription of tinted lenses and other requirements for students with dyslexia, the LEA may require a declaration that this provision is required solely for the student's studying needs, and not for general use (the cost of ordinary spectacles cannot be covered by DSA funds).

Students who are susceptible to visual discomfort may also benefit from screen filters for computers, changing the background or text colours on a computer screen when word processing,

---

[43] Testing kits and overlays for the treatment of visual discomfort are available from Cerium Visual Technologies, Appledore Road, Tenterden, Kent TN30 7DE, and also from I.O.O. Marketing Ltd, 56-62 Newington Causeway, London SE1 6DS. A visual screening checklist and further information on visual discomfort are available from the Adult Dyslexia Organisation (for address see Section 14.4).

photocopying texts and examination papers on tinted paper, and enlarged photocopies. Scanning material into computers and reprinting in doubling spacing or with different fonts can also be helpful. These students may be particularly sensitive to light, and especially to fluorescent tubes and neon lights that cause flicker, and may also find computer monitors that have a relative slow refresh rate (below 70 Hz) visually irritating. Such students may need to purchase natural daylight bulbs or appliances, and ensure that computer monitors are of appropriate standards to minimise discomfort.

9.2.3.3   *Student attitudes and preferences*

Support arranged for students with dyslexia must take account of their attitudes on a number of critical issues.

- Whether the student has the financial means (and inclination) to pay for the recommended support package.

- Whether the student has strong feelings about completing their degree 'on the same basis as everybody else'.

- Whether the student feels comfortable about teaching staff knowing of their difficulties.

- Whether the student has the time (and inclination) to learn how to use new technology and/or to attend support sessions. This includes complex applications such as voice-input systems, predictive typing systems and planning/organisational tools. Final year students may be particularly disinclined to spend precious time learning new skills.

- Whether the student has strong feelings for or against any item of technology – e.g. some students never become used to hearing their voice on a tape-recorder or to listening to synthetic voices; others find the glare of a computer screen uncomfortable.

- Whether the student is physically able to carry around portable computers or dictaphones, especially when added to other things which they need to carry.

- Whether the student can work with an amanuensis (scribe), proof-reader, mentor or other individual allocated to support them. It can be very difficult for some students to work with an amanuensis unless they can organise their thoughts very clearly and have some practice in this task. Personality clashes and misunderstandings are also a potential hazard.

Students may harbour misunderstandings about the roles of people assigned to support them and what certain items of support entail. A common misconception is that an amanuensis (scribe) should be able to change the wording so that the writing makes more sense, whereas in fact an amanuensis is permitted only to take down *verbatim* what the student says.

Students with dyslexia may also have idiosyncratic or misinformed notions of what will help them. Sometimes such ideas make the student unduly resistant to suggestions of alternative strategies. For example, one student with dyslexia firmly believed that because he had difficulties in taking good lecture notes, the only solution was for someone to be paid to attend lectures on his behalf and take notes for him. He was vehemently opposed to the alternative strategy of attending and tape-recording the lectures, listening to the recording later and stopping the tape when necessary in order to make notes. In the latter solution, the student would have heard the material more than once and would have gone through a process of organising it into note form, both of these activities being extremely beneficial to understanding and recall. The student's 'preferred' solution – having someone take notes for him – would not normally be advocated because it is inherently difficult to make sense of notes taken by another person, and because the student would miss the process of making notes, which is in itself an extremely valuable part of learning. With some persistence on the part of his study skills tutor, he was eventually persuaded to try tape-recording lectures and producing his own notes from the tapes. With practice and support, he is now using this method very effectively. As well as enhancing his learning, the experience has boosted his confidence, both in his own abilities and in the wisdom of his study skills tutor!

9.2.4   Administrative matters

9.2.4.1   Paying for evaluation of needs and provision of support

There should be an inquiry into the extent of funds which are likely to be available to the student through the DSA and of the types of support which are available within the institution or which can be bought in. Some HEIs have qualified support tutors who have experience in working with students with dyslexia; others must buy in services from outside the institution.

Where the student is eligible for the DSA, it would be reasonable for the student to claim the bulk of these additional expenses from this source. However, costs that arise from the provision of special facilities *associated with the student's course* (e.g. extra subject-specific tuition or subject-specific software) will not be covered by the DSA, and consequently these should be provided by the institution. HEIs should be aware that, at the present time, part-time students and overseas students are not eligible for the DSA, and may therefore be wholly reliant on what the institution can fund.[44]

It should also be noted that the DSA will cover costs of evaluation of needs (including technology assessment) but *not* the cost of a diagnostic assessment. However, where the professional carrying out a diagnostic assessment includes in his or her report components that deal with *needs* (e.g. recommended technology or study support requirements) then the portion of the cost which is attributable to those components of the assessment can legitimately be claimed against the DSA.

When considering applications for the DSA, some LEAs seem more reluctant to pay for study support than for equipment, even though an evaluation of needs may indicate that the former is more important than the latter in a particular case. The study support advocated should be claimed through the non-medical helpers' allowance section of the DSA; this would also appear to be the only channel for claiming for the cost of the assessment itself. It will be necessary to present a case to LEAs, outlining why a student needs extra support. Sometimes, LEAs assume that extra subject support is being requested (such as additional tutorials); this is not a permissible use of the DSA, however desirable it might be in some cases. It must be demonstrated that the specialist tuition and other recommendations are intended to address the effects of dyslexia.

The DSA can be paid direct to the student's institution (if the student requests this). The advantages of this are that the institution can manage resources being funded from the DSA more efficiently and extra paperwork for students with dyslexia is avoided. Support staff (either from within or from outside the institution) can be paid directly out of such resources.

HEIs should be aware that the HEFCE is currently investigating 'base level' provision for students with disabilities (see Section 1.1.4). The findings of this investigation are due later in 1998. The outcome of this may be an expectation (or insistence) that all HEIs provide certain minimal support for all students with disabilities independently of DSA awards. Some aspects of dyslexia support may come within such base level requirements, e.g. study skills support. It is also likely that a nationally coordinated DSA system will be established for England and Wales by 2000.

9.2.4.2   DSA applications

All HEIs should give advice and assistance to any student with dyslexia in the process of applying for the DSA, providing there is satisfactory evidence regarding the nature and severity of the student's dyslexia, and the existence of learning and support needs that would warrant such an application.

One of the reasons for setting up the Working Party and producing this report was to create guidelines and offer proposals that would eliminate the difficulties that sometimes occur when DSA applications are made by students with dyslexia (see Section 0). It would go a considerable way toward resolving many of the current problems in this area if, when considering applications for

---

[44] The Open University operates a scheme for Assessment of Technology Learning Support, which enables a small number of part-time students to be assessed as receive support, equipment and loans for purchase of computers.

DSAs from students with dyslexia, all LEAs not only adhered firmly to DfEE regulations on DSAs but also insisted that such applications are accompanied by the following documentary evidence:

- a professional report that conforms to the guidelines on diagnostic assessment of dyslexia given in Section 8.3

- information regarding the students' learning and support needs that has been prepared in accordance with the proposals on good practice given in this Chapter.

If such procedures were followed, then the processing of DSA applications in cases of dyslexia should be a great deal easier and fewer disagreements between LEAs and HEIs should arise. Moves towards standardisation of costs for specialist learning support should also help to eliminate disagreement and should enable LEAs to process DSA applications more swiftly.

The disparity between different LEAs in dealing with DSA applications has been the cause of much dissatisfaction on the part of many HEIs (see Sections 3.2.9 and 4.1.2.5). The implementation of a national body for administering DSAs is an obvious solution to this problem, which most HEIs would welcome.

9.2.5   *Support provision for students with dyslexia*

Some students with dyslexia will succeed without any additional support. There will be other students who will need some or all of the following additional facilities if their study is not to be adversely affected by their dyslexia:

- to be taught self management techniques

- specialist tuition to improve skills and essential subskills

- access to, and training in the use of, supportive technology

- other types of help such as readers and scribes if justified by the level of disability

- proofreaders

- referrals to specialists (such as optometrists with expertise in the visual correlates of dyslexia)

- sessions with counsellors

- information on support networks.

These provisions are outlined in more detail below. For the purpose of clarity, support has been divided here into three categories: study support, technology support, and other forms of support.

9.2.5.1   *Study support*

Many students with dyslexia require help with basic study skills, language and numeracy. This may include items such as help with personal management skills (such as organisational skills and assertiveness). There is sometimes confusion as to what such dyslexia support entails. This support is not subject-specific. It is concerned with the development of skills necessary to manage dyslexic thinking styles and difficulties within a higher education context, to enable students to recognise and work to their strengths, to enable access to the curriculum and to contribute towards achieving greater parity in assessment. Study skills work can be done both individually and in groups, in which students investigate learning strategies together. The latter can form part of an assessed module, with specific teaching input on matters such as: grammar, essay writing, oral presentation, organisation of information and ideas.

Staff familiar with the institution and the student's course of study should make recommendations for supporting student learning which are tailored to:

- the demands of the particular course

- the conditions pertaining on that course (e.g. modes of curriculum delivery, staff-student ratios, staffing patterns)

- the support ethos of the department.

It is helpful if the student is able to consider their priorities regarding the sort of help that they would value most; this helps them to negotiate when discussing their study needs with course staff. It is helpful if the institution can provide suggestions regarding different ways in which academic staff can help students with dyslexia, depending on the time and expertise available in the department (see Chapter 6).

Students with dyslexia often take more time to read; they may write more slowly and organise their materials in different ways. Essay writing can be particularly slow and stressful. Individual study support sessions may be required because generalised advice offered by a department may not take account of different learning styles. Feedback from academic staff about a student's written work can be particularly daunting to the student. Although academic staff will usually intend their feedback to be helpful, it may be seen by the student as excessively critical and this can have detrimental effects on the student's motivation. The study skills tutor may need to go through this feedback with the student, helping them to interpret it in a more positive light.

Effective study skills tutoring must combine an understanding of study skills techniques (especially those involving memory tasks, organisation and time management) with the ability to work alongside the student in identifying the various learning tasks relevant to each course of study. This process begins with identifying the skills required for a course – whether it be note-taking from lectures or handling particular styles of presentation – and progresses to a discussion of the particular difficulties each task presents the individual. The outcome should be the construction of both short- and long-term strategies. Students with dyslexia may not be fully aware of their particular areas of difficulty and of the value of multisensory techniques for learning.

Many of the problems in accessing information encountered by students with dyslexia stem from the mismatch between their individual thinking strengths and the expected pattern of thinking for a particular activity (Stacey, 1997, Wszeborowska-Lipinska and Singleton, 1999). West (1997) discusses the thinking strengths of many individuals who have dyslexia and who have a preference for visual processing (see Section 2.5). However, not all people with dyslexia have strengths in visual processing. Study skills tutors benefit from being aware of a wide range of 'intelligences' (Gardner, 1983) in order to help a student with dyslexia find the most suitable solutions to dyslexic problems. A mismatch of thinking strengths can affect the fluency of study for all students. For students with dyslexia, a mismatch can hamper the students' abilities to use coping strategies to manage their dyslexia (Stacey, 1998).

It is not within the bounds of this report to provide a manual of study skills support for students with dyslexia. Further information may be found in Gilroy and Miles (1996), Goodwin and Thomson (1991), Krupska and Klein (1995), Stephens (1996), and Waterfield (1995, 1998). There are some certificated courses in study skills tuition for students with dyslexia at higher education level: for further details see Section 14.7.

9.2.5.2 *Technology support*

Many students with dyslexia will require personal computers to work from in their own home so that they can work at the times of least interference from their dyslexic difficulties or external distraction. Such students should be supported wherever possible by a DSA. However, this will not meet all the technology support needs for students with dyslexia in any given institution. In terms of good practice, it is therefore recommended that all HEIs should provide:

- Technology facilities for the exclusive use of students with dyslexia or other disabilities as part of day-to-day studying. Such facilities should be conveniently and centrally placed (e.g. in or adjacent to the library) and be undisturbed, with natural daylight and little background noise.

- Technology support for lectures, e.g. electronic spelling checkers and tape-recorders (often on a loan basis).

- Technology support for examinations, e.g. computers for word processing of written examination answers.

Where technology support is being provided (whether on an individual or shared-use basis), training in using the technology is essential. It determines whether equipment is used to best advantage – or even whether it is used at all. Without appropriate training and guidance, some students are not able to begin to use recommended technology, or may use it in inappropriate ways which do not help their dyslexia. The training should include guidance on how to make optimum use of the technology, and how to incorporate the technology into other study skills.[45] Students need to be made aware of some of the pitfalls of using the technology they have been recommended, such as inappropriate use of tape-recorders in lectures and adding incorrectly spelled words to computer user-dictionaries, and be given assistance in devising strategies for dealing with these.

At the present time, the following list outlines some of the most useful items of technology for students with dyslexia. The last two items both contribute to preventing or alleviating visual discomfort (see Sections 2.3 and 9.2.3.2)

- standard word processing, with spell checking, thesaurus and printing

- portable electronic spelling checkers

- portable tape-recorders (for recording lectures)

- word prediction software (reduces amount of typing)

- voice-input software (text can be dictated to the computer instead of being typed in)

- text-to-speech software, so that the student can hear text being 'read' by the computer

- scanning facilities (usually complements text-to-speech software)

- planning tools (for creating mind-maps and charts, organising essays and notes)

- use of encyclopaedias and other reference material on CD-ROM

- access to the Internet to obtain information on the World Wide Web

- colour monitors (so that colour of the workspace background and print can be altered)

- large-screen monitors (17 inch or larger).

When recommending any of these, staff should be aware that the more sophisticated software packages (e.g. voice-input and text-to-speech programs) usually demand a computer hardware of a higher specification than is required by standard applications (e.g. standard word processing). The appropriate technical advice should be obtained to ensure that recommended software will run on the hardware that is available or also being recommended.[46]

No attempt has been made here to identify particular products in the above categories. The technology market changes rapidly and new products can swiftly supersede existing ones. Items which are deemed 'unreasonable' on financial grounds in one academic year, may become 'standard' by the next. A recent example of this has been the dramatic drop in prices of voice-input systems.

---

[45] A guide to the integration of technology within studying is provided in '*Study Skills with ICT (Information and Communications Technology)*' by Carol Kaufman and Chris Singleton, British Dyslexia Association, 1998.

[46] Advice on software and other technology to support students with dyslexia can be obtained from iANSYST Ltd., The White House, 72 Fen Road, Cambridge, CB4 1UN. Tel: 01223 420101. Fax: 01223 426644. Email: *sales@dyslexic.com*

Items which may have appeared 'unnecessary' only a year or so ago, such as CD-ROM drives, have swiftly become standard features of integrated computer packages. [47]

9.2.5.3   *Other types of support that may be required*

Study skills and technology support are by no means the only requirements of students with dyslexia. DSAs allow for covering the costs of some other types of support, provided a clear case is made on the DSA application. In addition, there are forms of support that can be provided by the institution, such as subject specific support and organisation of self-help groups. The following list is not exhaustive, but should give a good indication of the range.

a) **Examination support.** Additional costs of extra invigilation, amanuenses (scribes), readers, proof-readers, altering examination texts, use of computers in examinations, or other support, without which the student would be disadvantaged by their disability. (See Chapter 11 for further discussion of these issues.)

b) **Readers.** These may be necessary in order to read texts to the student, either in person or on to tape. Some students will be able to use human readers to supplement synthetic readers (scanner and text-to-speech software). Students need to make it clear to their readers what they find helpful. Students may also need to purchase an additional specialist dictaphone-tape-recorder for their reader, in order to tape-record texts for them, and copies of textbooks for the reader or RNIB service to use. It is important that the student has finance for additional tape-recorders, textbooks, photocopying and cassettes for the dictaphone. Readers may also be necessary for some students who experience visual discomfort (see Sections 2.3 and 9.2.3.2)

c) **Scribes (amanuenses).** These may be necessary in order to note down the student's ideas (for early drafts) and/or to write down final drafts verbatim. Scribes may be particularly important for students who have extreme difficulties when writing but who have oral strengths. The student may need support and guidance in how to work with a scribe. There are technological alternatives to scribes that have advantages in giving the student a greater degree of independence in learning, e.g. a student can learn to use a 'planning tool' (a piece of computer software that allows the student to create mind-maps and organise their written work), or can use a voice-input system to dictate essays into the computer.

d) **Proof-readers.** These may be necessary in order to correct minor technical errors, and are most appropriate for students with a high level of minor technical inaccuracy but whose phrasing is reasonable. Proof-readers can find it difficult to work with text where the meaning or sentence structure is confused or where the organisation of the writing is weak. Proof-reading works well for students whose difficulties are mainly in identifying spelling errors such as homophones. Combinations of different spelling checkers, text-to-speech software, support in identifying individual weaknesses in spelling, and proof-reading strategies, can circumvent the need for a proof-reader for many students. Such combinations give the student more independence of others in the long-term, although short-term personal support may be required.

e) **Library support.** Many students with dyslexia find using libraries difficult and stressful, and for these reasons may avoid use of a library, which will hinder their studies. Whilst it might be expected that libraries would themselves offer a certain amount of basic support to students with dyslexia, additional library support may be needed for students who experience extreme difficulties in making use of the library, especially on courses which require extensive use of library facilities (see Section 6.2.3.6). The additional support may include:

- extended loan periods for books and other library materials
- assistance with photocopying (possibly subsidised cost)
- preferential use of technology facilities in the library

---

[47] A comprehensive guide to assistive technology to support various disabilities (including dyslexia) is *'Special Access Technology'* by Paul Nisbet and Patrick Poon, Call Centre, University of Edinbugh, 1998.

- help in using micro-fiches

- books on tape

- assistance with scanning printed material

- help in finding books, journals, articles and abstracts.

Many of these special facilities will be appreciated by students with other disabilities. Some libraries have systems whereby students with dyslexia may identify themselves if they wish (e.g. using different coloured library cards) to obtain additional support, and where floor/section/aisle/shelf referencing is by colour, thus making it easier for students with dyslexia to locate books and materials.

f) **Optometrist assessment and tinted lenses.** For students who experience visual discomfort when reading for prolonged periods (e.g. blurring of text, disturbing sensations of text moving; eyestrain and headaches) there are a range of possible alleviating strategies. For further information, see Sections 2.3 and 9.2.3.2.

g) **Speech therapy and hearing.** Some students might find this helpful if they stutter or find speaking otherwise difficult, especially if oral presentation or group work forms a large part of their course. Some students are concerned about their hearing as they often seem to miss what other people are saying. Such individuals may need advice on what to ask for if they go for a hearing test, so that they are not merely tested for hearing loss. Many people with dyslexia experienced problems of 'glue ear' (otitis media) when they were children. This can impede the normal development of the ability to discriminate speech sounds. These difficulties may be combined with weaknesses of auditory sequencing in working memory. In such cases, individuals may find that similar-sounding words are confused in speech, with undesirable consequences (e.g. 'explain' vs. 'exclaim', or 'commend' vs. 'condemn'). Auditory discrimination training can sometimes be of benefit.

h) **Self-presentation skills.** These can be particularly important in giving the student the confidence to state their needs without appearing either demanding or as if their needs do not matter. Work on interpreting non-verbal cues, and timing skills and self-monitoring in conversation would be beneficial to some students. These can often be covered effectively in group workshops.

i) **Self-help groups.** Some students need encouragement to meet others for moral support and to share strategies.

j) **Mentoring.** Some HEIs operate mentoring systems (sometimes called 'buddy systems') where a new student with dyslexia is allocated a more experienced student who also has dyslexia as a mentor. The mentor is able to show the student how to access the facilities in the institution and (with appropriate training) provide a certain amount of study skills support.

k) **Subject-specific support.** Many students feel that they miss information in lectures or have difficulties learning course material or acquiring specific skills as a result of their dyslexia, and want additional support within their own subject. When a case can properly be made that the dyslexia is the cause of the problems and that a general dyslexia support tutor could not be expected to have the expertise to teach the required skills, the cost should arguably be met by the DSA. Currently, however, the cost of this is not usually recoverable from the DSA: HEIs are expected to provide for this. In many case, it can be difficult for many academic staff to find the time offer a great deal of additional support to individual students, although some departments employ postgraduate students to give subject-specific support. Alternatively, courses with a number of students with dyslexia may be able to set up study or discussion groups.

l) **Additional textbooks and photocopying.** It is important that students with dyslexia have access to their own copies of books, articles and other texts in order to use interactive reading strategies (such as marking texts and colour-coding passages) and so they can read at their own pace. Those using readers need to have copies of texts to loan to the reader. For articles and some other texts, students may need to make enlarged photocopies on to tinted paper. Extended library loans, whilst useful, are not adequate substitutes for such strategies. Evaluation of learning needs should indicate the students for whom additional texts and photocopying are essential. Academic staff may have to be explicit about essential reading so that students are able to purchase texts or employ readers most appropriately. LEAs should make DSA funding available to cover such additional costs.

m) **Books about dyslexia, spelling and study skills**. Many dyslexic people have been given very little information about what dyslexia is or what it means for their future options. This lack of information can make students unnecessarily anxious and confused about what they should do or are capable of achieving. Students with dyslexia are entitled to claim from the DSA for reasonable costs incurred in purchasing books which will help them to understand their difficulties, to improve spelling, grammar and punctuation, or to enhance their study skills.

n) **Extended degree.** Students with dyslexia may need to study full-time, covering a reduced number of options, for a longer period. For example, a three-year course could be extended to a four-year course of study.

9.2.6 *Responding to individual needs*

Support for any disability, including dyslexia, should be carefully matched to the needs and attitudes of the individual student (see Section 9.2.3). There is sometimes a misconception that the principal (or only) 'solution' to provision for students with dyslexia is a computer. Although computers often make a great deal of difference to the studying of students with dyslexia, in fact a far wider range of responses is usually called for. Some general strategies have been outlined above. Suggestions for dealing with individual dyslexic difficulties are covered below.

9.2.6.1 *Difficulties in processing aural information*

Many students with dyslexia have problems in listening to lectures and taking notes simultaneously. In such cases the following solutions are suggested.

- A good-quality tape-recorder to play back lectures later, and pick up what they have missed. This should be a sturdy piece of equipment – ideally one that takes standard tape cassettes – with a counter, facilities to slow down the speech, and to insert sound markers on the tape to help them find their place. A supply of tape cassettes, rechargeable batteries and a battery recharger should be included in the recommendations for the equipment.

- Working with two tape-recorders may be helpful to some students. One should be of good quality so that it is does not pick up too much background noise in lectures and seminars. Cheap recorders can be a false economy because if the tapes are hard to listen to, the students do not use them. Students can play back the first tape, and summarise onto the second recorder. This makes the amount of taped material more manageable.

- Dyslexia support on: advance preparation for lectures; note-taking strategies; and how to make the most of lectures.

Guidance or training in using the equipment is essential. For example, students need guidance in how to combine selective use of the tape-recorder with advance preparation for the lecture. They need to develop note-taking strategies before, during and after the lecture, as well as acquiring effective listening skills and ways of using the information that is on tape. Without this, the tape-recorder can become a study hazard rather than a study aid. Students can find lectures boring and drift off rather than listening. Some students attempt to transcribe the whole lecture from tape, which generates far too much written material for them to work with and may result in leaving little or no time for other aspects of studying. Listening, thinking and writing structured notes is advocated rather than straight transcription. Some students accumulate banks of tapes they have not listened to, which can lead to panic and distress when preparing for examinations. Students realise they have insufficient time to listen to all the tapes, but cannot find the information they need.

9.2.6.2   Reading Difficulties

Students with dyslexia can display a wide range of problems with reading. In many cases, reading can be fairly accurate provided the student has time to read slowly and re-read difficult material. With large amounts of reading to get through – especially with limited time – the student's comprehension of the material may suffer. In some cases prolonged reading may create visual discomfort, causing headaches, blurred vision or eyestrain (visual discomfort; see Sections 2.3 and 9.2.3.2).

There are various strategies that can be tried to deal with these difficulties:

Mild to moderate reading difficulties:

- Students with dyslexia benefit from having their own copies of textbooks and articles, so that they can take their time to read and absorb the material. This involves additional expenses in purchasing texts and photocopying books and articles. It is important for students to have access to texts as they need them, and for them to use necessary interactive reading strategies such as the DARTS technique (margin summaries), bookmarking (insert key points on a 'book-mark' into key pages) and highlighting key words. This is an additional cost for students with dyslexia and therefore financial assistance from the DSA is appropriate.

- Enlarged photocopies of texts can be easier for some students to read. They can help to prevent or alleviate visual discomfort. Again, there will be an additional expense which should be claimed against the DSA.

- Some students find it easier to read if the text is photocopied on to tinted paper, or by using coloured filters. The colour can help to prevent or alleviate visual discomfort. Tinted paper is usually more expensive than white paper, and it is therefore reasonable to claim financial help for this from a DSA.

- Enlarged computer screens can help student who need to read in larger fonts.

- Two tape-recorder technique. If the student reads fluently and quite accurately but without understanding, they may benefit from reading aloud on to tape, playing this back and summarising on to a second tape-recorder (see Section 9.2.6.1).

- Where appropriate course materials exist on CD-ROM, a computer with CD-ROM facilities may be needed. By means of visual, auditory and interactive media, CD-ROMS can help the student to access basic concepts of the subject and to see how a subject is structured.

- Students who prefer to listen to texts may be able to get similar books to those they need via the *National Listening Library*. There is a charge for this, which could be accommodated within the DSA.

Severe reading difficulties:

- Students with extremely severe dyslexia and/or extreme visual discomfort can benefit from a scanner combined with text-to-speech software. This is the preferred solution that is recommended for students whose reading is extremely slow or inaccurate or who cannot focus on the page for any length of time. There are considerable advantages in terms of independence of learning using this method compared with using a human reader. The scanner needs to work from very good copy – some photocopied material will not scan well. Hence the student could incur additional costs of books and materials, and may need to claim for these. Students may be able to make use of shared facilities for this and/or take scanned material home on disc to use with a personal copy of a text-to-speech program. If a student is on a course with very heavy reading demands (e.g. humanities), a personal scanner for use at home may be more appropriate.

- In cases of severe handicap, some students may need to employ a human reader. Some students take to the synthetic voice of a text-to-speech program very well, others find it very difficult to listen to for extended periods, and for them a human reader may be the only answer. Usually it is best for material to be read on to tape, so that it can be played back as many times as the student requires. They may also need a reader for texts which do not scan into the computer, or to read new vocabulary.

- Students with extreme visual discomfort syndrome or who have difficulties reading print smaller than font size 11 and who have a doctor's certificate to this effect, are regarded by the RNIB as 'partially sighted' and can use the RNIB facilities for students. The RNIB provides a form to complete.[48] Students with visual discomfort can also benefit from technology which helps partially sighted students, such as print enlargers or very sophisticated text-to-speech systems such as ONMI-3000. These can be expensive but some HEIs have purchased such facilities for shared use.

9.2.6.3   Writing difficulties

Many students with dyslexia have problems of organisation composition, handwriting, punctuation and redrafting. If such difficulties are relatively mild, then use of a word processor, which saves constant redrafting, may be the only support required. In cases where there are more severe organising difficulties, the following strategies are suggested.

- Use of a computer with word-processing facilities saves constant redrafting.

- Use of a tape-recorder (preferably with foot-controlled switch) to compose orally before writing on to the computer.

- Use of the program *Texthelp!* to listen to writing being read back, so student can hear what has been typed and detect errors.

- Specialist tuition to develop study strategies and improve basic skills.

- The student may need support in developing mindmaps on large sheets of paper, using colour. If the student is happy to use computer software for this there are several packages available.[49]

- In extreme cases, a scribe or a proof-reader might be needed, especially if the student's oral expression is reasonably good. Some students also have difficulties expressing their ideas orally, and need support to clarify their thinking so that they can work effectively with a scribe. In practice, it is extremely difficult to support students if they have both severe difficulties expressing themselves both orally as well as in writing. This is particularly the case with respect to examinations and assessment. Some courses with a practical or artistic component may be able to devise alternative forms of assessment.

9.2.6.4   Spelling difficulties

Where problems are solely (or mainly) weak spelling, the following approaches should be considered:

Weak but phonetic spelling and a low error rate:

- Portable spelling checker (such as the *Franklin Language Master*). There is a model with voice facility which can be recommended. Models with a 'confusables' button enable the student to identify homophones (e.g. 'their' vs. 'there') more easily.

Weak spelling and high error rate:

- *Franklin Language Master* (or other portable spelling checker), plus word-processor with spelling check. Study support to develop more effective spelling strategies.

---

[48] For address, see Section 14.4.

[49] Recommended programs are listed in *'Study Skills with ICT (Information and Communications Technology)'* by Carol Kaufman and Chris Singleton, British Dyslexia Association, 1998.

Weak, non-phonetic or high error-rate spelling:

- Computer with word-processing package, spelling checker and dictionary. Text-to-speech facility (e.g. *TextHELP!)* enables the student to hear their errors. Predictive typing (e.g. *TextHELP!, Telepathic II, Penfriend).* Portable spell-checker (e.g. *Franklin Language Master*). Study support to develop more effective spelling strategies.

Extremely poor spelling and copying:

In this category would be placed those students whose spelling displayed a high error rate and non-phonetic spelling errors of a kind not likely to be picked up by a spelling checker, and who have very weak abilities at detecting errors.

- Computer with word-processing package, spelling checker and dictionary. In addition to that recommended above, a scanner might be helpful. Students can then scan texts into their computer, put the text through the spelling checker and add new words to the spelling dictionary.

- *ACE Spelling Dictionary* (Moseley, 1995). This uses an index that is purely sound-based. To locate the spelling of a word, the user first identifies the *sound* of the first syllable of the word and then – by means of the index of picture-sound matches – identifies the first letter of the word. This, in turn, refers them to the correct page in the dictionary, where the words are sorted into categories according to the number of syllables. Use of this dictionary requires good auditory discrimination and organisational abilities (both of which may be weak in many dyslexics) but provides a very effective solution to poor spelling for many individuals.

All students with spelling difficulties:

- *S.O.S. technique* (Simultaneous Oral Spelling). This involves repeating the names of the *letters* of the target word as they are written. With dedication and regular rehearsal over a period of time, this multisensory approach can enable students to learn to spell subject-related or other important words that are frequently (or habitually) mis-spelled.

9.2.7 Severity of dyslexic difficulties and support needs

In some cases the student's dyslexia is relatively mild or the student has already developed fairly effective compensatory skills and strategies (for further discussion on these issues, see Section 8.3.3.2). In these cases, the dyslexia may not affect course work to a great extent, and a recommendation for an application for DSA may be inappropriate. The student may benefit from other kinds of support such as sympathetic consideration of errors by teaching staff, alternative examination arrangements, support groups, moral support or counselling, or study skills support to fine-tune their study strategies. However, most university work involves a great deal of writing and is therefore likely to present additional work and time commitments from students with dyslexia compared to the bulk of their peers. These difficulties could be alleviated by the availability of word processing facilities (including spell-checker, thesaurus, and dictionary) to which the student has easy access at their peak working times.

Both the diagnostic assessment and the evaluation of needs should take account of the nature and severity of the student's dyslexic difficulties (see Section 8.3.3). Furthermore, it is entirely proper that such information is considered by the LEA when making decisions about the appropriateness of the provision being requested in a DSA application. In general, it will probably be the case that the more severe the difficulties, the greater will be the amount of DSA funding allocated to support the student, because the more severely affected student may need more sophisticated technology and a greater range of other support, such as study skills tuition, scribes and readers.

However, it would be quite improper for any LEA to impose *pre-determined limits* on funding for students with different levels of severity (e.g. to reject as routine DSA applications in 'mild' cases or to place an arbitrary upper limit on the funding to which students who are classed as 'mildly' or 'moderately' affected will be considered eligible). While the 'mild', 'moderate' and 'severe' classification is a pragmatic acknowledgement of the varying degrees of impairment and differing support needs of students with dyslexia, it too crude to be consistently related to the costs of support. Furthermore, LEAs are under a public duty to use proper discretion in the award of DSAs. To do other than consider each and every case on its individual merits would not be a proper exercise of discretion on the part of an LEA and could be subject to the legal challenge of judicial review.

Nevertheless, by LEAs and HEIs working together, a degree of standardisation of provision can be achieved, which would be to the benefit of all concerned, *provided that the possibilities for arguing a case for non-standard provision still remain*. In some HEIs, the *amount* of study skills support that is recommended is geared to the severity of the student's difficulties (as classified in the diagnostic assessment and/or evaluation of needs). While the use of this procedure should not be regarded as prescriptive (since there will be individual cases which merit an entirely different approach) it should make the task of the LEA Awards Officer more straightforward. Once the diagnostic evidence and classification of the student has been accepted by the LEA, then a corresponding range of support recommendations can be swiftly agreed between the LEA and the HEI as being appropriate for that student. The adoption of standardised procedures should cut down the amount of disagreement between HEIs and LEAs and enable many students with dyslexia to receive the support they require with less delay and frustration. If the *cost* of study skills support (e.g. the rate per hour) was also subject to standardisation, a further potential cause of delay and/or disagreement would be removed.

9.3 Recommendations on evaluation of needs and provision of support

1. The Government and Higher Education Funding Councils should accept and implement Recommendation 6 of the Dearing Committee regarding the provision of funding for institutions to provide learning support for students with disabilities.

2. The Government should accept and implement Recommendation 6 of the Dearing Committee regarding the extension of the scope of Disabled Students' Allowances so that these are available to part-time students, postgraduate students and those who have become disabled who wish to obtain a second higher education qualification.

3. With regard to evaluation of the learning and support needs of students with dyslexia, it is recommended that:

    a) All HEIs should have a policy and set of procedures for evaluation of the learning and support needs of students with dyslexia.

    b) Where the HEI does not have on its staff a professional with competence in evaluating the learning needs of students with dyslexia, then the student should be referred to such a person outside the HEI.

    c) The evaluation of learning and support needs should be based on a student's current problems and educational setting and, in the first instance, carried out as early as possible during a student's course, and thereafter should be updated as and when necessary.

    d) All HEIs should give advice and assistance to any student with dyslexia in the process of applying for the Disabled Students' Allowances, providing there is satisfactory evidence regarding the nature and severity of the student's dyslexia, and the existence of learning and support needs that would warrant such an application.

4. With regard to provision of support for students with dyslexia, it is recommended that:

    a) All HEIs should have, either on the staff or otherwise available to students, at least one tutor with training and/or experience in supporting students with dyslexia and all students with dyslexia should be made aware of that tutor.

    b) After a place in the HEI has been offered to a student with dyslexia and until the results of a diagnostic assessment are available, preliminary support should be available, funded by the institution.

c)	After the results of a diagnostic assessment are available, full support should be made available, based on the results of that diagnostic assessment and upon an evaluation of the student's needs by a competent professional. Wherever possible, that support should be funded by Disabled Students' Allowances.

d)	Support for students with dyslexia should be given with due regard to the proposals on good practice given in Section 9.2 of this report.

e)	Support for students with dyslexia should be acknowledged to concern the whole institution and not simply the support services. This will include lecturers and tutors, library and computer staff, and administrative staff.

f)	There should be a permanent base for the dyslexia support, which wherever possible should be centrally located within the institution and easily accessible to students.

g)	All HEIs should make reasonable efforts within their resources to develop facilities within their institution that can be used for the support of students with dyslexia, such facilities to include shared technology and group study skills support, particularly for students with dyslexia who are unable to obtain Disabled Students' Allowances.

5.	When considering applications for Disabled Students' Allowances from students with dyslexia, all LEAs should expect such applications to be accompanied by evidence regarding the students' learning and support needs that is in accord with the proposals on good practice given in Section 9.2 of this report.

6.	When considering applications for Disabled Students' Allowances from students with dyslexia, LEAs should *not*

a)	reject applications solely because there is a lack of evidence that the student's difficulties were identified earlier in education; nor

b)	impose upper limits on the amounts of financial support that will be given in cases of dyslexia where the condition is judged to be less than severe.

10 Counselling students with dyslexia

10.1 Issues, problems and challenges

10.1.1 The need for counselling support

Students with dyslexia in higher education may need varying degrees of counselling support. First, like many students who arrive with a need to develop learning skills and an anxiety about the future, they will often require general help with study and managing university life. Second, because students with dyslexia may bring with them a backlog of unhelpful coping strategies and damaged self-esteem, they may need professional counselling to prevent the repetition and continuation of these disadvantages (Goodwin, 1996). Many students with dyslexia have experienced considerable stresses in their academic studies before reaching higher education, which may in turn lead to excessive fears about being able to cope with student life. Some stresses may relate to the students' anticipatory fears about the response of the academic community to their dyslexia. They may remember previous years of struggle, of adult hostility and/or indifference to their dyslexia, and away from the familiar support of their family, the challenge may at times seem overwhelming (Gilroy and Miles, 1997). Mature students with dyslexia may encounter additional stresses arising from having children who are also dyslexic, or who may have had to come to terms relatively late in life with a revised self-image as a result of diagnosis of dyslexia.

10.1.2 Awareness and communications

Counsellors need to be aware of the particular difficulties of having dyslexia in an institution, whether they are professional counsellors or persons using counselling skills as part of student support generally. Counsellors who are not fully aware of the issues surrounding dyslexia may inadvertently give unhelpful advice or instigate inappropriate interventions. Symptoms such as anger, depression and anxiety may be misattributed to general life difficulties or personality traits without realising that dyslexia and the frustration that so often accompanies it may be primary factors.

Difficulties can start with communications. Even finding out about counselling advice from a notice board can be difficult for some students with dyslexia – notice boards can be unsystematically arranged and less than helpful in their display. Students have to be organised to write down useful dates and other relevant information. Provision of written information about counselling services in student support or advice booklets is a good idea, but can also be ineffective if it is too lengthy, or buried within other text that makes it difficult for students to notice or locate.

10.2 Proposals on good practice

10.2.1 General principles

Counselling which recognises the individual nature of dyslexia and the stress that it can cause is needed to underpin all strategies. In order to address counselling needs effectively, every HEI should have at least one student counsellor available who has specific knowledge and/or experience of dyslexia counselling. In addition, *all* counsellors working with students in higher education should have at least *some* awareness of the impact of dyslexia on everyday activities as well as educational ones.

Counselling support in higher education needs to encompass an understanding of the stresses experienced by students with dyslexia in relation to their university life and to their ability to develop successful learning strategies. It needs to be student-centred at an individual personal counselling level as well as offering flexible support (Goodwin, 1998). The counsellor needs to understand that presenting difficulties of stress may be specifically related to dyslexia as opposed to any other stress-related-symptoms.

Counselling needs to be available on a long-term basis as well as for immediate crises. If immediate crises can be dealt with promptly, they can often be prevented from seriously disrupting a student's study and from stirring up bad experiences from the past (e.g. of severe teacher criticism or bullying from other pupils when in school). While all students with dyslexia are liable to reactivation of bad past experiences, newly identified students seem to be especially vulnerable. When memories of bad past experiences do interfere with a student's studies, long-term counselling may be essential. Further details are given in the following sections of this Chapter.

Counselling and study skills support for students with dyslexia are very closely linked; in some HEIs, they are carried out by the same person. The distinction between the two jobs needs to be maintained. Where the two jobs are carried out by different people, each person needs to be aware of the work of the other and of the overlap.

10.2.2 Counselling newly arrived students

Students with dyslexia may arrive in higher education experiencing a wide range of stresses and worries. Some may have recently undergone a range of assessments and tests and may feel disappointed that the identification process has not brought great relief but rather what appear to be diminished prospects of success. Others, whose dyslexia has yet to be identified, may arrive fearing that the difficulties they have managed to cope with at school will become so great at university that they may not be able to study effectively. Some students with dyslexia assume that because they have successfully gone through a selection process to get on a higher education course they have therefore been assessed as being capable of completing that course. This is not always so, and it certainly does not follow that if students have met entry requirements of the practical or vocational type that they are necessarily fully prepared for higher education. Clearer information (preferably always written) needs to be available regarding admissions. More thought needs to be given to preparing students with dyslexia for higher education, both in dealing with the problems of living and working within a large and complex institution, as well as meeting the demands that their particular course(s) will place on them. In part, this preparation might be achieved by means of an interactive video programme.

Counsellors working with newly arrived students need to be practical and offer strategies for students to develop so they can cope with finding unfamiliar staff in unfamiliar buildings and knowing which staff they should contact. The counsellors should also participate in staff development so that staff are more aware that students with dyslexia will often avoid seeking help, because they are lacking in confidence or confused about who to ask and may mask their fear with apparent indifference. The initial period at university or college places heavy demands on memory, organisation and orientation, which are particularly stressful areas for the students with dyslexia and academic staff need to be aware of this.

10.2.3 Counselling newly identified students

Students who have recently been identified as having dyslexia may have priority needs for counselling because they need to come to terms with new aspects of themselves, which they may not have appreciated (or perhaps only dimly appreciated) before. The discovery that one has dyslexia can produce feelings of relief, but it can also generate anxieties. Students exhibit confusion and loss of confidence because they have only a vague understanding of the nature of the condition at this early stage. They may have inaccurate preconceptions about what having dyslexia is likely to mean for them. A change in self-image is called for and a period of adjustment to a new identity, which can be painful. During this time, the individual may become excessive self-centred and preoccupied, which may alienate friends and create additional stresses.

Some students with dyslexia may have been living stressfully with their 'secret' for some time, or may have been in denial of it. When eventually they decide to come and seek help they can feel a loss of face and anger with themselves that their dyslexia has 'overcome' them. They may be quite abrupt or apparently rude because facing up to their problems is so painful.

Mature students, especially, may have worries about whether their children may also have dyslexia and what this will mean for their family as a whole. One mature student cried for days after being informed that she had dyslexia, not because of changes to her own self-image, but because 'she now understood in a much deeper way' what her daughter (now aged 20) who was also dyslexic, had suffered throughout schooling. She identified with her own child in a much more significant way than before and this stirred up deep seated emotions in her.

As well as understanding and practical counselling, all these students need helpful information about what dyslexia is, and about the strategies that can be developed to circumvent its effects. Counselling support should be offered in parallel with study skills support.

10.2.4 Stress management

Students with dyslexia can be prone to stress caused by a wide variety of problems, including:

- not being able to complete all the reading required (because of slow reading ability)
- taking longer to write essays
- worrying about spelling and grammatical structure of written work
- general disorganisation of life, academic work, lecture notes and other material
- forgetting appointments, such as tutorials and supervisory meetings
- getting behind with assessed work, such as practical reports.

These problems have implications for study skills support as well as for counselling support. The former will generally tend to focus on explicit strategies for addressing particular problems. The latter is likely to allow the student the opportunity to explore their own feelings about their difficulties and come to terms with them, thus helping to relieve stress. Sometimes, these functions may be combined where a dyslexia support tutor has counselling experience as well as training in study skills tuition.

Students with dyslexia are often working at their limits. Most students, or academics, will recognise the way that, under pressure, the most organised individual with a reasonably good memory, can become unable to cope, remember or handle normal working tasks – as if for a brief moment they have gone 'blank' and cannot retrieve even the simplest information. It is likely that some students with dyslexia will experience this level of stress, not once or twice a year, but on a daily basis. This may arise in situations such as getting to the right room with the right papers on time, filling in forms and cheques or attempting to take notes or prepare an essay. It may also occur on some days more than others (the good day/bad day syndrome), most usually because of extreme tiredness and stress. Stress management can be invaluable in helping students cope and a counsellor needs to work closely with students identifying useful approaches. A wide variety of techniques may usefully be explored, including relaxation therapies (e.g. yoga or deep breathing techniques); creative visualisation; focus on possible changes to diet; improved exercise and general relaxation. Role models of successful dyslexic people can help them view themselves in a more positive light.

Personal counselling will often involve both stress management and study skills work but the approach of considering the whole person should underpin the processes. A person-centred approach can facilitate this and may encourage students to discover their own ways of learning and understanding themselves, in the safe environment provided by a counsellor who accords them empathy and positive self-regard. The counsellor needs to listen with care to the student's anxieties. Some students may be so angry and frustrated that work needs to be done on the student's morale and anxiety at a more specialist counselling level before the student feels able to look at, say, language skills. Others may need to look at structural approaches to general study skills first, which offer immediate relief to anxious students. Many students who used the Dyslexia Unit at Bangor University spoke of the great sense of relief they felt in having at last a meaningful discussion about the problems of being dyslexic (Gilroy and Miles, 1997). Sometimes a more directive approach may emerge from working with a student where the counsellor becomes a more general advisor and advice is given about particular problems. The counsellor may work with a student on how the difficulties of study can be communicated to the teachers concerned, and occasionally this may involve some advocacy or explanatory intervention on the student's behalf. Building inner confidence enables a student to overcome stress and needs to be part of any support offered to students with dyslexia.

The students with dyslexia may also create stress for members of staff. It has also been found that a whole-institution perspective to stress management can be effective for staff as well as students. This can be achieved through provision of staff development courses on stress management techniques, so that academic staff cannot only help themselves and each other, but also learn ways of reducing the stress on students with dyslexia (Reid and Hinton, 1996).

10.2.5 *Counselling at examination time*

When assessment takes the form of written examinations, levels of stress and anxiety may become acute and immobilise the dyslexic student. Whilst academic departments in HEIs are becoming more aware of special examination requirements, some students do not claim them and struggle on with increasing helplessness. People who are highly anxious are especially vulnerable to panic. Students with dyslexia often experience high levels of anxiety during activities that demand rapid and accurate information processing. Written examinations are among the most taxing of such tasks. Panic can set in and students may experience total 'blankness', when coping strategies fail and the task seems impossible.

To address these difficulties, counselling support may be needed at the personal level. This can help to boost the student's self-esteem, reduce examination anxiety and manage stress when revising and during examinations. It is important that students have worked with a counsellor or support tutor to identify what their particular examination fears are. These may be fears about misreading questions (e.g. see the vignette 'Laura' in Chapter 2) or about going 'blank' during the examination, or a variety of other concerns. In dealing with these, the counsellor needs to be aware of specific strategies that have been advocated by the student's study skills tutor and which the student is being encouraged to use in order to cope with the problems. Similarly, the counsellor needs to be aware of provisions that have been agreed with the examinations office to help prevent such problems (see Chapter 11).

10.3   Recommendations on counselling students with dyslexia

1.   Every HEI should have at least one student counsellor available who has specific knowledge and/or experience of dyslexia counselling.

2.   All counsellors working with students in higher education should have some awareness of the impact of dyslexia on everyday activities as well as educational ones.

3.   Counselling for students with dyslexia should be:

     a)   available for immediate crises and for long-term problems;

     b)   an integral part of the support service within the institution; and

     c)   available as a priority to students recently identified as having dyslexia.

4.   The student's confidentiality must be respected at all times and information exchanged with academic or other staff of the institution only by permission of the student and always with absolute discretion.

11 Examinations and assessment

11.1 Issues, problems and challenges

11.1.1 Academic standards and equal opportunities

The grade and certificate awarded at the end of the course more often than not determines the next stage in any student's life and can have far reaching consequences. The particular difficulties experienced by able students with dyslexia, including slow, inaccurate reading and writing skills, poor spelling, and weak memory and organisational skills, can place these students at a disadvantage, not only in conventional written examinations but also in other forms of assessment as well. It has long been recognised that some adaptation of the examination system is appropriate in order to try to create what is often referred to as a 'level playing field', without which these students would be disadvantaged in the examination situation. Such adaptations are variously described as 'special arrangements', 'special provision' or 'accommodations', the latter being an expression generally used in the US. The earlier term 'concessions' is falling into disuse as it has connotations of a privilege being granted.

The provision of additional time in GCSE and 'A' level examinations for students with dyslexia has been established practice for many years (see Hedderley, 1996; Joint Forum for GCSE and GCE, 1997; Pumfrey and Reason, 1991). The national survey revealed that almost all HEIs also provide additional time in written examinations for students with dyslexia, and some HEIs make further special provision for these students, including allowing the use of amanuenses and word processors in examinations (see Section 3.2.10).

Provision of special examination arrangements for students with dyslexia creates a tension between two important principles in higher education: (i) maintaining academic standards and (ii) ensuring equal opportunities. Both these principles must be stringently upheld. When considering what special examination provision would be appropriate for students with dyslexia, it is essential to ensure, as far as possible, that neither principle is violated. This is not an easy task.

The maintenance of academic standards is often a major concern associated with the examination and assessment provisions for students with dyslexia in higher education. Academic staff, especially those who have limited understanding of the nature and effects of dyslexia, may be uneasy about whether allocation of additional time or other special arrangements to students with dyslexia in examinations is fair. A closely associated worry is the need for consistency of provision across the higher education sector, e.g. academic staff may be concerned whether a given amount of additional time is appropriate, or whether it might be too much or too little. The grade and certificate awarded at the end of a course are intended to signify a certain level of knowledge, competence in applying that knowledge, and ability to communicate. Considerable diligence is taken by examination boards to ensure that grades correspond to expected academic standards. Care is also taken to achieve comparable standards among different institutions, which is maintained by the system of external examining.

Much of the foregoing impinges on the debate about 'graduateness', which has already been discussed in Section 1.1.5.1. *The Working Party rejects the view that students with dyslexia who have met the academic entry requirements to higher education cannot subsequently meet the criteria to become graduates because they have difficulties in literacy.* Provision of special arrangements in examinations and assessments for students with dyslexia does not imply a lowering of academic standards. The aim is to establish equitable circumstances under which students with dyslexia can demonstrate their accomplishments. But if the demands of a higher education course exceed the student's abilities to cope with the examination requirements given appropriate provision and institutional support, a student with dyslexia may well not be successful in higher education. Unless the student with dyslexia develops and can deploy effective coping strategies that enable him/her to pass examinations and produce the intellectual competencies expected of a graduate in work situations, the award of a degree or other higher education qualification is without value. *The Working Party unequivocally accepts that the currency of degrees must be maintained in the interests of all parties concerned with higher education and its graduates.*

There is a further problem which relates to examinations and academic standards – should the fact that a student with dyslexia had additional time in examinations be recorded on the student's degree certificate or conveyed to prospective employers in references? These particular issues are considered further in Chapter 12.

11.1.1.1   *Verbal versus non-verbal skills and examinations*

Many individuals with dyslexia report that they often rely on processing information in non-verbal ways because their verbal information processing skills are restricted (see Chapter 2). This alternative strength in thinking may be exploited when studying (Stacey, 1997; Wszeborowska-Lipinska and Singleton, 1999). An important objective of support for students with dyslexia is to encourage them to study by alternative methods of learning that draw on their cognitive strengths, e.g. developing non-verbal rather than verbal skills through visualisation strategies and mind-mapping. Having allowed them to develop and use their alternative thinking strengths for studying, the educational system still predominantly uses verbal methods for examinations and assessments. If the mode of final assessment is conventional (i.e. emphasising verbal information processing) and no account is taken of dyslexic weaknesses or learning styles, the grade obtained may not give a very accurate picture of the most important abilities of the student, the knowledge and understanding that has been gained during the course.

Very broadly, the issues, problems and challenges surrounding examination and assessment of the work by students with dyslexia are, in essence, the *adaptation* of a system that uses verbal skills as its major means of communication so that it does not disadvantage these students. However, as far as equal opportunities are concerned, it would arguably be more equitable to develop alternative but equivalent methods of assessment that used non-verbal skills as well as verbal ones, so that students with dyslexia could demonstrate their knowledge and competencies in different ways. That is a much wider issue requiring research that is outside the scope of this report.

11.1.2 *Can a 'level playing field' be created?*

For people with dyslexia, written examinations present a situation in which they are required to demonstrate their talents and learned capabilities using a medium (recall and written expression under conditions of extreme time pressure) *which impinges directly on the core of their disability* (memory and written language). Without some special arrangements, such candidates would be disadvantaged in comparison with other candidates who do not have this disability.

11.1.2.1   *The rationale and constraints of additional time*

Allowing additional time in written examinations is the most common and, indeed, the most widely accepted, method of trying to ensure equal opportunities for students with dyslexia. How efficacious is this solution, in practice? Additional time can compensate to some extent for the slow speed of reading and writing of these students, although legibility of handwriting – in cases where this is a problem – will in generally be only marginally improved. Additional time can also alleviate the pressure of time that can be antagonistic to recall of information and structuring of written answers, and will often help to lower stress levels. However, additional time will not eradicate these students' memory difficulties entirely or cure their chronic spelling problems. Neither will it enable these students to rectify all their mistakes in the structure of essays.

Hence the practice of allowing additional time, whilst offsetting the adverse effects of dyslexia in examinations to a considerable extent, does not, by itself, entirely satisfy *all* concerns about equal opportunities. The problem arises largely because the disability directly affects the medium in which the examination is taking place. There would seem to be two possible solutions to this: (a) change the medium (e.g. by word processing or tape-recording answers) or (b) request examiners to make allowances for the disability when marking scripts of students with dyslexia (e.g. by recommending that they discount errors of spelling and punctuation and are tolerant of poor grammar). Both these solutions are already in use in many HEIs at the present time. Both require administrative modifications to examination procedures and have staffing and resource implications, whether in providing equipment, transcribing tape-recordings, or in providing marking guidelines and ensuring that such guidelines have been applied.

Although it is true that standards in higher education incorporate the general expectation that all graduates will be able to communicate effectively in writing, in practice the translation of that general expectation into marking practices of specific examiners may vary considerably. The importance of spelling and sentence construction as factors in the effectiveness of written communication may vary from subject to subject, and even from examiner to examiner, but rarely are conventions on the marking of spelling and grammar made explicit to students. This is particularly the case in conventional written examinations, in which, owing to pressure of time, misspelled words and poorly constructed sentences are not uncommon. Some examiners will attribute such errors to the exigencies of the examination situation and ignore them; other examiners may be less understanding. Reports of diagnostic assessments of students with dyslexia frequently advocate that examiners should give sympathetic consideration to infelicities of spelling and grammar, but that cannot be guaranteed, especially if the script is not identified as being that of a dyslexic student, and examiners are not prepared to be sympathetic.

It may be contended that it is impossible for examiners to *ignore* grammatical errors when marking students' work, since such errors are liable to affect the meaning of the prose. It is now widely accepted in linguistics and psycholinguistics that syntactical processes (i.e. word order) and semantics are not altogether independent, but interact to some degree (Harley, 1995; Simpson, 1994). Ignoring the grammar when marking would arguably be tantamount to reconstructing the meaning, in which case examiners would be marking their own interpretation. In practice, however, there is a fair amount of ambiguity in language and in many cases more than one interpretation can be placed on a sentence or string of words (Norris, 1987). In order to resolve such ambiguities, the listener or reader is forced to consider alternative meanings of words and phrases, bringing into play their own knowledge of the language and of the context (Mitchell, 1987, 1994). Hence all reading of text inevitably calls for a certain amount of reconstruction. In general, written examination answers probably demand rather more reconstruction on the part of the reader because they have been hurriedly written and have undergone little, if any, editing.

The crux of the matter, therefore, is not whether examiners are able to make allowances for poor construction of sentences in written examination answers (because they almost certainly do), but whether a somewhat greater tolerance should be shown towards students who are known to have dyslexia.

11.1.2.2   *Should allowances be made in marking?*

Whether examiners *should* make specific allowances in marking the examination papers of students with dyslexia is a thorny issue and one that generated probably the greatest debate within the Working Party. Broadly, there are two schools of thought. One school maintains that the process of marking work should in principle always be carried out in ignorance of the identity of the student concerned, and regardless of whether or not the student has a disability of some kind. To violate this principle is to create a situation in which bias for or against the student may come into play. Adherents to this view maintain that any accommodations for disability should properly be made in relation to the process of examination itself (e.g. by allowing additional time or modifying the method of examination) and in the deliberations of examination boards. To encourage differential marking practices would imply special pleading as well as potentially creating a situation of double compensation, which would be inequitable to other candidates.

The opposing school of thought argues that *even with* provision of additional time, conventional written examinations still disadvantage students with dyslexia for three main reasons.

First, because writing is the medium of assessment. Advocates of this view maintain that assessing students with dyslexia by means of written examinations is inherently inequitable in view of their disability. Hence it is argued that unless some allowance is made for the medium of assessment, then the examination will be unfair to students with dyslexia. Allowance of additional time results in only marginally improvements in spelling, grammar and punctuation, because most students with dyslexia cannot with complete reliability identify *correct* spelling, grammar and punctuation, especially under conditions of time pressure. If legibility of handwriting is a major problem this, too, is unlikely to be greatly improved by allowance of additional time: it is exceptionally difficult for adults to change their handwriting style because it is encoded in automatic motor memory.

The second reason is that if students with dyslexia think that their literacy skills are being marked, they may tend to concentrate more on the process of writing *itself* (such as legibility and punctuation) rather than on the *meaning* which they are trying to put across. Consequently, the quality of their ideas may be less evident in their answers and the mark awarded will be unlikely to reflect their abilities.

The third reason concerns the changes that higher education in the UK has undergone in recent years, which have affected the efficacy of traditional special arrangements for students with dyslexia. There has been an increasing move towards modular course structures with examinations at the end of each module, rather than at the end of the year or the end of the whole course (which was the convention in the past). In many HEIs, these developments have gone hand-in-hand with implementation of a two-semester system, replacing the old three-term structure of academic years. Methods of teaching in higher education are changing over time: traditional lectures, tutorials and practical are being augmented by a range of other learning activities, especially those that exploit information and communications technology. Use of methods of assessment other than traditional written examinations has steadily increased. Marks that contribute towards final degree class are often now accumulated each term or semester.

Hence where forms of assessment *other than* traditional written examinations are being employed (which is increasingly the case in higher education in the UK) it is increasingly difficult to rely exclusively, or even primarily, on additional time to compensate for the disabilities of students with dyslexia.

11.1.2.3   *Anonymity and differential marking practices*

Differential marking practices for students with dyslexia already take place in many HEIs to some extent, either informally (because the examination script is identified by name) or formally (e.g. by use of stickers put on scripts that identify that this work is that of a student with dyslexia). However, the use of anonymous marking schemes for written examinations (and sometimes assessed course work) is steadily increasing in higher education. Institutions may be resistant to the identification of students with dyslexia by means of stickers on scripts, because it is believed that this contravenes the principle of anonymity.

In fact, many of the special arrangements made for disabled students *already contravene this principle*. For example, in cases where tape recording or word processing has been agreed as an alternative medium of communication in examinations, anonymity will *almost inevitably be broken*. Word processed answers will be in printed, rather than the hand-written, format used by the remainder of the class. Tape recorded answers will have to be transcribed – a job usually carried out by an audio typist – and these will also be in printed format. It will therefore be clear to the examiners that this student is different or 'special' in some way. Since students with disabilities currently make up only about 4% of all students in higher education, it will often be straightforward for examiners to identify the students concerned.

Furthermore, answers that have been dictated into a tape recorder, when transcribed, will not usually have explicit punctuation and will often be lacking observance of the grammatical rules used in written communication. This is because speech and writing are quite different modes of communication, with different 'standards'. The typist may endeavour to insert punctuation (in the same way that an amanuensis sometimes does) but unless the actual words are changed (which is strictly prohibited) the text will not necessarily be grammatical. When marking such transcriptions, examiners will inevitably be faced with the task of discounting such infringements of grammar while concentrating on the content of the text. In other words, a differential marking practice will be in operation.

Use of amanuenses for students with dyslexia is a relatively common special provision, especially for candidates with very slow writing speeds or handwriting difficulties. But this may confer an unexpected *advantage* for the student with dyslexia, since use of an amanuensis effectively resolves spelling difficulties (assuming that the amanuensis has adequate spelling skills). So (largely) does the use of a word processor, assuming the spelling checker is employed.

A dilemma therefore arises: students with dyslexia will generally be compensated to a much great degree by using an *alternative method of communication* in examinations, such as an amanuensis, tape recorder or word processor (the latter especially when it is their 'normal' mode of writing). Should such special arrangements be restricted only to *some* students with dyslexia (e.g. the more 'severe' cases), or permitted for all? If the latter, this could present major administrative problems, since an average-sized university will expect to have about 50 dyslexic students requiring special arrangements *each examination session* (a session usually being either morning or afternoon) throughout a typical examination period of 3 weeks. A further complication is that individual rooms would have be provided (and separate invigilators) when tape recording or amanuenses are being used, and even in the case of word processing when voice recognition systems are being used to input text. Few, if any, HEIs would be able to cope with such demands.

There is a strong case for treating students with dyslexia in the same way as other disabilities when it comes to making special examination arrangements. That is, to evaluate *individual needs* and implement provisions which will be equitable whilst preserving academic standards. Since many accepted special arrangements for a variety of disabilities already breach the 'principle' of anonymity and incorporate, implicitly or explicitly, adaptations to marking practices, it is difficult to sustain the objection to a formalised scheme view whereby all dyslexic students have the option of being identified as having dyslexia and their examiners being asked to discount errors of spelling, grammar and punctuation. This also has the advantages of ease of administration and lower cost, compared with solutions involving alternative media, such as amanuenses, word processors and tape recorders.

11.1.3 *Problems experienced by students in examinations and assessments*

This section describes some of the problems in examinations and assessments reported by students with dyslexia and highlighted by dyslexia support tutors. Note that 'examinations and assessments' includes class tests, practical assessments, presentations, written assignments, dissertations and assessed essays, all of which can sometimes involve as much (or even more) reading and writing under timed conditions than conventional examinations. Not all students will necessarily experience the same problems and each student may experience different problems on different occasions. These problems are by no means unique to students with dyslexia, and many students who do not have dyslexia report similar problems from time-to-time.

It is important to distinguish between the *direct* disadvantaging effects of dyslexia on a student in examinations and assessments, and the *indirect* effects. Direct effects concern the established cognitive characteristics of dyslexia (e.g. inefficiency in working memory and limitations in phonological processing ability) and the known educational concomitants of these (e.g. difficulties in reading and writing, and in the organisation of information). Indirect effects arise because students perceptions of their own limitations (e.g. through past experience) can cause apprehension, stress or even panic when confronted with examinations or assessments. Such emotions can have far-reaching consequences for these students' functioning. Excessive stress can be an indirect effect of dyslexia (Miles and Varma, 1995). Since all students can suffer from stress-related problems from time-to-time it may be considered unfair to try to make allowances for such indirect effects of dyslexia *over and above* what special provisions are already permitted to compensate for the direct effects of dyslexia.

11.1.3.1   *Organisational difficulties*

- Problems for students with dyslexia can initially occur with filling in forms (such as requests for additional time) and returning them by the due date.

- On the day of the examination finding the right place, getting there on time and finding the correct seat within the examination room can all cause problems. Anxiety about these matters may create additional stress.

- Organisation within the examination itself (such as managing the time in which to write answers) may also create difficulties for students with dyslexia.

- Noise can be particularly stressful for some students with dyslexia who report that they have very low noise distraction thresholds.

11.1.3.2   *Reading*

- Some students with dyslexia report that their biggest dread is misreading the instructions on the question paper, so answering the wrong question.

- Some students with dyslexia who have a tendency to misinterpret written information may choose a question on an unfamiliar topic rather than one on a topic they know well, if the former involves reading less text.

- Coping with multiple-choice papers requires three skills which are typically weak in the case of students with dyslexia: rapid and accurate reading of relatively large amounts of text; sufficient working memory to retain the question while evaluating possible answers, and the ability to locate the correct place quickly and accurately on the answer grid.

- The longer time which it often takes students with dyslexia to complete the reading preparation for written assignments may be a significant factor contributing to failure to meet deadlines for submission of assessed work.

- Many students with dyslexia suffer from visual discomfort (see Section 9.2.3.2), so that after a period of time, the text on the examination paper and/or the script that the student is writing, may appear blurred, indistinct or cause headaches or unpleasant visual sensations. This may also disincline such students to read over or check their examination answers.

- In most examinations students are permitted to write on the examination paper. Occasionally this may not be allowed (e.g. in a multiple choice paper where the student is required to mark answers on a separate answer sheet, or where the paper involves large amounts of quoted text and copies are re-used for reasons of economy). In such cases, if students with dyslexia are not permitted to write on the examination paper this may be an additional handicap to them. In dealing with large amounts of text such restrictions may adversely affect reading comprehension and so undermine their confidence. In the multiple-choice examination they may be liable to transcription errors, e.g. deciding that they will choose a given answer, but marking the number of a different answer on the sheet.

11.1.3.3   *Writing and spelling*

- Limited automaticity of writing skills forces students to focus on the process of writing *itself* (such as legibility and punctuation) rather than on the *meaning* which they are trying to put across. They may easily lose track of what they are trying to say in their answers, or inadvertently miss out words.

- Most individuals with dyslexia have poor spelling, and may waste valuable time in puzzling over how particular words are spelled.

- Some students with dyslexia have poor handwriting and must concentrate most of their intellectual effort on trying to write legibly. Others have very slow handwriting and cannot get all their ideas onto paper in the time allowed.

- Many students with dyslexia find it hard to organise their thoughts into a structured essay. Although many have mastered this problem by using a word processor, the institution may be reluctant to allow this in written examinations.

- Because writing is a relatively slow process for many students with dyslexia, they will typically take longer to complete essays and other assessed written work, which may lead to problems in meeting deadlines and interfere with other important aspects of their courses.

11.1.4 Determining appropriate provision

The standard response to the difficulties encountered by students with dyslexia in examinations is to allow additional time. 99% of HEIs responding to the national survey stated that this was their policy (see Section 3.2.10). In about 40% of institutions the amount of extra time allowed is standard for all students with dyslexia in that institution, regardless of the nature or extent of their dyslexic difficulties; in the remainder, the time allowed varied from case to case. In those institutions in which it is standard, there is variation across HEIs, with about 50% institutions allowing an additional 10 minutes per hour and 50% allowing an additional 15 minutes per hour.[50]

Whether there should be national consistency in examination provision for students with dyslexia, and the extent to which examination provision should be dependent on the nature and extent of the student's particular difficulties, are important matters that the Working Party has addressed. In particular, although provision of a standard amount of extra time for all students with dyslexia might appear to be the fairest solution all round, its appropriateness must be questioned in the light of known variations in both nature and severity of the condition (see Section 8.3.3.1). It also runs counter to the principle of providing for *individual* needs in all cases of disability. Where HEIs adopted a varied approach to examination provision for students with dyslexia, most (83%) reported that this was 'dependent on the diagnostic assessment report'.

11.1.5 Resource issues

A significant problem for HEIs in making provision for students with dyslexia in examinations is resources. There are manpower costs of organising special provision and of invigilating examinations (especially in cases when students with dyslexia have been allocated additional time or separate examination rooms). In addition, there are space costs in providing separate examination rooms where these are deemed to be necessary (e.g. where an amanuensis is being used), and other costs (e.g. for provision of special equipment or facilities, such as word processing, where needed).

There are various other methods of assessing the work of students, including class tests, practicals, dissertations and presentations. Each method may cause particular communication difficulties for individual students with dyslexia. Tutors need to be aware of the problems that students with dyslexia are likely to encounter in these activities so that they can allow for them as fairly possible, without making the students uncomfortable about any special arrangements that are provided. This has resourcing and organisational implications for staff development. Funding implications are addressed in Chapter 9.

11.2 Proposals on good practice

It is important to recognise that special examination arrangements are but *one aspect* of the much wider support in learning that students with dyslexia require if they are going to be able to make the best of their studies and perform up to standard in examinations and assessments.

---

[50] In GCSE and A level examinations, 25% additional time is usual (Joint Forum for GCSE and GCE, 1997).

11.2.1 Course aims and objectives

Ideally, the first step in addressing the problem of examination provision for students with dyslexia (or for any disabilities) is not the consideration of the examination, nor of the student, but of the course itself. Having clear course aims and objectives helps to clarify what methods of examination and assessment would be most appropriate. The exposition of these aims and objectives helps students to prepare more effectively for examinations and other forms of assessment. In particular, course aims should state the relative importance in the course of:

- learning facts, concepts, theories and procedures

- applying such learning to show understanding and the ability to solve problems

- using argument and criticism

- showing originality of ideas

- use of written language

- use of oral language

- use of non-verbal skills, such as practical competencies and production of diagrams.

The examination and assessment system should refer to these course aims. For example, in a given course the first four of the above skills might each amount to 20% of the requirements of the course, with the last three amounting to the final 20% between them.

Having stated course aims, the task of considering the extent to which accommodation can be made for students with disabilities in examinations and assessments becomes more straightforward. In the example given above (in which less than 20% of the course requirements relate to written language skills), students with dyslexia, who would be expected to have difficulties with written language, could perhaps be assessed by other means (such as oral examination), without affecting the integrity or quality of the course. In some institutions, oral examinations still form an integral part of the process of examining students, while in others they have fallen into disuse.

When addressing the problem in this manner – by first analysing course aims and objectives – we inevitably find ourselves confronted with the question: what are the most appropriate methods of assessment on this course for *all* students? Perhaps a written examination is not the most appropriate but continues to be used *only because* it is traditional and also convenient.

11.2.2 Preparation for examinations

11.2.2.1   Student-related preparations

The nature of the degree course taken and the mode(s) of examination and assessment involved are important issues that must be addressed at the start of (or prior to) an undergraduate's studies. Waiting until examinations or course work submission times draw near makes it more difficult for problems to be dealt with satisfactorily and appropriate arrangements to be made. As is the case with other disabilities, special provisions can undoubtedly ease the problems experienced by students with dyslexia in examinations and go some way towards offsetting the disadvantages of dyslexia, but they do not remove such problems altogether. To a considerable extent, the solution lies in the preparation of students with dyslexia in order for them to cope with examinations. This has resource implications for learning support well before examinations.

All requests for adapted examination and course work arrangements should be backed up by appropriate documentation. In many institutions this will come from the student services section of the institution. Relevant information from various professional reports (such as psychologists' reports and reports of evaluation of support needs) should also be taken into consideration. The most suitable arrangement should be chosen by discussion with the student, the dyslexia support tutor and/or disability officer, taking into account the policy and guidelines of the institution. Consultation with the course tutor and/or the examinations officer may also be necessary. Students with dyslexia and the members of the academic staff who teach and examine them need to understand the adapted arrangements – not only to appreciate what examination arrangements are available for students with dyslexia, but also know how these arrangements can be accessed.

For some students, 'practice' examination experiences are very useful in enabling the student to develop their individual coping strategy and to feel more confident. Accurate information can 'de-mystify' the marking and assessment procedure. Anxious students may make false assumptions about the level of competence required. Knowing what examiners are looking for in examination scripts, how marks are put together, what abilities and standards are required, can help to reassure students that they are not expected to be perfect and that their writing will be sympathetically regarded.

Many useful suggestions for students with dyslexia in preparing for examinations are to be found in Gilroy and Miles (1996).

11.2.2.2   Staff-related preparations

Examination structure, mode and content should be clearly and explicitly related to course aims and objectives. When writing questions for examination papers, academic staff should be mindful of the course objectives as well as considering their impact and possible interpretation from the students' points of view.

Examination questions and essay titles that are clearly and directly written ease the reading problems of most students with dyslexia. The physical appearance and layout of examination papers can be altered to help reading problems through use of coloured paper, clear and adequately-sized fonts (size 12 or larger) and well spaced-out questions. Multiple-choice examinations can sometimes be changed to become short answer papers. Frequently, the examination requirements of a course will allow many variations from the traditional 'unseen' written paper to be developed.

Where it has been decided that examiners are to be notified when marking the work of students with dyslexia, effective procedures (such as stickers on examination scripts) have to be established to deal with this. Such procedures should include issuing to examiners recommendations to disregard errors of spelling and punctuation and to be tolerant of poor grammar.

11.2.3 Deciding on type of provision

11.2.3.1   General principles

For practical purposes, a distinction may be drawn between 'group provisions' and 'individual provisions'. 'Group provisions' refers to special arrangements that can generally be accommodated fairly easily within conventional arrangements for examinations, including using the same examination rooms and invigilators. In other words, the dyslexic candidate will be sitting examinations together with a group of other students, which may include non-dyslexic students. 'Individual provisions' refers to special arrangements that cannot generally be accommodated within conventional arrangements for examinations, e.g. use of amanuenses, word processors or dictated examination answers. These will usually require separate examination rooms and alternative arrangements for invigilation.

The suitability of group or individual provisions depends on the nature of the individual student's difficulties. A student may need different provisions for different types of examinations. The most suitable arrangements should be chosen through discussion with the student, the support tutor, the examinations office and the course tutor. Information from various professional reports (e.g. diagnostic assessment and evaluation of needs) should be taken into consideration.

From the institution's point of view, the most cost-effective solution is a system of general group provisions that are flexible enough to cater for the majority of students with dyslexia. Some students will have particular needs that can be meet by additional provisions within the general system. Some students will have needs that are not met by the general provisions; these students will need provisions specified individually for them, which may or may not require alternative arrangements for examination rooms and invigilation. The overall aim of this division into two categories is to use the limited resources of the institution as productively as possible. Group provisions tend to demand fewer resources per student than individual ones. Reserving the possibility of applying individual provisions where these are appropriate means that the greater needs of some students can still be accommodated.

11.2.3.2   Group provisions

Fairly simple group arrangements which can assist many candidates with dyslexia, and which can be administered in a conventional examination situation without great difficulty, include the following.

- Provision of additional time (see Section 11.2.3.4).

- Use of various techniques to assist reading, including: coloured overlays, photocopying of the exam paper on to tinted paper, or enlargement of the exam paper. These may also allay the student's anxiety that they will misread a question and avoid them spending undue amounts of time re-checking it.

- Arranging particular seating positions in order to minimise disturbance by noise or light difficulties.

- Permission to use spelling dictionaries or portable electronic spelling checker.

- Provision of rough paper (if not normally provided) and/or permission to write on examination papers (if not normally permitted). These provisions help to cut down the working memory demands on candidates with dyslexia.

- Permission to indicate the correct answer to multiple choice questions on the question paper itself, rather than on a separate grid, in order to avoid the candidate marking answers in the incorrect place.

- Use of a examination room in which there are likely to be fewer distractions, e.g. a smaller room rather than a large hall.

11.2.3.3   Individual provisions

When students needs are not met by the group system, the appropriateness of the following special arrangements may all need to be considered. In general, it will be the more severely affected candidates that will require individual provisions such are those listed below. Any new method that is adopted needs to be practised with the student beforehand, under mock examination conditions.

- Methods that avoid the candidate with severe writing problems having to produce hand-written answers, including oral examination, tape recording of answers, use of an amanuensis (scribe), use of a conventional word processor, and use of a voice-activated word processor.

- Methods that avoid the candidate misreading questions, including tape recording of questions.

- Methods that reduce distractions, including papers being taken in a quiet room, separate from the main examination room.

- Methods that reduce excessive fatigue and/or stress, including avoiding too many hours of examinations in the same day, providing short breaks during examinations, and giving at least one day's rest in between successive examinations.

- Transcription and assistance with computer-marked answer sheets.

- Individual supervision of examinations involving calculations to check that digits are not transposed or omitted when copying from the question paper or electronic calculator.

11.2.3.4   Additional time

Additional time in written examinations for candidates with dyslexia is a very well-accepted provision in examinations at higher education level, as well as in GCSE, 'A' level and many other public examinations. Additional time can serve many functions, including the following.

- Reduction (but not elimination) of stress.

- Increased time to read questions, reducing (but not eliminating) the possibilities of misreading.

- Increased time to think about and structure answers, which can compensate to some extent for organisational difficulties.

- Increased time to recall facts, compensating to some extent for memory difficulties.

- Increased time to write answers, reducing (but not eliminating) the production of poorly structured, ungrammatical answers, and compensating to some extent for slow or painful handwriting. (Note that this will not usually improve legibility of handwriting to any great degree.)

- Increased time to use spelling aids (such as a spelling dictionary or portable spelling checker). Rarely will the provision of additional time, by itself, enable the dyslexic to improve spelling to any significant degree. Spelling aids can be useful, but use of a dictionary on a frequent basis in examinations is not recommended because students with dyslexia often have great difficulty using a dictionary effectively. It is also liable to disrupt their chain of thought. Hence students should be discouraged from spending excessive amounts of time trying to produce correct spellings. This can divert a great deal of time and energy away from the main purpose of the examination.

- Increased time to check over the content of answers, which may result in *some* improvement in the detection and correction of errors, but will not eliminate all (or even the majority of) errors since most dyslexics are very inadequate proof readers.

During the consultation process carried out by the Working Party, several dyslexia tutors reported that dyslexic students, when allowed extra time, tend to function much better *but do not necessarily use the additional time.* They are more able to relax and concentrate on careful reading of the question and planning out the answer without the growing panic that they will run out time. As a result they may well produce satisfactory answers in the nominal time of the examination.

When separate examination accommodation is not available, some institutions prefer to allocate additional time at the beginning of examinations rather than at the end. This approach may reduce the effects of disturbance from other students entering and leaving the examination room, but it depends to a large extent on circumstances. There may be less notice taken by other students of the extra time allocated to dyslexic candidates when the students all leave the examination room together than when some are left behind.

The Working Party has considered very carefully the issue of how much additional time should be allowed in written examinations. It has already been pointed out that, at present, about 40% of institutions allow a standard amount of extra time, which is usually either 10 or 15 minutes per hour. In GCSE and 'A' level examinations, 15 minutes per hour (25% additional time) is the norm. In about 60% of HEIs, the amount of extra time allowed varies from case to case. In Section 8.3.3.3, it was argued that since dyslexia is a condition that varies in severity, personnel carrying out diagnostic assessments and evaluations of learning and support needs should distinguish between dyslexic students on the basis of the severity of the effects of their dyslexia. The Working Party believes that this distinction should be maintained in making special examination provision. *The imposition of blanket arrangements for additional time for all students with dyslexia in an institution is contrary to the fundamental requirement that in all cases of disability, arrangements should be on an individual basis dependent on needs.* Adherence to this principle is expected of LEAs when making decisions about DSA awards for any disability, and of HEIs when providing study skills support for students with dyslexia. It should also be the case for examination provision.

In order to maintain consistency across the sector, and consistency with other categories of examinations in the public sector, the Working Party recommends the following *minimum amounts* of additional time for candidates with dyslexia when sitting written examinations.

- In cases where the effects of the dyslexia are **mild**: *a minimum of 10 minutes per hour.*

- In cases where the effects of the dyslexia are **moderate**: *a minimum of 15 minutes per hour.*

- In cases where the effects of the dyslexia are **severe**: *a minimum of 15 minutes per hour.*[51]

It should be remembered that the labels 'mild', 'moderate' and 'severe' are approximations that are intended to reflect individual variation in the effects of dyslexia and in the degrees of compensation that individuals with dyslexia can bring to bear in given situations. Hence all cases should be considered on their individual merits and a *greater allowance* of additional time will sometimes be necessary, together with other appropriate arrangements.

The Working Party recognises that in some HEIs there may be administrative resistance to the implementation of a sliding scale of additional times that is dependent upon severity and other individual factors. Standard provision for all students with dyslexia may be preferred because it is easier to manage. However, for students with disabilities other than dyslexia, individual examination arrangements based on need will usually be the norm, and there is a strong case for applying the same procedures and principles to *all* disabilities. On the other hand, in some institutions, staff resources may at present be insufficient to provide individual evaluation of examinations requirements for *every* student with dyslexia. In such circumstances, the following compromise may be suggested. All students with dyslexia should be offered the *minimum* amount of additional time allowed for a student in the 'mild' category (i.e. 10 minutes per hour) or, alternatively, the standard amount that the institution allows (provided this is not less than 10 minutes per hour). Individual students who feel that they require *more* additional time than this may then apply to the disability officer, dyslexia tutor or other member of staff charged with this responsibility, in order to have their examination needs evaluated and arrangements will then be made on the basis of the outcome of that evaluation.

In cases where the effects of the dyslexia are *severe*, a greater allowance of additional time will often be necessary. It should be borne in mind that when greater than 25% additional time is allowed (15 minutes per hour), this could be counterproductive for some students. Furthermore, the duration of the examination may then have been so lengthened as to cause excessive fatigue. Few examinations at higher education level are greater than 3 hours in duration, which, with 25% additional time, will extend to 3 hours 45 minutes. A longer duration than that would probably require breaks and would also present difficulties for many candidates in sustaining concentration and mental effort. Where examinations are of shorter nominal duration (e.g. 2 hours), greater than 25% additional time will not usually create such problems for the student and may therefore be considered more appropriate.

Where examinations involve reading large amounts of text (e.g. case studies or lengthy quotations from texts), the amount of extra time should always be considered very carefully in relation to the student's reading speed. It is important to allow adequate time for the candidate to assimilate the required information from the text.

In general, allowance extra of time should be given *in addition to* other special arrangements, *not instead of* such arrangements. The amount of extra time that is given, and the other special arrangements, should be decided by consultation with the student, the student's tutor and/or examiner, the dyslexia support tutor and/or disability officer, and the examinations officer of the institution. Evidence from reports of diagnostic assessment and evaluation of learning and support needs should be taken into account. When calculating additional time, any fractions of minutes should be rounded up to the nearest minute.

11.2.3.5   *Use of word processors in examinations*

Word processors are increasingly permitted for examinations. 85% of HEIs answering a question on this in the national survey (N = 150) reported that they allowed this, although how frequent it is within individual institutions is not known. Some institutions are able to make use of a room

---

[51] For a description the categories 'mild', 'moderate' and 'severe' and discussion of the evidence supporting this approach, see Section 8.3.3.3. Note that the allocation of a *minimum* of 15 minutes additional time per hour for both the 'moderate' and 'severe' categories is deliberate but, in most cases, students whose dyslexia is rated as 'severe' will require an individual evalution of their examination requirements, which may result in a greater allowance of addition time.

containing several computers for examination purposes and use network machines with partitioned hard disks, which are organised so as to prevent students having access to illicit material. Some institutions can provide individual computers. Under exceptional circumstances, students are allowed to use their own computers, provided appropriate checks are made. Students need to know which machines will be available in order to be familiar with them, especially with the keyboard and software. Care has to be taken to prevent the possibility of cheating, and a computer technician needs to be available in case there is a computer fault.

Use of word processors in examinations is a provision that should be more widely used. Students with dyslexia develop essay writing skills, beyond touch typing, that capitalise on computer facilities. To remove these skills from them by requiring examinations to be hand-written does not help them fully to demonstrate the knowledge and competencies they have acquired. Voice-activated word processing is being increasingly advocated for students with dyslexia. Using such an application – sometimes referred to as 'voice input' or 'voice recognition' – the student can dictate into the computer, thus avoiding the need for typing or use of an amanuensis, which is usually more expensive. However, voice input creates a problem for accommodation, as separate rooms will be needed to avoid disturbing other candidates. Nevertheless, as a general matter of principle, it should be acknowledged that to deny students with dyslexia access to their 'normal' mode of writing is to create a further disadvantage for them in examinations.

However, use of computers in examinations still presents some dilemmas, particularly computer where packages of software support with enhanced features are concerned. An example is *textHELP!* – which is now one of the most widely recommended pieces of software for students with dyslexia.[52] As well as providing spell-checking, text-reading and other useful facilities, when used with a word processor this program includes a word prediction facility, which enables much faster writing, as the computer 'guesses' what word the student wants to use next. After practice with the individual student, the program becomes increasingly accurate at word prediction for that student, thus making writing much easier. Arguably, students with dyslexia who make regular use of *textHELP!* have made this their 'normal' mode of writing. But should they have access to its facilities in an examination? Disability officers in many HEIs have expressed concerns that the use of these type of facilities would confer an *unfair advantage* on students with dyslexia. Clearly, developments in technology that may impact on examinations need to be studied very carefully.

11.2.3.6   Invigilators

During the consultation process, a few dyslexia tutors commented that invigilators can have considerable influence on the performance of some students with dyslexia. Such concerns are probably not exclusive to students with dyslexia, but may be more pronounced in dyslexic students. Debilitating memories of past examination experiences can be evoked by an unwitting chance remark by an invigilator. The way the invigilator moves around the room or interacts with individuals can affect the students' way of working. A calm atmosphere and a sympathetic attitude can allow students to settle down to work well. By participating in staff development, invigilators can gain an understanding of dyslexia and of the effects that it can have on examination performance.

11.2.3.7   Re-sit candidates

Special consideration is needed for candidates with dyslexia who have repeatedly failed examinations or substantially underachieved due to an immobilising level of stress or panic symptoms. Such candidates will often be required to re-sit examinations, which may increase stress even more. A review of the adequacy of special arrangements will usually be necessary, as well as consultation with the student. Some students with dyslexia are prone to misread words on examination papers – again, often because of stress or panic – and so misunderstand the intention of the questions. Tape recording of questions can be one solution to this problem (see Section 11.2.3.3).

---

[52] *textHELP!* is produced by Lorien Systems, Enkalon Business Centre, 25 Randalstown Road, Antrim, Co. Antrim, BT41 4LJ, Northern Ireland. Tel: 01849 428105 Fax: 01849 428574. E-mail: *info@loriens.com*

Issues that often need discussing or working on with the student include stress reduction techniques, time management, and the extent to which the paper is a test of factual knowledge as opposed to understanding and/or application of that knowledge. Examiners could consider to what extent the examination is intended to test memory *per se* and whether memory aids (e.g. a list of key words or formulae) might be appropriate for all students (see also Section 11.2.1).

11.2.4 Course work assessment

Course work takes many forms, and it is impractical within this report to try and cover every form of assessment. Any method of assessment can be dealt with by:

- looking at the problem in the light of the difficulties that students with dyslexia are likely to experience

- considering what adaptations would allow those students to use appropriate strategies that capitalise on their alternative thinking strengths, without giving them an unfair advantage

- providing constructive, understandable feedback so that students can evaluate those strategies and progressively improve their skills.

For the purposes of illustration, we have considered course work under three headings: written work, class work and presentations.

Written work. Written work is usually set with deadlines, and for various reasons students with dyslexia may have more difficulties with meeting deadlines than other students. It is helpful if deadlines are staggered to avoid too many occurring at the same time. Unless there are extenuating circumstances, delaying deadlines is not usually helpful as it often creates problems later on. The problems resulting in the unmet deadlines need to be anticipated and a suitable study organisation implemented rather than the deadlines being adjusted.

Assessed class work. Where assessed class work has a time limit this should be adjusted in line with the extra time for examinations. Assessed class work takes many different forms, e.g. practical tests, tests using projected slides, and case studies. It is not always easy to arrange provisions that allow students with dyslexia to demonstrate knowledge and skills in such a way that they are not exposed as being different. A suggestion would be allowing all students to use an outline crib sheet in assessed class work. This may not make very much difference to the performance of non-dyslexic students, who will probably be able to remember the necessary material satisfactorily, but it can make a substantial difference to a dyslexic student, removing the worry of forgetting essential points and allowing them to concentrate on demonstrating their practical skills, understanding of the subject matter, and interpretation of information.

Presentations. Some students with dyslexia have no difficulty with oral presentations while others cope poorly. Students need to be reassured that they are being marked for ideas, informed critical acumen, the ability to address complex problems and their overall communication skills, and that obvious dyslexic problems (e.g. lexical access or 'word finding' difficulties) will be discounted.

11.2.5 Marking practices and examination boards

Practice with respect to marking the assessed work of students with dyslexia varies considerably between HEIs. Some institutions have marking regulations restricting the marks that can be allocated to literacy skills, some instruct markers to focus on ideas, some rely largely on provision of additional time and otherwise only take dyslexia into consideration for borderline cases in meetings of examination boards. In course work, as in written examinations, if students with dyslexia think their literacy skills are being marked, they may tend to concentrate more on those and consequently the quality of their ideas may not be evident in the work presented. In addressing these issues, examination boards need to consider course aims and how assessment can best be matched to those aims, including what proportion of marks are to be allocated to quality of English (see Section 11.2.1), as well as ways in which course structure and regulations for the accumulation of credits and grades might disadvantage students with dyslexia. In the words of Gilroy and Miles (1996), the most important thing is to '...ensure that [examination Boards] do not unwittingly mark a candidate down for lack of skills which they would agree on reflection to be irrelevant' (p. 184).

It has already been pointed out that in some HEIs, it is the practice that work (whether examination script or other assessed material) is labelled as that of a student with dyslexia. The arguments surrounding this issue are presented in Section 11.1.2. In institutions that have adopted anonymous marking, this may be perceived to create problems. However, the relative merits of identification versus anonymity should be considered, and the importance of equal opportunities for disabled students brought into the debate. It would not be unreasonable to take the student's preferences into account because anonymity is primarily for the benefit of students. Some students with dyslexia may prefer their work to remain anonymous along with that of other candidates, others may prefer that examiners know that they have dyslexia, even if that may compromise the anonymity of their work. In some institutions in which anonymous marking has been introduced there are reports of students choosing to identify themselves as dyslexic by writing a statement to this effect on the script so that examiners are aware that their handwriting, spelling and punctuation may be deficient. Although examiners can be instructed to disregard such declarations, it is clearly better to have an institutional solution to the problem.

It may be argued that any adjustments to marks should be made by boards of examiners rather than by individual examiners. Prior to the introduction of modular course systems, examinations were usually structured in a way that permitted this, at least to some extent. Particular attention was paid to borderline cases where it was conceivable that they would be upgraded as a result of further consideration of their disability, over and above the special arrangements that have already been implemented for them. Since examination scripts were still to hand at the time examination boards were being held, it was possible in such cases to recover the examination scripts and other assessed work of the student and re-examine them (and, in some cases, ask the external examiner to mark them), before deciding upon the final degree class to be awarded to the student. At this stage, any aspects of disability that had not been allowed for in special examination arrangements (such as problems of handwriting, spelling or punctuation) could be taken into account in the decision process.

The modular course structures which are becoming the norm in UK higher education can make it difficult for boards of examiners to give fullest consideration to students with dyslexia whose results make them borderline cases. In modular systems, examiners are less likely to know all the students they are examining (because students can often select from a wide range of modules offered across the institution), and so there may be no member of the board of examiners to comment on how a particular disability may have affected a particular student's results. The flexibility permitted to examination boards in the past is increasingly not the case today. The board's freedom of decision and action may be restricted by previous stages of the qualification process, e.g. passing or failing given numbers of modules at certain levels in previous years of the course. Alteration of marks or grades by the board may not be permitted under the institution's regulations. Even though a board of examiners may desire and would be permitted, to re-examine previous work, in order to check whether dyslexic students have been marked down for poor written language skills or not given due credit for ideas and understanding, in practice this may be impossible because the work in question cannot be located or because of time and resource constraints. Finally, there are no rules or guidelines about how much a student's marks should be adjusted in order to make an equitable allowance for their particular disabilities.

A case may therefore be made for adoption of a scheme of identifying the work of dyslexic students, and advising examiners, when marking, to make allowances for *specific dyslexic difficulties*.[53] Rather than adjusting marks and being faced with the almost impossible task of deciding how much adjustment would be fair (as would be the case at the examining board stage), they are being asked to discount, as far as possible, errors in spelling, grammar and punctuation, and instead to mark for content and ideas. In many institutions this will be simply formalising a process that already takes place covertly. It also avoids the undesirable situation of students unilaterally

---

[53] It is recognised that this may not be possible where the quality of written expression is one of the principal focuses of the examination (e.g. in English language).

identifying themselves as dyslexic on otherwise anonymous examination scripts, in a manner that could be difficult for examiners to verify and which may result in some examiners making allowances and others not.

Wherever a labelling scheme is adopted, the extent to which this will compensate for the student's difficulties should be weighed up against any other special arrangements that are being considered. Appropriate guidelines need to be given to examiners, e.g. in the form of a slip attached to the work. Examiners should also be made aware what other special arrangements have been accorded to the candidate, so that inappropriate or excessive allowances are not made in the marking process. Issues that examiners wish to discuss on this should be raised *before* the examination is taken, or work handed in, to avoid misunderstandings. The object should be to ensure that work is *marked for content, ideas and critical acumen* and that any allowances in marking are fair and are for aspects of the performance of dyslexic candidates that cannot be compensated by other means.

Students with dyslexia should always be given the option of whether they wish their work to be identified or not. As with all disability matters, every care should be taken to ensure confidentiality, e.g. by returning work to the student privately rather than by a procedure in which other students would be able to see the dyslexia label.

On occasions, examiners may detect no symptoms of dyslexia in an examination script or in some other piece of work. This lack of apparent dyslexic symptoms should not be taken as evidence that the dyslexia has been 'cured' or that the disability was a myth. Work that shows few signs of dyslexia may evidence the efficacy of the support and special arrangements being provided for the student. HESA statistics show that, in terms of degree classes at graduation, the performance of students with dyslexia is not altogether different from that of other students. Furthermore, where appropriate support provision is available, there are indications that the proportion of students with dyslexia achieving 'good' degrees (i.e. first class and upper second) more closely resembles that of the whole cohort (see Section 1.1.5.1).

11.3   Recommendations

1.   Every HEI should have a written policy on the examination and assessment of students with dyslexia ('the examinations policy').

2.   The examinations policy should:

      a)   acknowledge that academic standards are paramount and that special arrangements in examinations and assessments are for the purpose of establishing equitable circumstances for these disabled students;

      b)   be compiled having due regard to the Working Party's proposals on good practice given in Section 11.2 of this report;

      c)   cover all special examination arrangements and marking regulations;

      d)   cover all work that is submitted for marking, including class tests, practicals and dissertations;

      e)   be binding on all faculties, schools or departments within the institution;

      f)   specify the responsibilities of the student and the institution for communication with respect to special arrangements;

      g)   embody provision for monitoring the system of special arrangements; and

      h)   refer to the institution's policy with respect to identification of dyslexia.

3.   When additional time in written examinations is being allowed for candidates with dyslexia, due regard should be given to the Working Party's recommendations on amounts of additional time in relation to the severity of effects of dyslexia, given in Section 11.2.3.4.

4. When courses or modules are being planned, consideration should be given to the relative importance of written language, and whether forms of assessment other than written examinations would be appropriate, especially for students with dyslexia.

5. Academic staff should endeavour to write examination questions, essay titles and instructions clearly and directly, being mindful of the difficulties that some students with dyslexia may experience in reading such material.

6. Examination invigilators should be given training in how to deal with dyslexic students in examination conditions.

7. Where a scheme of identification of the work of students with dyslexia is being adopted, examiners should satisfy themselves that the regulations are being fairly administered so that both undue allowances and overstrict marking are being avoided.

8. Within the staff development which HEIs provide on dyslexia, guidance should be given on how to mark the examination scripts and assessed work of students with dyslexia (especially where spelling, grammar and punctuation are concerned) and how most usefully to give feedback to such students about their work.

9. As far as possible, students with dyslexia should be allowed to find and use a mode of assessment in which they are competent and confident, and which takes into account their individual difficulties.

12 Careers advice for students with dyslexia

12.1 Issues, problems and challenges

There are a number of problems that students with dyslexia encounter when seeking a suitable career, and several pertinent issues that HEIs need to consider in this connection.

- When it comes to choosing careers and seeking employment, some students with dyslexia will not want to make any concessions to their dyslexia. Their personality and interests may make them determined to achieve their career goals, whatever these may be, despite their dyslexic difficulties.

- Students with dyslexia may, or may not, have a realistic understanding of the problems which they are likely to encounter in trying to get into their chosen career and of the challenges which will confront them if and when they achieve that goal.

- Some professions may be reluctant to accept individuals with dyslexia, however determined those individuals may be and despite qualifications obtained in higher education. The case of Duncan reported in Section 2.6.1.4 illustrates the anxiety felt by many students with dyslexia over whether to disclose their dyslexia to a potential employer.

- Some students with dyslexia may be inclined to avoid careers that require advanced written language skills. Instead they may be attracted to careers that they believe will minimise the adverse effects of dyslexia and/or capitalise on their cognitive strengths, e.g. architecture, engineering, arts and design.

- Employers are likely to want to know whether a candidate is likely to require special facilities in order to operate effectively in a given post. Employers may also have concerns about meeting their obligations under the *Disability Discrimination Act 1995*.

- When writing references, academic staff may be concerned about whether it is right (or even whether they are under a duty) to inform potential employers that the student has dyslexia, and/or that additional time was given in examinations.

12.2 Proposals on good practice

People with dyslexia are to be found in jobs across the whole occupational spectrum. Dyslexic people can be businessmen or women, teachers, academics, scientists, engineers, architects, designers, social workers, prison and probation officers, managers in industry, the retail sector, banking and commerce, employed in entertainment and the creative arts, computer programmers, as well as being found in many other occupations. Not all of these people will have had a formal assessment of their dyslexic difficulties; nevertheless, they have often developed compensatory strategies and developed effective ways of handling their dyslexia.

12.2.1 Encouraging staff and student awareness

Students and careers advisers should be made aware that dyslexia is not necessarily a barrier to success in any occupation. Careers staff should note that in order to achieve in higher education, a dyslexic student will have had to be adaptable, develop coping mechanisms and will have shown a high degree of persistence. These are traits that are assets in the job market.

> *'Dyslexic people are not intellectually deficient, they are not odd and they are by no means inadequate workers. They may have to organise their lives differently from others, but that*

does not mean that they perform any less. Indeed, in many instances, it will be found that the problems they meet are little different from those met by everyone else – but they are exaggerated and made more obvious.' (Hales, 1995).

The above quote sums up the philosophy behind careers advice for students with dyslexia, which should focus on the problems that people with dyslexia are likely to encounter and solutions to these.

One of the first places that a student with dyslexia will usually go to for careers advice is the University Careers Service. There should be at least one member of the careers advice staff in each institution who will take primary responsibility for students with dyslexia and find out about the condition. But it is also important that all careers advisors are given some dyslexia awareness training as part of general or specialist staff development. It is a good idea to compile an information package for students and staff on the nature of dyslexia, and its likely effects on people in different types of employment, with experiences drawn from dyslexic people in all walks of life. Members of staff belonging to the institution who have dyslexia may be pleased to be invited to contribute to this, discussing how they progressed through the early stages of their career. The pack should include information about relevant legislation, including the *Disability Discrimination Act 1995,* and about grants, advice and services that are available through the Department of Education and Employment, e.g. Placing Assessment and Counselling Teams (PACTs), Disability Employment Advisers and Committees for the Employment of People with Disabilities.[54]

The *Disability Discrimination Act 1995* makes it unlawful for an employer to discriminate against a disabled person –

a) in the arrangements which he makes for the purpose of determining to whom he should offer employment;

b) in the terms on which he offers that person employment; or

c) by refusing to offer, or deliberately not offering, him employment.[55]

This provides some measure of protection for applicants with dyslexia. In addition, many larger employers operate an Equal Opportunities policy that incorporates disability awareness and personnel with specific managerial responsibility for disability matters. Some of these companies are members of the Employers' Forum on Disability.[56]

12.2.2 The careers consultation process

At an early stage in higher education, firm decisions about career pathways will not often be made, but early discussion about a wide range of career possibilities and postgraduate training for people with dyslexia can give great encouragement. The earlier career choices are made, the better the opportunity to tailor higher education towards the desired goal. Ideally, careers advice should be taken well before the student's final year in higher education. This allows more time to examine alternatives that may not have previously been considered, and may avoid students with dyslexia having false preconceptions about barriers to employment, which could be demotivating in their studies. Dyslexia support tutors should therefore encourage students to consult the Careers Service as early as possible.

Before entering into the details of job applications, students with dyslexia should consider:

• the implications of telling people about their dyslexia

• whether it is relevant that they should reveal this information

• how they will explain their dyslexia, should this arise.

---

[54] See *'Employing people with disabilities: sources of information and advice.'* available from the Employment Service, Disability Services Branch, Courtwood House, Silver Street Head, Sheffield S1 2DD.

[55] At the present time, businesses employing less than 15 employees are exempt from this legislation.

[56] For address see Section 14.4.

In general, it is better to disclose dyslexia than to conceal it, but this should be a matter about which the student must decide personally. It is highly probable that sooner or later any graduate with dyslexia will, in their employment, find themselves having to do a task that presents some problems because of their dyslexia. If they make errors, and their employer does not realise that the cause of the errors was dyslexia (rather than, say, negligence) then the subsequent consequences for their employment are probably better if they had disclosed their dyslexia at the outset. Many firms now include questions about disability on application forms.

Careers advice staff should be aware that students with dyslexia may lack confidence and self esteem despite their achievements in higher education. They may decide to avoid certain areas of work because of their dyslexia when, in fact, the occupation in question does not require the advanced literacy skills that the students may feel they lack. It is important to talk through reasons for preferences carefully so that a potentially successful match between a job and the student's knowledge, skills and abilities is not missed. Careers advice should not reinforce the false perception that there are large numbers of occupations that people with dyslexia should avoid.

However, consideration of employment possibilities must also be realistic. A student might realise that certain jobs, such as those that involve learning many names in a short space of time, being able to read labels under pressure, working against time to prepare reports, might not be very suitable. When thinking about future jobs, dyslexic students will therefore need to look carefully at themselves. In summary, students should carry out a personal assessment of:

- their intellectual strengths and weaknesses

- their interpersonal skills and limitations

- their motivation and interest

- whether positive motivation improved their skills of dealing with dyslexic problems

- what they found difficult on their higher education course(s)

- what coping strategies they have developed

- how hard they have worked

- what they have achieved during their time in higher education

- what other achievements outside higher education they have made.

They might also ask peers, by whom they will have been observed during work and leisure, to give a dispassionate, third-party perspective on their strengths and limitations. Following this, it will then be necessary for the student, together with the careers adviser, to consider the outcomes of this personal evaluation in relation to specific employment possibilities. This will help them to judge what the likely difficulties of particular jobs will be and what solutions could be adopted to deal with them. One common factor is that of time pressure in the employment situation. For example, a dyslexic person may have been an excellent researcher during their university studies, provided they have had ample time to complete the work. In the occupational setting, individuals may well find themselves under considerable time pressure, and under those circumstances find it difficult to produce good results.

Consequently, the next stage of the process should involve the students thinking realistically about the following:

- each job under consideration, and the extent to which it links with the individual's strengths and weaknesses

- the types of communication (e.g. oral, written, computer networks) and other demands which the job is likely to involve

- the types of pressure (e.g. time, rapid recall of information) that are likely

- the types and number of people they will be dealing with

- how they will cope with difficulties and manage the stresses of the job.

The purpose of this reflection is not to solve all work-related dyslexia problems before they arrive (because this is rarely, if ever, possible). Rather, the purpose is to acquire a range of approaches and a degree of understanding of work issues so that the transition to employment will be successful.

Students will also need to discuss their future with tutors, especially those who may be called upon to supply references.

12.2.3 *Making job applications and preparing for interviews*

When applying for a job, students with dyslexia will need assistance in constructing a CV, and help in completing application forms. They are under no obligation to declare that they have dyslexia, but should explore with the help of the Careers Adviser the likely advantages and disadvantages of not declaring this. It should be remembered that the *Disability Discrimination Act 1995* offers some protection against discrimination. Any statement about the student's dyslexia should include reference to effective strategies that the person has developed to compensate.

Good interview skills are vital. Oral fluency will demonstrate to employers the student's abilities and can compensate for weaker literacy skills. It is important that the student practises interview techniques in order to be able to cope with the stress that is almost inevitable in this situation. Careers staff could provide assistance with this practice, perhaps on a group basis. Students will need to know how to deal with rapid questioning and may need to work out how to get over possible mispronunciations. They will need to consider how to respond to questions about their dyslexia, should this be mentioned. They will also need to indicate to a future employer how they will cope in certain situations.

Psychometric assessment is increasingly used in employment selection (especially by larger companies). The University Careers Service should try to offer help with preparation for this type of testing, which could be problematic for a dyslexic person. Verbal reasoning tests may not do justice to a dyslexic person's capabilities; ideally, a non-verbal test should be also used but that may mean asking for special provision, which could be counterproductive. However, in selection processes for careers in some parts of the public sector, as well as for major companies, requests for special arrangements for candidates with dyslexia or other disabilities when taking psychometric tests are not uncommon. Such requests will usually be considered sympathetically (especially when accompanied by a letter from the university). This action will be particularly important where large amounts of reading and/or writing are required, when it would be reasonable to request additional time.

12.2.4 *Writing references for applicants who have dyslexia*

Referees have a duty to be honest but fair in what they say about students in references, including those for prospective employment or further courses of training. If required to answer specific questions in providing a reference, they must answer truthfully to the best of their knowledge. If asked for a general reference, without specific questions, they should do their best to give a fair and balanced picture of the student's achievements and capabilities, including limitations as well as strengths. It would be unethical and dishonest to give a reference that is misleading regarding the student's abilities. At the same time, there may be personal or private matters regarding the applicant, about which the referee may have knowledge, but which it would be improper for a referee to mention. Such private matters would include the student's personal or family relationships and sexual preferences.

Dyslexia is a disability and there is no duty on the individual to declare a disability to anyone. The government's code of practice on disability is clear that disabled people are not obliged to reveal a disability to their employer or potential employer.[57] In this sense disability is private, and the individual is entitled to keep it private and to decline permission for another person to disclose such

---

[57] '*The Disability Discrimination Act 1995: Code of Practice for the elimination of discrimination in the field of employment against disabled persons or persons who have had a disability.*' Department of Education and Employment, 1996.

information. Nonetheless, employers, in order to meet their obligations under the *Disability Discrimination Act 1995,* may rightfully decide that they need to know which of their employees has any disability, and thus they would be entitled to take appropriate steps to encourage (but not to force) disclosure. If the person does declare that they have a disability, this information should be regarded as confidential within the company employing the person, and only those company personnel who need to know should have access to this information. If the person decides to declare to a specific person or institution that they have a disability (e.g. to their employer), this information will become non-private while still remaining confidential. It does not necessarily become entirely public.

If the student has made their disability known to their HEI, and has requested support and special arrangements in examinations because of that disability, their disability is no longer completely private, but, like the situation that exists in employment, such information remains a matter of confidentiality. Students still have a right of confidentiality such that they must give permission before knowledge of their disability is conveyed to any third parties. Within the institution, it is usually impossible to implement effective support and make special arrangements for examinations unless certain members of staff are aware of the student's disability. By giving permission for this, it does not mean that the student has waived his or her rights to confidentiality in other respects. Members of staff are not entitled to reveal this information to third parties, either inside or outside the institution, other than to those who (a) *need to know* in order to effect the support or other arrangements (e.g. examinations officers, LEA Awards Officers) or (b) *are entitled to know* in order to ensure that academic standards are maintained and equal opportunities provided (e.g. personal academic supervisors, members of Boards of Examiners). Prospective employers do not come within those categories, and therefore without the student's permission, referees are not entitled to reveal that the student has a disability.

The conclusions of the foregoing may be argued to conflict directly with the duty on those supplying references to be honest and truthful and neither to mislead prospective employers nor those making selections for entry to further courses of training. The only way that this situation can be resolved is for the referee to consult with the applicant regarding the wording of the reference where the student's dyslexia is concerned. With the student's permission, the referee may also wish to consult with the institution's dyslexia support tutor or disability officer. If, after such consultation, the referee believes that it is essential to mention in the reference that the student has dyslexia, they should make this clear to the student and seek the student's permission. The student is entitled to refuse permission, in which case the referee would be entitled to decline to supply a reference. The student may therefore need to think carefully about which members of the academic staff they should ask to supply references. This could be problematic when a reference is expected from certain staff (e.g. heads of departments).

While referees are entitled to state that, in their opinion, the applicant is not suitable for the job in question, it would be unethical for referees to refer to a student's dyslexia only in a negative light. If the dyslexic student has progressed successfully through higher education he or she will inevitably have developed strategies for managing their dyslexia, and have shown determination, persistence and probably many other desirable qualities as well. These should also be mentioned in the reference, otherwise a misleading impression will be given. Referees should bear in mind that the support and special examination arrangements afforded to students with dyslexia are provided in order to compensate for a disability and to create a level playing field for assessment purposes. Use of phrases such as 'being given concessions', 'special support' or 'needing extra time in examinations', without explaining the purpose of any support or special arrangements, and the student's entitlement to these, would also be grossly unfair. An example of a more helpful form of expression for this purpose is the following: '*This person has dyslexia, which is a registered disability. Within this institution, he/she has been given the support to which they are entitled as a disabled student under the equal opportunities policy of the institution. This has enabled him/her to develop strategies for managing the effects of their dyslexia effectively and to demonstrate his/her knowledge and abilities to a high/satisfactory/adequate standard.*' The reference should then go on to explain briefly what dyslexia is and what implications it has for the particular employment, what the student's strengths and limitations are, and aspects of the student's abilities that may benefit from assistance and/or training when employed (e.g. using a dictaphone or electronic organiser for taking notes). The institution's dyslexia support tutor or disability officer may be able to help with wording of this part of the reference.

12.3 Recommendations

1. Careers Advice Services in all HEIs should:

    a) have at least *one* student careers adviser with explicit knowledge and/or experience of dyslexia as it relates to the employment of graduates;

    b) endeavour to ensure that all careers advisers in the Service have some awareness of the problems and needs of students with dyslexia in relation to employment; and

    c) give special assistance to students with dyslexia in making applications for employment and in preparing for interviews and occupational selection processes.

2. Students with dyslexia should be encouraged to:

    a) seek careers advice as early in their courses as possible;

    b) choose careers that fit their interests and skills, rather than making a choice mainly on the basis of avoiding literacy-related problems in employment; and,

    c) disclose their dyslexia in making applications for employment (but they should not be compelled to do so).

3. When supplying references for any student with dyslexia, academic and other HEI staff should:

    a) consult with the student, and (with the student's permission) other relevant personnel concerning the student's dyslexia and the likely impact that it will have on the occupation in question;

    b) give information in references on the student's strengths as well as limitations;

    c) not reveal in the reference that the student has dyslexia unless the student gives permission for them to do so; and,

    d) if the student's dyslexia is revealed in the reference, mention ways in which the student has developed strategies to compensate for their dyslexia and how these might be of assistance to the student in employment.

4. All careers staff specialising in advising students with dyslexia should be aware of those few professions where there are reservations about allowing people with dyslexia to train for or enter those professions.

13 Conclusions

13.1 Overview of the report

13.1.1 Aims

The aims of this Working Party were to survey the present support for dyslexic students in Higher Education and, after consultation and consideration of evidence, to produce guidelines and proposals on good practice, so that support can be developed in consistent, appropriate and cost-effective ways. The Working Party has taken into account recommendations on disability provision given in the Report of the National Committee of Inquiry into Higher Education, *Higher Education in the Learning Society* (Dearing, 1997), and the DfEE response to the Dearing Report (DfEE, 1998) as well as considering issues of academic quality and 'graduateness', and the impact of the *Disability Discrimination Act 1995*.

13.1.2 The nature of dyslexia

Dyslexia is a complex constitutional condition that is found in about 4% of the population, and which primarily affects acquisition and use of written language, memory and organisational skills. It is a legally recognised disability. Research into the nature and causes of dyslexia is on-going and as yet there is no one model that all professionals in this area agree upon.

Nevertheless, there is considerable evidence regarding the following:

- the neurological bases of dyslexia

- the cognitive characteristics of dyslexia

- the educational and behavioural outcomes for the person with dyslexia

- the positive aspects of dyslexia.

Each of these aspects has implications for the development of effective systems of identification and support of students with dyslexia in higher education. The lack of a uniform model of causation should not be allowed to obstruct the development of provision for students in higher education who have dyslexia and who may require support in order to learn and study effectively and take their places in the workforce.

13.1.3 Evidence

Proportionately, dyslexic students represent the largest and most rapidly increasing group of disabled students in higher education. The steady increase in students with dyslexia over recent years should be regarded as encouraging and in keeping with moves to improve access to higher education for people with disabilities. The national survey of HEIs carried out by the Working Party, to which 83% of HEIs in the country responded, revealed that the incidence of dyslexia in higher education may be estimated at about 1.2% – 1.5% of students (see Chapter 3). By the time they reach adulthood, most individuals with dyslexia have acquired some awareness of their strengths and limitations, and have developed an array of compensatory strategies to enable them to manage their lives. These strategies can be augmented by support and guidance within the higher education setting to enable students with dyslexia to use their abilities fully. Current discussions within higher education regarding the qualities of 'graduateness' do not take into account the existence of high levels of talent that can be masked by dyslexia. Examination of the degree class results of students with dyslexia reveals that overall about 40% obtain 'good' degrees (i.e. first or upper second class honours), with indications that in universities where there is a good record of dyslexia support this proportion is somewhat higher. This, and other evidence regarding the success of graduates with dyslexia in various occupations, indicates that dyslexia is not an insurmountable barrier to academic or career success (see Section 1.1.5.1).

Consultation by the Working Party with representatives from HEIs and LEAs revealed a range of complex concerns about the increase in numbers of students with dyslexia in higher education, and the resultant impact which that was having on facilities for psychological assessment, DSA applications, learning support, examination provision and HEI finances (see Chapter 4). These may be briefly summarised as follows.

Widening access to higher education for students with dyslexia raised concerns about equal opportunities and academic standards. Obtaining official recognition of a student's dyslexia through a diagnostic assessment, sometimes following other screening procedures, is often found to be problematic. The subsequent identification of the special needs of students with dyslexia, and the provision of the support which they require, often creates resourcing problems. Students identified as having dyslexia, or considered as possibly having dyslexia, typically face more than academic stresses. Problems of equity arise in the organisation of examination and assessment arrangements. Finally, are the legitimate interests of students and potential employers compatible?

13.1.4 Support developed so far

Despite legitimate and continuing controversies concerning the nature, aetiology, identification, prognosis, incidence and alleviation of dyslexia, the condition is a legally recognised disability in the UK. In higher education, there is a consequential increased recognition of, and support for, dyslexic students by a variety of means, including the Disabled Students' Allowances (DSAs).

The Working Party's survey shows that a good beginning in the identification and support of students with dyslexia has been made in many institutions, but there are considerable variations among the systems that have been developed so far (see Chapter 3). At present, policies and provision for dyslexic students in higher education varies markedly between institutions. Fewer than half of all HEIs have trained specialist staff to provide the necessary support and counselling. Fewer than half of all HEIs provide students with dyslexia access to assistive technology that could substantially facilitate their studies. The majority of institutions reported that the operation of the DSA system for students with dyslexia was unsatisfactory in many respects. This is perceived to arise from inconsistencies in diagnostic assessment and because of lack of knowledge on the part of LEA Awards Officers about dyslexia and how students with this disability can be supported. The Working Party has sought to remedy both these deficiencies: firstly, by creating guidelines on diagnostic assessment, and secondly, by sending a copy of this report to all LEAs for use by Awards Officers.

13.1.5 Issues, problems and challenges

How adequately do HEIs address the challenges represented by a significant, and increasing, number of dyslexic students? What can be done to improve support for such students within HEIs? What guidelines are necessary in order to facilitate the development of effective and consistent provision across the sector?

In each of the following eight areas of concern regarding students with dyslexia, the Working Party has sought to discuss the key issues, problems and challenges that confront the sector:

- institutional and national policy (Chapter 5)
- staff development and institutional awareness (Chapter 6)
- admission to higher education (Chapter 7)
- identification of students with dyslexia (Chapter 8)
- evaluation of needs and provision of support (Chapter 9)
- counselling of students with dyslexia (Chapter 10)
- examinations and assessment (Chapter 11)

- careers advice for students with dyslexia (Chapter 12).

Consideration of these matters provides insights into the complexities, and often controversial nature, of the issues.

13.1.6 *Proposals for good practice and recommendations on policy*

For each of the eight areas of concern listed in the previous section, the Working Party gathered, collated and distilled the different components of good practice which have been developed in different institutions. In many instances, the Working Party also had to investigate professional practices and opinions in various specialised fields, including educational psychology, disability assessment, staff development and training, counselling and careers guidance. These proposals on good practice are intended as a resource to assist staff as they develop their support for dyslexic students. In relation to identification of students with dyslexia, it was necessary for the Working Party to carry out a rational evaluation of the different approaches that currently operate, in order to produce clear guidelines for good practice that are designed to assure quality and consistency in diagnosis. Finally, the Working Party has set out recommendations in each area, and these will have implications for policy making and implementation in all HEIs. In putting forward these recommendations the Working Party has, at all times, sought to balance the equal demands of equality of opportunity and the maintenance of academic standards.

13.1.7 *Priorities in support for students with dyslexia*

Institutions who are in the early stages of developing their systems for identification and support of students with dyslexia want to know where to begin, which are the most important matters to address and what are the most effective strategies to implement. Such knowledge is particularly useful to institutions that find they have resourcing problems and therefore, the Working Party has put forward the following priorities.

Immediate priorities are:

- establishing a policy on dyslexia for the whole institution

- developing a programme of staff awareness on dyslexia, especially for key staff such as admissions tutors, examination officers and invigilators, counsellors and careers advisers

- instigating special examination and assessment arrangements for students with dyslexia

- employing a support tutor and counsellor for students with dyslexia

- providing assistance to students with dyslexia when making DSA applications.

Second stage priorities are:

- covering the cost of diagnostic assessment for students with dyslexia

- providing technological support and training

- developing a regular programme of study skills tuition

- creating a screening programme for students who are suspected of having dyslexia

- considering how library facilities can be adapted or augmented in order to assist students with dyslexia

- creating guidelines for the marking of work of students with dyslexia.

Much of the support for dyslexic students is vital for their progress and is also good practice for all students. This perspective on support can sometimes help to dispel the resistance of over-worked tutors and non-academic staff.

13.1.8 Financial implications

An important consideration of this Working Party has been the financial implications of any recommendations on policy or proposals on good practice for students with dyslexia. Although all HEIs are under a duty to provide equal opportunities for all students with disabilities, including those with dyslexia, and are required to publish a Disability Statement detailing their policies and practices, the provisions required to assure equal opportunities inevitably have costs attached to them. The majority of HEIs have very tight budgets, with little excess income over already-committed expenditure to devote to support of disabled students. Senior managers will consequently be zealous in their search for the most cost-effective solutions, and the Working Party has been mindful of this. None of the recommendations or proposals made in this report have been put forward in a economically inexpedient manner. But thus far, no comment had been made about the *overall* costs that an HEI might expect to incur by making appropriate provision for its dyslexic students. In this section, we attempt to address this matter but it must be stressed that all calculations are purely illustrative and have been made solely with the intention of giving HEIs a very broad indication of likely costs.

As with most other aspects of higher education, the major costs will arise from skilled personnel. The core personnel will be the disability officer (or coordinator) and the dyslexia tutor (or adviser). These will usually require ancillary personnel, such as secretarial and, possibly, technical staff, the latter being necessary if the institution's disability provision includes a fair amount of specialist technology.

13.1.8.1   The costs of a Disability Officer

The post of disability officer, although central to the implementation of policies and procedures, is not one that arises solely (or even primarily) as result of provision to students with dyslexia. It is now widely recognised that every HEI should have a member of the administration who has overall as well as day-to-day responsibility for *all* students with disabilities. This post has been referred to in this report as the 'disability officer', but Skill (1997) used the term 'disability coordinator'. The principal duties of the disability officer will normally include:

- advising the institution on the implementation of the *Disability Discrimination Act 1995*

- preparing and keeping up-to-date the Disability Statement of the institution

- advising and implementing the institution's policy and procedures on disability

- liaising with all academic and academic support units throughout the institution in order to ensure implementation of the institution's policy and procedures on disability

- providing advice to students with disabilities, both within the institution and seeking admission to the institution, including advice and support in the application for DSAs where appropriate

- preparing and delivering staff development on disability matters

- managing any resources of the institution that are specifically for use by disabled students

- providing advice to examinations staff and examination boards regarding special arrangements in examinations for disabled students.

In addition, disability officers may also carry out evaluations of needs for disabled students prior to application for DSAs, and dyslexia screening, provide they are suitable qualified and experienced for these tasks. The duties listed above are described and discussed in the *Coordinator's Handbook* (Skill, 1997).

It can be seen that these duties require considerable knowledge and expertise in the area of disability generally. All HEIs have need of such a post, regardless of whether they wish to go further and adopt the policies and implement the procedures on dyslexia advocated in this report. A university of average size (15,000 students) can expect to have about 570 disabled students, of which each year about one-third will be new to the institution and so will probably require a greater amount of support.[58] It can be seen that addressing and monitoring the support needs of this body of students, as well as dealing with the administrative and liaison responsibilities of the post, will be a full-time job. Given the expertise required in such a post, appointment on university administrative or academic-related scales at least at Grade 2 (range about £17,000 to £25,000) will be called for. Depending on experience and qualifications, a somewhat higher appointment may be appropriate or necessary.

HESA data supplied to the Working Party on students graduating in 1997 indicated that about 22% of all disabled students have dyslexia (see Section 1.1.5.1). This would suggest that perhaps about a quarter of the disability officer's time would be devoted to this category of student. However, 52% of all disabled students fall into the category known as 'unseen disabilities' (e.g. diabetes, epilepsy, asthma). Students in this category typically demand less of the professional time of a disability officer because, by this stage in education, the majority of persons with these disabilities have usually acquired reasonably efficient ways of managing their disability and, in general, their disability will not have such a great impact on their studies as other disabilities would. If, simply for the sake of argument, this category was removed from the calculations then students with dyslexia would amount to about 45% of all disabled students. This indicates that dealing with dyslexic students is likely to take up a larger proportion of the time of a disability officer than their incidence would at first suggest.

Furthermore, the national survey carried out by the Working Party found that 43% of students with dyslexia in higher education are diagnosed *after* admission (see Section 3.2.3). Initially, at least. such students are likely to have somewhat greater needs for advice and support than are students whose dyslexia was recognised prior to entry to university, because they have to come to terms with their newly-discovered disability. In particular, they are likely to have greater counselling needs (see Chapter 10).

Taking into account all the factors considered above, it may therefore be reasonably estimated that about 40–50% of the overall time of a disability officer will be employed in addressing, in one way or another, the needs of students with dyslexia. Basing calculations on the mid-point of the salary scale quoted above, and allowing for on-costs of 25% for national insurance and pension, it may therefore be reasonably estimated that the cost to the average HEI in respect of the disability officer's time devoted to students with dyslexia will be in the region of £10,000 – £13,000 per annum.

13.1.8.2   The costs of a Dyslexia Tutor

The recommendations of the Working Party also call for the employment of a tutor or adviser specifically to support students with dyslexia by giving instruction on study skills and assistance with studying generally (see Section 5.3, Recommendation 4, and Section 9.3, Recommendation 4a). The duties of such a post may also include dyslexia screening, liaison with academic staff, delivering staff development on dyslexia, administration and involvement in policy-making. A suitably qualified and experienced dyslexia tutor might also carry out diagnostic assessments (see Section 8.3.1).

Given that the overall incidence of dyslexia in higher education has been estimated at between 1.2% and 1.5% (see Section 3.2.3), an average university, with about 15,000 students, will have about 180–225 students with dyslexia. Elementary arithmetic indicates that one dyslexia tutor in such an establishment would have, on average, 11 minutes or thereabouts to spend with each dyslexic student each week. In practice, not all students with dyslexia require weekly support and in some cases it is possible to give tuition in study skills on a group basis.[59] However, significant numbers of students

---

[58]   This is based on the estimate of 3.8% disabled students in higher education However, figures on the overall incidence of disablity in higher education are obscured by inadequate record-keeping in many HEIs, variation in definitions of disability and by the large number of students for whom disability status is unknown. Dearing (1997) estimates that the overall rate is about 3.8% (based on HESA figures for first year students in 1996). This figure is consistent with HESA data supplied to the Working Party on students graduating in 1997, which gave an overall incidence of 3.7% (see Section 1.1.5.1).

[59]   At Oxford Brookes University, there is a taught module on English and Study Skills specifically for students with dyslexia, with about 12–15 students per year enrolled.

with dyslexia do require individual support, even if this is given less often than once per week. The minimum duration for individual support is 30 minutes, and sessions of one hour are the norm. It can therefore be seen that, at the very least, an average HEI will require the services of a full-time dyslexia tutor during the teaching period.

The expertise required in such a post is comparable to that of a disability officer, and thus, appointment on an equivalent university scale and grade would be appropriate (i.e. administrative or academic-related scales at least at Grade 2; range about £17,000 to £25,000). Depending on experience and qualifications, a somewhat higher appointment may be appropriate or necessary. If the contract of appointment refers only to the teaching period (30 weeks per year), the overall cost will be in the region of £16,000, based on the mid-point of the range specified and allowing for 25% on-costs to cover national insurance and pension.

At the present time, many HEIs employ dyslexia tutors on an hourly or daily rate, funded directly by DSAs, so the institution does not have to bear any of the personnel costs (although other costs, such as provision of facilities, may be incurred by the institution). This approach is not altogether satisfactory, for while it may provide assistance to many dyslexic students who are in receipt of DSAs, large numbers of other dyslexic students who need this type of support will be left out, including those who are not eligible for DSA (e.g. part time, foreign or postgraduate students), or who have obtained a DSA, but have been unsuccessful in securing financial provision for study skills support under the Non-Medical Helper's Allowance component of the DSA (see Sections 9.1.2.2 and 9.2.4.1).

13.1.8.3   *Other likely expenditure and recoverable costs*

To administer a service for students with dyslexia involving about 50% of the disability officer's time, plus a full-time dyslexia tutor during the teaching period, will require the services of secretary or clerical assistant on at least 50% time. Assuming that such a post will be on at least Grade 3 of the university clerical scales (starting salary about £11,000), and allowing for 25% on-costs to cover national insurance and pension, the cost to the institution of this post will be in the region of £7,000.

Estimating other costs, such as office accommodation and ancillary costs, is more difficult, but a reasonable estimate can be obtained by using the current overheads rate for university contracts (46% on staff costs). Since the personnel costs described in this section total about £34,500, the overhead would be a further £16,000 or thereabouts, making £50,500 in total.

The cost of dyslexia screening (see Section 8.2.6) may be covered within the salaries of the disability officer and/or the dyslexia tutor. The cost of diagnostic assessments (see Section 8.3.4.6) may also be covered within the salary of the dyslexia tutor if that person has appropriate qualifications and experience (see Section 8.3.1). However, assuming for the moment that dyslexia screening and diagnostic assessments represent *additional* costs to the institution, these may be estimated at about £2,000 for screening (see Section 8.2.6) and £9,000 for diagnostic assessments, the latter figure being based on an estimate of 60 diagnostic assessments per year (see Section 8.1.1) at an average cost of £150 each (see Section 8.1.7). These items add a further £11,000 to overall costs. To this must be added costs of equipment (such as computers) and recurrent costs (such as stationery and test materials). Assuming that such costs do not exceed £5,000 per annum, we arrive a round figure of approximately £66,500 per year to fund a basic service for students with dyslexia in a university of average size. This amount would cover 50% of a disability officer's time, a full-time dyslexia tutor, half-time secretary or clerical assistant, overheads and recurrent costs, and provision for dyslexia screening and diagnostic assessments. The cost per each student provided for will be about £330 per annum.

A proportion of these costs (possibly half or even more) may be recoverable by the institution, depending on the expertise of the staff and the efficiency of the organisation. If the disability officer or dyslexia tutor carries out evaluations of needs and prepares reports for DSA purposes, then the cost of these (usually about £300 each) can be claimed against the DSA. In an average-sized university, roughly 50–60 reports on support needs for students with dyslexia would be expected each year, which could yield an annual income of over £15,000. In addition, a fair proportion of dyslexic students would be expected to secure Non-Medical Helper's Allowances to cover study skills tuition.

If study skills tuition was given one hour per week (30 hours per year) at a flat rate of only £25 per hour (which is a very modest estimate: some private dyslexia tutors will charge more than this), this would generate income of £750 per annum per student. If more than about 30 students were receiving tuition on this basis, additional dyslexia tutors would be needed to teach them. However, in principle, income from the Non-Medical Helper's Allowance component of the DSA should cover the salary of at least one dyslexia tutor, provided that the system is efficiently managed. Further cost savings can be made by negotiating discounted fees for diagnostic assessments on the basis of group rates or block-booked arrangements, and some institutions ask students to pay a proportion of the cost of dyslexia screening and/or diagnostic assessment.

The figures quoted in this section are indications of likely expenditure and income based on reasonable estimates derived in some cases from data and calculations referred to elsewhere in this report. They should serve as a useful starting point for discussion within any institution that is considering establishing or improving provisions for students with dyslexia. *However, the figures given here are not recommendations, nor must they be relied upon.*

The costs of establishing and maintaining a satisfactory service for students with dyslexia that is consistent with the recommendations made in this report are not inconsiderable. However, efficient management should enable a fair proportion of those costs to be recovered. Above all, this expenditure should be seen as an integral and essential part of the institution's general commitment to securing equal opportunities for all disabled students and honouring its implied responsibilities under the *Disability Discrimination Act 1995.*

13.2   The future

13.2.1 Research and development requirements

Although a great deal has been achieved in the last decade, there are significant areas that still need research and development. Much of the research that has been carried out up to now has focused on the literacy problems of children. More work now needs to be done on how dyslexia affects the lives of adults, on how their coping strategies alter their problems and needs. Identification procedures need to be upgraded to cover the complexities of dyslexia in adults. In order to achieve compatibility of standards, in identification, in training of support personnel and in support systems, there needs to be an organisation that takes responsibility for good practice and that has power to enforce good standards. Dyslexic adults are in a better position than many children to share their experiences with each other and with the supporting professionals. The information they can contribute will enhance the understanding of dyslexia by the population at large. As is the case in many areas of disability, the lack of understanding by others can be a major contribution to the problems of dyslexic people.

The principal research and development needs may be summarised as follows.

- Improved identification procedures that are appropriate for adults with compensated dyslexia.

- Development and validation of new psychometric tests and other assessment techniques that are appropriate for use at higher education level.

- Improved training for dyslexia support staff and for counsellors, including accredited diploma courses.

- Creation of training programmes for suitably qualified and experienced non-psychologists in the assessment of students with dyslexia in higher education.

- Promotion of a better general understanding of dyslexia amongst staff and students in higher education, and amongst the population generally.

- Establishment of an umbrella body to monitor provision and accredit training.

13.2.2 Reforming policy and provision for all students with disabilities in higher education

Higher education in the UK is currently undergoing a period of transition and is the subject of intense public and government scrutiny. League tables of universities are emerging and the relative importance of research excellence and teaching quality are widely debated. Finances are becoming tighter and institutions are finding that they have to fund an increasing proportion of their activities by commercial means. The recommendations of the Report of the National Committee of Inquiry into Higher Education (Dearing, 1997), the subsequent government reactions to that report (e.g. DfEE, 1998), and various legislative proposals in relation to access and support of talented students with disabilities aspiring to enter higher education, are all under public discussion. The time is therefore opportune to consider reforms of policy and practice regarding disabled students in higher education.

The remit of the Working Party was specifically to address policy and provision for students with dyslexia in higher education, not to consider the mechanisms for funding and support of all disabilities. But dyslexia cannot be viewed in a vacuum. We have inevitably had to take into account the arrangements for students with *other disabilities* in higher education, as well as the various practices concerning the identification and support of individuals with special needs in *other stages* of education. In so doing we have come to the conclusion that there is a strong case for considering a more coherent and explicit national policy to support all talented disabled students in higher education, including those who are dyslexic. Can this be done with HEIs that are self-governing organisations? These issues have been discussed in some detail by Pumfrey (1998), who concludes that such a development is possible, dependent on the priority accorded by government, the redeployment of existing resources and the cultural, social and economic costs and benefits involved.

Insofar as provision within higher education is concerned, there are many similarities between dyslexia and other disabilities, e.g. evaluation of needs, application for DSA, particular technology support, and special examination arrangements. But there are also a few important differences that should be acknowledged. With other disabilities (unlike dyslexia) the diagnosis is rarely contentious and the recommendations on the DSA application not often disputed. Few disabilities other than dyslexia have associated with them a need for a specific teaching input (i.e. study skills tuition). Consequently, even though this teaching input provides significant enhancement of learning capacity, the legitimacy of its inclusion within DSA claims is often contended. It is to be hoped that the publication of this report will do much to resolve such disputes. If the Working Party's recommendations on guidelines for identification of students with dyslexia are widely adopted, this should go a considerable way towards dispelling the anxieties of LEA Awards Officers and others with responsibility for public funds in this area.

Nevertheless, it should be stressed that this report does not seek to establish dyslexia as a special case over and above any other disability. The Working Party recognises that any changes to policy for students with dyslexia that are to have widespread and long-term effects must be firmly embedded within general policy for all disabilities, both in individual institutions and within the whole higher education sector. The Working Party's recommendations on institutional and national policy set down in Section 5.3 reflect that concern. Disability Statements published by HEIs should clearly evidence their assurances on promoting equal opportunities and their commitment to making provisions that are appropriate to all disabilities.

Insofar as support for disabilities and special needs in other stages of education are concerned, there are practices which the higher education sector could find instructive. In further education, disability support is primarily the responsibility of the institution. Following the removal of further education colleges from the local government system, the field of current provision for students with learning difficulties and/or disabilities in further education has been comprehensively addressed in the Tomlinson Report (FEFC, 1996). Its emphasis on the importance of 'Inclusive Learning' is based on explicit principles, many of which can be seen to apply to all students at all stages of education. However, considerable caution should be exercised before applying the further education model in its entirety to higher education and abandoning direct funding to the talented dyslexic student via the DSA system. Many support tutors within further education are envious of the level of provision that is made possible by the DSA in higher education. The relative merits of the two support systems that operate in further education and higher education have never been adequately explored despite their co-existence for several years.

Many of the greatest detractors of the DSA system are to be found outside HEIs. For example, LEA Awards Officers take for granted that it is likely to be more cost-effective for HEIs to supply the technology on a shared basis rather than provide the technology on an individual basis, funded by the DSA. However, it has been asserted that if this were to be done technology-based solutions for dyslexic students would be less responsive to individual needs than at present. The question as to whether such equipment would be as available for home use, where many disabled students are able to work most effectively, has also been raised. The contention that the technology will be of value for longer periods and serve the needs of a greater number of disabled students if it remains the property of the institution, is suspect. For example, most three-year-old computers are worth relatively little because of the rapidity of developments in computer technology. Arguably, they would continue to be used for somewhat longer if owned by the disabled student.

In the earliest years of a child's life and during the primary and secondary stages of education there is an existing model for special educational needs and disabilities that might have application within higher education.[60] This model is set down in the *Code of Practice on the Identification and Assessment of Special Educational Needs* (DfE, 1994). Dyslexia is included as an example of specific learning difficulties. Within the school system, five stages of special educational needs provision were established. The first three of these are school-based. Formula funding to cover these three stages was devolved to mainstream schools. For individuals whose special educational needs were persistent or severe, a further stage of assessment, which is the responsibility of the LEA (Stage 4), could lead to the issuing, or otherwise, of a formal Statement of Special Educational Need (Stage 5).[61] At Stage 5, the responsibility for funding additional support lies with the LEA.

The first three stages of this five-stage model opened up mainstream school-based special education provision to any child with special educational needs. The move was intended to encourage early and effective intervention, thereby reducing pressures to provide formal Statements (which is a complex, time-consuming and costly process) and the resources that, in law, followed the issuing of a Statement. Although this system has its weaknesses, arguably it has improved the manner and effectiveness with which special educational needs have been addressed in schools. Its major strength is that provision is possible for pupils other than those whose special educational needs are shown to be sufficiently severe and long-standing to require a formal Statement.

In higher education, the DSA represents the formal entitlement of a student to additional resources that are not the direct financial responsibility of the institution, and so may be regarded as roughly equivalent to a Statement of Special Educational Needs within the primary and secondary sectors (Stage 5 of the *Code of Practice*). The diagnostic assessment of dyslexia in higher education loosely corresponds to Stage 4 (except that at present the cost of diagnostic assessment is borne by the student or the institution rather than an external source). The similarities between the two systems are sufficient to give encouragement to the notion of extending the *Code of Practice* model to higher education. Stages of identification and support of students with dyslexia (and, indeed, other disabilities or special needs) corresponding to Stages 1, 2 and 3 could be created within higher education, which would be the responsibility of HEIs to finance and administer, along the same lines as currently operate within further education. For example, students with minor hearing loss, slight visual impairment or borderline dyslexia may not qualify for a DSA. But they still have special needs that should be recognised and addressed within their institution. With appropriate organisation, support for students with these disabilities can be made and this will not necessarily cost a great deal, e.g. enlarged photocopies of OHP transparencies used in lectures or seminars, tape-recording of lectures and tutorials, or tolerance of spelling errors.

---

[60] Special educational needs are defined in the Education Act, 1996, Part IV, Chapter 1, Section 312, in terms of 'significantly greater difficulty in learning than the majority of children of the same age' and/or having 'a disability which either prevents or hinders the child' from making use of the educational facilities of the school.

[61] In Scotland, the Statement of Special Educational Needs is called the 'Record of Needs'.

In several HEIs, nascent systems of this type are already in place, including disability tutors in departments, schools and faculties, whose brief it is to be aware of the needs of students with disabilities and to advise colleagues on how best these students can be supported. Many HEIs have already made considerable provision out of their own budgets for disabled students, of whom a considerable proportion are not eligible for DSAs. Such provision includes establishing centres where advice and support can be accessed and assistive technology is available for use by disabled students. However, to finance such a scheme on a national basis, some of the disability funding that currently goes into the DSA system would need to be diverted to HEIs directly, via the Higher Education Funding Councils. Monies allocated for disability support in institutions would need to be ring-fenced and their application monitored.

In conclusion, a combination of procedures modelled on the *Code of Practice,* together with institutional funding mechanisms similar to those applied in further education, and reform of the DSA system, offers possibilities for positive and cost-effective progress in support for all students with disabilities in higher education. More coherent, explicit policies and practices based on common principles that are seen to be fair, across the whole system of education, could be developed.

13.3 Postscript

Both economically and culturally, widening access to higher education matters. Equal opportunities and anti-discrimination legislation encourage the entry of talented but disabled students into higher education. When a disability such as dyslexia prevents the recognition of talent by educational organisations, the nation and the individual lose.

The recommendations and proposals in this report are designed to encourage HEIs to address with confidence the issues that confront them concerning dyslexia. The proposals on good practice put forward by the Working Party offer bases for development of equitable, efficient and cost-effective systems for the identification support of students with dyslexia, which do not compromise academic standards.

Gradually, as more dyslexic students in higher education are given appropriate support, academic tutors and the general public will come to recognise the intelligence, talents and abilities of these students rather than noticing the masking effects of dyslexia. Support for dyslexic students will be accepted as providing equal opportunities for students with genuine needs. It will be realised that many of the changes of practice in teaching and learning that are vital for dyslexic students can also be beneficial for other students. It will also be increasingly appreciated that the country as a whole can benefit substantially from the alternative intellectual strengths possessed by people with dyslexia.

In higher education, or at any stage of education, not to recognise talents that are obscured by dyslexia or any other disability is an unnecessary and socially unjustifiable waste of human resources.

14 Appendices

14.1 References

Aaron, P.G. , Phillips, S. and Larsen, S. (1988) Specific learning disablity in historically famous persons. *Journal of Learning Disabilities,* 21, 523-545.

American Psychiatric Association (1994) *Diagnostic and Statistical Manual for Mental Disorders* (4th Edition) [DSM–IV] Washington, DC: American Psychiatric Association.

Ashton, (1996) In defence of discrepancy definitions of specific learning difficulties. *Educational Psychology in Practice,* 12, 131-140.

Ayres, A.J. (1985) *Developmental Dyspraxia and Adult Onset Dyspraxia.* Torrance, CA: Sensory Integration International.

Beaton, A., McDougall, S., and Singleton, C.H. (Eds.) (1997a) *Dyslexia in literate adults.* (Special issue of the *Journal of Research in Reading,* 20, 1). Oxford: Blackwell.

Beaton, A., McDougall, S. and Singleton, C. H. (1997b) Humpty Dumpty grows up? Diagnosing dyslexia in adulthood. *Journal of Research in Reading,* 20, 1-12.

Beech, J.R. (1997) Assessment of memory and reading. In J. Beech and C.H. Singleton (Eds.) *The Psychological Assessment of Reading.* London: Routledge, pp. 143-159.

Beech, J.R. and Singleton, C.H. (Eds.) (1997a) *The Assessment of Reading.* London: Routledge

Beech, J. and Singleton, C. H. (1997b) The psychological assessment of reading: theoretical issues and professional solutions. In J. Beech and C.H. Singleton (Eds.) *The Psychological Assessment of Reading.* London: Routledge, pp. 1-26.

British Dyslexia Association (1995) *The Dyslexia Handbook.* Reading, Berks: BDA.

British Psychological Society (1998) *Dyslexia, Literacy and Psychological Assessment.* Draft Report of the Working Party of the Division of Educational and Child Psychology. Leicester: British Psychological Society.

Brown G.D.A. and Ellis, N.C. (Eds.) (1994) *Handbook of Spelling.* Chichester: Wiley.

Closs, A., Lannen, S. and Reid, G. (1996) Dyslexia in Further and Higher Education: a franmework for practice. In G. Reid (Ed.) *Dimensions of Dyslexia.* Vol. 1. Edinburgh: Moray House, pp. 447-467.

Cornelissen, P., Bradley, L., Fowler, S. and Stein, J. (1991) What children see affects how they read. *Developmental Medicine and Child Neurology,* 33, 755-762.

Cornelissen, P., Bradley, L., Fowler, S. and Stein, J. (1992) Covering one eye affects how some children read. *Developmental Medicine and Child Neurology,* 34, 296-304.

Cornelissen, P., Bradley, L., Fowler, S. and Stein, J. (1994) What children see affects how they spell. *Developmental Medicine and Child Neurology,* 36, 716-727.

Cornelissen, P., Munro, N., Fowler, S. and Stein, J. (1993) The stability of binocular fixation during reading in adults and children. *Developmental Medicine and Child Neurology,* 35, 777-787.

Crombie, M. and Reid, G. (1994) 5–14 Programme and specific learning difficulties. In E. Jordan (ed.) *A Curriculum for all? 5–14 and Special Educational Needs.* Edinburgh: Moray House Publications.

Dearing, R. (Chair) (1997) *Higher Education in the Learning Society.* Report of the Committee of Inquiry into Higher Education. London: Department for Education and Employment.

De Fries, J.C., Alarcón, M. (1996) Genetics of specific reading disability. *Mental Retardation and Developmental Disabilities Research Reviews*, 2, 39-47.

De Fries, J.C., Alarcón, M. and Olson, R.K. (1997) Genetic aetiologioes of reading and spelling deficits: developmental differences. In C. Hulme and M. Snowling (Eds.) *Dyslexia: Biology, Cognition and Intervention*. London: Whurr, pp. 20-37.

DfE (1994) *Code of Practice for the Identification and Assessment of Special Educational Needs*. London: Department for Education.

DfEE (1998) *The Learning Age and Higher Education in the 21st Century: Response the Dearing Report*. London: Department for Education and Employment

Edwards, J. (1994) *The Scars of Dyslexia*. London: Cassell.

Elliott, C. D. (1990) *Differential Ability Scales*. New York: Psychological Corporation.

Elliott, C.D., Murray, D.J. and Pearson, L.S. (1979) *British Ability Scales*. Winsdor, Berks: NFER–NELSON.

Elliott, C. D., Smith, P. and McCulloch, K. (1996) *British Ability Scales II*. Windsor, Berks: NFER–NELSON.

Ellis, A.W., McDougall, S.J.P. and Monk, A.F. (1996) Are dyslexics different? *Dyslexia*, 2, 31-58 and 59-68.

Evans, B.J.W. (1997) Assessment of visual problems in reading. In J. Beech and C.H. Singleton (Eds.) *The Psychological Assessment of Reading*. London: Routledge, pp. 102-123.

Evans, B.J.W. and Drasdo, N. (1990) Review of ophthalmic factors in dyslexia. *Ophthalmic and Physiological Optics*, 10, 123-132.

Evans, B.J.W., Drasdo, N. and Richards, I.L. (1996) Dyslexia: the link with visual deficits. *Ophthalmic and Physiological Optics*, 16, 3-10.

FEFC (1996) *Inclusive Learning: Report of the Learning Difficulties and/or Disabilities Committee* (The Tomlinson Report). Coventry: Further Education Funding Council.

Fisher, A.G., Murray, E.A. and Bundy, A.C. (1991) *Sensory Integration, Theory and Praxis*. Philadephia: F.A.Davis.

Fleming, K.I. and Singleton, C.H. (1997) *Dyslexia Sub-types and Birth Difficulties*. Paper presented at the Fourth International Conference of the British Dyslexia Association, University of York, April 1997.

Frederickson, N. and Reason, R. (1995) Discrepancy definitions of specific learning difficulties. *Educational Psychology in Practice,* 10, 195-205.

Friel, J. (1997) *Children with Special Needs: Assessment, Law and Practice*. (4th edition) London: Jessica Kingsley.

Frith, U. (1997) Brain, mind and behaviour in dyslexia. In C. Hulme and M. Snowling (Eds.) *Dyslexia: Biology, Cognition and Intervention*. London: Whurr, pp. 1-19.

Frith, C. and Frith, U. (1996) A biological marker for dyslexia. *Nature*, 382, 19-20.

Galaburda, A.M. (Ed.) (1993) Dyslexia and Development: Neurobiological Aspects of Extra-ordinary Brains. Cambridge, MA: Harvard University Press.

Gardner, H (1983) *Frames of Mind: the theory of multiple intelligences*. New York: Basic Books.

Gilroy, D. E. (1993) *Dyslexia and Higher Education*. Bangor: Dyslexia Unit, University of Bangor.

Gilroy, D. E. and Miles, T. R. (1996) *Dyslexia at college*. (2nd edition). London: Routledge.

Goodwin, V. (1996) Counselling dyslexic students in higher education. In C. Stephens (Ed.) *Dyslexic Students in Higher Education*. Huddersfield: University of Huddersfield with Skill (National Bureau for Students with Disabilities), pp. 55-56.

Goodwin, V. (1998) Person-centred conselling for the dyslexic student. In J. Waterfield (Ed.) *Dyslexia in Higher Education: Learning along the continuum.* (Proceedings of the 2nd International Conference on Dyslexia in Higher Education) Plymouth: University of Plymouth, pp. 28-29.

Goodwin, V. and Thomson, B. (1991) *Adult student and dyslexia: a resource book for adult students and staff.* Milton Keynes: The Open University.

Hales, G. (Ed.) (1994) *Dyslexia Matters.* London: Whurr.

Hanley, J.R. (1997) Reading and spelling impairments in undergraduate students with developmental dyslexia. *Journal of Research in Reading,* 20, 22-30.

Harley, T.A. (1995) *The Psychology of Language: From Data to Theory.* Hove: Erlbaum.

Hedderley, R (1996) Assessing pupils with specific learning difficulties for examination special arrangements at GCSE, 'A' level and degree level. *Educational Psychology in Practice,* 12, 36-44.

HEFCE (1995) *Access to Higher Education: Students with Special Needs.* (HEFCE Report on the 1993–94 Special Initiative to Encourage Widening Participation for Students with Special Needs.) Bristol: Higher Education Funding Council for England.

HEFCE (1996a) *Access to Higher Education: Students with Learning Difficulties and Disabilities.* (Report of the 1993–94 and 1994–95 HEFCE Special Initiatives to Encourage Widening Participation for Students with Disabilities.) Bristol: Higher Education Funding Council for England.

HEFCE (1996b) *Special Initiative to Encourage High Quality Provision for Students with Learning Difficulties and Disabilities.* Circular 9/96. Bristol: Higher Education Funding Council for England.

HEFCE (1996c) *Special Initiative to Encourage High Quality Provision for Students with Learning Difficulties and Disabilities(SLDD): Funded Projects.* Circular 23/96. Bristol: Higher Education Funding Council for England.

HEFCE (1998) *Disability Statements: A guide to good practice.* Bristol: Higher Education Funding Council for England.

HESA (1997) *Students in Higher Education Institutions: HESA Data Report 1996/97.* Cheltenham: Higher Education Statistics Agency.

HESA (1998) *Analysis of Degree Classes of Students with Disabilities in Higher Education Institutions, 1996/97.* [Special data report prepared by HESA for the National Working Party on Dyslexia in Higher Education.] Cheltenham: Higher Education Statistics Agency.

HEQC (1996) *What are graduates? Clarifying the attributes ofr gradutaeness – A paper to stimulate discussion.* London: Higher Education Quality Council.

Horne, J.K and Singleton, C.H. (1997) *Assessment of dyslexia in higher education.* Paper presented at the Fourth International Conference of the British Dyslexia Association, University of York, April 1997.

Hulme, C. and Snowling, M. (Eds.) (1997) *Dyslexia: Biology, Cognition and Intervention.* London: Whurr.

Hynd, G. W. and Hiemenz, J.R. (1997) Dyslexia and gyral morphology variation. In C. Hulme and M. Snowling (Eds.) *Dyslexia: Biology, Cognition and Intervention.* London: Whurr, pp. 38-58..

Irlen, H. (1991) *Reading by the Colors: Overcoming dyslexia and other reading disabilities through the Irlen method.* New York: Avebury Publishing.

Joint Forum for GCSE and GCE (1997) *Candidates with Special Assessment Needs: Special Arrangements and Special Considerations (Regulations and Guidance for 1998).* Cambridge: Joint Forum for GCSE and GCE.

Kaufman, C. (with C.H Singleton and J. Hutchins) (1998) *IT for dyslexic adults*. Reading: British Dyslexia Association.

Kaufman, C. and Singleton, C.H. (1998) *Study skills with ICT*. Reading: British Dyslexia Association.

Kingslake, B. (1982). The predictive (In) Accuracy of On-entry to school screening procedures when used to anticipate learning difficulties. *Special Education,* 10, 23-26.

Klein, C. (1993) *Diagnosing Dyslexia: A guide to the assessment of adults with specific learning difficulties*. London: Basic Skills Agency.

Krupska, M. and Klein, C. (1995) *Demystifying Dyslexia*. London: London Language and Literacy Unit.

Lovegrove, W. (1994) Visual deficits in dyslexia: Evidence and implications. In A. Fawcett and R.I. Nicolson (Eds.) *Dyslexia in Children: Multidisciplinary perspectives*. New York: Harvester Wheatsheaf, pp. 113-136.

McLean, B. (1997) *The Dyslexia Test*. Farnham, Surrey: Helen Arkell Dyslexia Centre.

McLoughlin, D., Fitzgibbon, G. and Young, V. (1994) *Adult dyslexia: assessment, counselling and training*. London: Whurr.

McLoughlin, D. (1997) Assessment of adult reading skills. In J. Beech and C.H. Singleton (Eds.) *The Psychological Assessment of Reading*. London: Routledge, pp. 224-237.

McGuire, J.M., Madaus, J.W., Litt, V. and Ramirez, M.O. (1996) An investigation of documentation submitted by university students to verify their learning disabilities. *Journal of Learning Disabilities,* 29, 297-304.

McNab, I. (1994) *Specific Learning Difficulties: How severe is severe?* Assessment Briefing Paper. Windsor, Berks: NFER–NELSON.

Matty, J. (1995) *Dyslexia: signposts to success. a guide for dyslexic adults*. Reading, Berks: British Dyslexia Association.

Miles, T. (1982, 1997) *The Bangor Dyslexia Test*. Wisbech, Cambs.: LDA.

Miles, T. (1993) *Dyslexia: the pattern of difficulties* (2nd edition). London: Whurr.

Miles, T. and Miles, E. (Eds.) (1992) *Dyslexia and Mathematics*. London: Routledge.

Miles, T. and Varma, V. (Eds.) (1995) *Dyslexia and Stress*. London: Whurr.

Mitchell, D.C. (1987) Reading and syntactic analysis. In J.R.Beech and A.M.Colley (Eds.) *Cognitive Approaches to Reading*. Chichester: Wiley, pp. 87-112.

Mitchell, D.C. (1994) Sentence parsing. In M.A. Gernsbacher (Ed.) *Handbook of Psycholinguistic Research*. SanDiego: Academic Press, pp. 375-410.

Morgan, E. and Rooney, M. (1997) Can dyslexic students be trained as teachers? *Support for Learning,* 12, 28-31.

Moseley, D.V. (1997) Assessment of spelling and related aspects of written expression. In J. Beech and C.H. Singleton (Eds.) *The Psychological Assessment of Reading*. London: Routledge, pp. 204-223.

Neale, M.D. (1966, 1989). *Neale Analysis of Reading Ability*. Windsor, Berks: NFER-NELSON.

Nicolson, R.I (1996) Developmental dyslexia: part, present and future. *Dyslexia,* 2, 190-207.

Nicolson, R.I. and Fawcett, A.J. (1990) Automaticity: a new framework for dyslexia research. *Cognition,* 30, 159-182.

Nicolson, R.I., and Fawcett, A.J. (1994) Comparison of deficits in cognitive and motor skills in children with dyslexia. *Annals of Dyslexia,* 44, 147-164.

Nicolson, R.I. and Fawcett, A.J. (1995) Dyslexia is more than a phonological disability. *Dyslexia,* 1, 19-36.

Nicolson, R.I. and Fawcett, A.J. (1997) Development of objective procedures for screening of dyslexic students in higher education. *Journal of Research in Reading,* 20, 77-83.

Nicolson, R.I., Fawcett, A.J. and Miles, T.R., (1992). *Adult Dyslexia Screening Feasibility Study.* (Report to the Employment Department) Sheffield: University of Sheffield.

Nisbet, P and Poon, P. (1998) *Special Access Technology.* Edinburgh: CALL Centre, University of Edinburgh.

Norris, D. (1987) Syntax, semantics, and garden paths. In A. W. Ellis (Ed.) *Progress in the Psychology of Language,* Vol. 3. Hove: Erlbaum, pp. 233-252.

Orton Dyslexia Society (1994) A new definition of dyslexia. *Bulletin of the Orton Dyslexia Society* (now the International Dyslexia Association), Fall, 1994.

Orton Dyslexia Society Research Committee (1994) Cited in G. Reid Lyon: Towards a definition of dyslexia. *Annals of Dyslexia,* 45, 1995, 3-27.

Potton, A., (1983). *Screening.* London: Macmillan.

Pumfrey, P.D. (1985) *Reading: Tests and Assessment Techniques* (2nd Edition). London: Hodder and Stoughton.

Pumfrey, P.D. (1996) Challenges and responses. In C. Stephens, (Ed) *Dyslexic Students in Higher Education.* Skill and University of Huddersfield, 1996, pp. 5-9.

Pumfrey, P.D. (1998) Reforming policy and provision for dyslexic students in higher education: Towards and national code of practice. *Support for Learning,* **13**, 87-90.

Pumfrey, P.D. and Reason, R. (Eds.) (1991) *Specific learning difficulties (Dyslexia): challenges and responses.* London: Routledge.

Rack, J. (1997) Issues in the assessment of developmental dyslexia in adults: theoretical and applied perspectives. *Journal of Research in Reading,* 20, 1997, 66-76.

Raven, J. C. (1958) *Standard Progressive Matrices.* London: H.K.Lewis.

Rayner, K. and Pollatsek, A.(1989) *The Psychology of Reading.* Hillsdale, NJ: Erlbuam.

Reid, G. (1998) *Dyslexia: a practitioner's handbook* (2nd Edition). Chichester: Wiley.

Reid, G. and Hinton, J.W. (1996) Supporting the system: dyslexia and teacher stress. In G. Reid (Ed.) *Dimensions of Dyslexia,* Vol 2. Edinburgh: Moray House Publications, pp. 393-402.

Riddick, B., Farmer, M. and Sterling, C. (1997) *Students and Dyslexia: Growing up with a specific learning difficulty.* London: Whurr.

Ripley, K. Daines, B., and Barrett, J. (1997) *Dyspraxia: A guide for teachers and parents.* London: David Fulton.

Sawyer, C.E., Francis, M.E. and Knight, E. (1992) Handwriting speed, specific learning difficulties and the GCSE. *Educational Psychology in Practice,* 8, 77-81.

Sawyer, C.E., Gray, F. and Champness, M. (1996) Measuring the speed of handwriting for GCSE candidates. *Educational Psychology in Practice,* 12, 19-23.

Siegel, L.S. (1989a) IQ is irrelevant to the definition of Learning Disabilities. *Journal of Learning Disabilities,* 22, 469-478.

Siegel, L.S. (1989b) Why we do not need intelligence test scores the definition and analyses of Learning Disabilities. *Journal of Learning Disabilities,* 22, 514-518.

Siegel, L.S. (1992) An evaluation of the discrepancy definition of dyslexia. *Journal of Learning Disabilities,* 25, 617-688.

Simpson, G.B. (1994) Context and the processing of ambiguous words. In M.A. Gernsbacher (Ed.) *Handbook of Psycholinguistic Research.* SanDiego: Academic Press, pp.359-374.

Singleton, C.H. (1988) The early diagnosis of developmental dyslexia. *Support for Learning*, 3, 108-121.

Singleton, C.H. (1995). Issues in the diagnosis and assessment of dyslexia in Higher Education. In J.Waterfield (Ed.) *Dyslexia in higher education: Learning along the continuum. Proceedings of the First International Conference on Dyslexia in Higher Education, 1994.* Plymouth: University of Plymouth, pp. 11-18.

Singleton, C.H. (1996) Dyslexia in Higher Education – Issues for policy and practice. In C. Stephens, (Ed) *Dyslexic Students in Higher Education.* Skill and University of Huddersfield, 1996, pp. 10-16.

Singleton, C. H. (1997a) Screening early literacy. In J. Beech and C.H. Singleton (Eds.) *The Psychological Assessment of Reading.* London: Routledge, pp. 67-101.

Singleton, C. H. (1997b) Computerised assessment of reading. In J. Beech and C.H. Singleton (Eds.) *The Psychological Assessment of Reading.* London: Routledge, pp. 257-278.

Singleton, C.H., Trotter, J.M. and Smart, E. (1998) *Pre-assessment Screening for Dyslexia In Higher Education.* Interim report on a project funded by the Higher Education Funding Council for England. Hull: University of Hull.

Singleton, C.H. (1998a) Higher Education – what's going on? *Dyslexia Contact*, 17(1), 36-7.

Singleton, C.H. (1998b) Dyslexia in higher education:policy, provision and practice. In J.Waterfield (ed.) *Dyslexia in higher education: Learning along the continuum. Proceedings of the Second International Conference on Dyslexia in Higher Education, 1996.* Plymouth: University of Plymouth, pp. 9-16.

Skill (1997a) *Disability Directory for LEA Awards Officers.* London: Skill (The National Bureau for Students with Disabilities).

Skill (1997b) *The Coordinator's Handbook.* London: Skill (The National Bureau for Students with Disabilities).

Snowling, M. (1995) Phonological processing and developmental dyslexia. *Journal of Research in Reading,* 18, 132-138.

Snowling, M. and Nation, K. (1997) Language, phonology and learning to read. In C. Hulme and M. Snowling (Eds.) *Dyslexia: Biology, Cognition and Intervention.* London: Whurr, pp. 153-166.

Snowling, M., Nation, K., Moxham, P., Gallagher, A. and Frith, U. (1997) Phonological processing skills of dyslexic students in higher education: a preliminary report. *Journal of Research in Reading,* 20, 31-41.

Solity, J. (1996) Discrepancy definitions of dyslexia: an assessment through teaching perspective. *Educational Psychology in Practice,* 12, 141-151.

Stacey, G. (1996) Organising thoughts to improve study skills. In C. Stephens (Ed.) *Dyslexic Students in Higher Education.* Huddersfield: University of Huddersfield with Skill (National Bureau for Students with Disabilities), pp. 51-54.

Stacey, G. (1997) A dyslexic mind a-thinking. *Dyslexia*, **3**, 111-119.

Stacey, G. (1998) Equal opportunities and staff concerns. In J. Waterfield (Ed.) *Dyslexia in Higher Education: Learning along the continuum.* (Proceedings of the 2nd International Conference on Dyslexia in Higher Education) Plymouth: University of Plymouth, pp. 71-79.

Stanovich, K. (1991) Discrepancy definitions of reading disability: has intelligence led is astray? *Reading Research Quarterly,* 26, 7-29.

Stein, J.F. (1991) Vision and language. In M. Snowling and M. Thomson (Eds.) *Dyslexia: Integrating theory and practice.* London: Whurr, pp. 31-43.

Stephens, C. (Ed.) (1996) *Dyslexic Students in Higher Education.* Huddersfield: University of Huddersfield with Skill (National Bureau for Students with Disabilities).

Thomson, M. (1993) *Developmental Dyslexia.* (3rd edition). London: Whurr.

Tonnesson, F.E. (1997) How can we best define dyslexia? Dyslexia, 3, 78-92.

Turner, M. (1997) *Psychological Assessment of Dyslexia.* London: Whurr.

Waterfield, J. (Ed.) (1995) *Dyslexia in Higher Education: Learning along the continuum.* (Proceedings of the 1st International Conference on Dyslexia in Higher Education) Plymouth: University of Plymouth.

Waterfield, J. (Ed.) (1998) *Dyslexia in Higher Education: Learning along the continuum.* (Proceedings of the 2nd International Conference on Dyslexia in Higher Education) Plymouth: University of Plymouth.

Wechsler, D. (1981) *Wechsler Adult Intelligence Scale – Revised* (WAIS–R). New York: Psychological Corporation.

Wechsler, D. (1987) *Wechsler Memory Scale – Revised* (WMS–R). New York: Psychological Corporation.

West, T.G. (1997) *In the Mind's Eye.* (Updated edition) New York: Prometheus Books.

Wilkins, A. (1995) *Visual Stress.* Oxford: Oxford University Press.

Wilkins, A., Evans, B.J.W., Brown, J., Busby, A., Wingfield, A.E., Jeanes, R and Bald, J. (1994) Double-blind placebo-controlled trials of precision spectral filters in children who use coloured overlays. *Ophthalmic and Physiological Optics*, 14, 365-370.

Wilkinson, G.S. (1993) *Wide Range Achievement Test* (3rd edition, revised). Delware: Jastak Associates.

Willows, D.M., Kruk, R.S. and Corcos, E. (eds.) (1993) *Visual Processes in Reading and Reading Disabilities.* London: Erlbuam.

Wolfendale, S. and Corbett, J. (1996) *Learning Support in Higher Education.* London: Cassell.

Wszeborowska-Lipinska, B. A. and Singleton, C. H. (Submitted) Learning styles in developmental dyslexia.

Zdzienski, D. (1997) *StudyScan.* Limerick: ISL.

14.2 Degree classes of students with dyslexia

UK Domiciled Students Graduating 1996/97: Analysis by Disability, Gender and Length of Course [Source: HESA, 1998. For discussion of these data, see Section 1.1.5.1.]

CATEGORY	Sex	Course	First	Upper Second	Lower Second	Third / Pass	Unclas-sified	TOTALS
Dyslexia	Female	ThreeYr	18	192	210	46	10	476
		FourYr	5	64	55	9	8	141
		Total	23	256	265	55	18	617
		Percent	3.73	41.49	42.95	8.91	2.92	**39.32**
	Male	ThreeYr	22	235	338	82	34	711
		FourYr	12	90	92	26	21	241
		Total	34	325	430	108	55	952
		Percent	3.57	34.14	45.17	11.34	5.78	**60.68**
	Total		**57**	**581**	**695**	**163**	**73**	**1569**
	Percent		**3.63**	**37.03**	**44.30**	**10.39**	**4.65**	**0.80**
Other Disabilities	Female	ThreeYr	150	1089	888	137	63	2327
		FourYr	50	396	305	46	36	833
		Total	200	1485	1193	183	99	3160
		Percent	6.33	46.99	37.75	5.79	3.13	55.79
	Male	ThreeYr	120	759	743	191	72	1885
		FourYr	47	250	228	66	28	619
		Total	167	1009	971	257	100	2504
		Percent	6.67	40.30	38.78	10.26	3.99	44.21
	Total		**367**	**2494**	**2164**	**440**	**199**	**5664**
	Percent		**6.48**	**44.03**	**38.21**	**7.77**	**3.51**	**2.90**
No Disabilities	Female	ThreeYr	3538	26798	21631	3011	1580	56558
		FourYr	1916	14826	10129	1271	1152	29294
		Total	5454	41624	31760	4282	2732	85852
		Percent	6.35	48.48	36.99	4.99	3.18	52.88
	Male	ThreeYr	3687	20235	20722	5318	2003	51965
		FourYr	2334	10490	8680	1998	1030	24532
		Total	6021	30725	29402	7316	3033	76497
		Percent	7.87	40.16	38.44	9.56	3.96	47.12
	Total		**11475**	**72349**	**61162**	**11598**	**5765**	**162349**
	Percent		**7.07**	**44.56**	**37.67**	**7.14**	**3.55**	**83.02**

CATEGORY	Sex	Course	First	Upper Second	Lower Second	Third / Pass	Unclas- sified	TOTALS
Unknown	Female	ThreeYr	570	4145	2685	458	367	8225
		FourYr	510	2622	1623	359	199	5313
		Total	1080	6767	4308	817	566	13538
		Percent	7.98	49.99	31.82	6.03	4.18	52.12
	Male	ThreeYr	519	2961	2897	929	355	7661
		FourYr	540	2078	1502	489	168	4777
		Total	1059	5039	4399	1418	523	12438
		Percent	8.51	40.51	35.37	11.40	4.20	47.88
	Total		**2139**	**11806**	**8707**	**2235**	**1089**	**25976**
	Percent		**8.23**	**45.45**	**33.52**	**8.60**	**4.19**	**13.28**
All students	Female	Total	6757	50132	37526	5337	3415	103167
		Percent	6.55	48.59	36.37	5.17	3.31	52.76
	Male	Total	7281	37098	35202	9099	3711	92391
		Percent	7.88	40.15	38.10	9.85	4.02	47.24
GRAND TOTAL			**14038**	**87230**	**72728**	**14436**	**7126**	**195558**
GRAND PERCENT			**7.18**	**44.61**	**37.19**	**7.38**	**3.64**	**100.00**

NOTES

1. 'Other disabilities' includes all HESA disability categories other than dyslexia, i.e. blind and partially sighted; deaf and hearing impaired; wheelchair user and mobility difficulties; personal care support; mental health difficulties; unseen disabilities (e.g. diabetes, epilepsy, asthma); multiple disabilities; and miscellaneous disabilities.

2. The category 'Unknown' refers to students for whom information on disability status is not available.

3. Figures include all students graduating from 3-year and 4-year first degree courses, whether on a full-time, part-time or sandwich basis. Data from students on postgraduate courses are not included.

4. 'Unclassified' refers to degrees that are not subject to a classification, e.g. medical and general degrees.

5. In HEIs where second class honours are undivided, these figures have been amalgamated with the lower second category.

6. In the percent rows under the 'degree class' columns, the figures are for each degree class as percentages of the *category total*; in the 'total' column, the figures are for each disability category as percentages of the *overall total* number of students graduating.

7. The category 'Dyslexia' does not include students with dyslexia whose condition has been diagnosed *after* entry to higher education (see Section 3.2.3).

14.3 Results of the National Survey on Dyslexia Provision in Higher Education

For explanation of how this survey was conducted, see Section 3.1. Questionnaires were sent to all institutions offering higher education courses in the UK. The total number was 234, comprising 44 'Traditional' universities (TU), 48 'New' universities (NU; i.e those established as universities since 1990), and 142 Colleges offering higher education courses (Col).

195 responses were received (83% response rate), which comprised 41 (21%) Traditional Universities, 45 (23%) New Universities, and 109 (56%) Colleges.

Part 1 - Admissions Policy

1. Does your Institution admit students registered as dyslexic to all courses?

> 193 responded to this question (1% no response):
>
> | **181 (94%) Yes** | **12 (6%) No** |
> |---|---|
> | 37 (90%) TU | 4 (10%) TU |
> | 41 (91%) NU | 4 (9%) NU |
> | 103 (96%) Col | 4 (4%) Col |

2. If "No" please explain any exceptions:

> 10 (out of 12) responded to this question (17% no response):
>
> | 6 (3%) Teaching | 3 (7%) NU; 3 (3%) Col |
> |---|---|
> | 3 (2%) Medical/Pharmacy | 2 (5%) TU; 1 (2%) NU |
> | 1 (<1%) TEFL | 1 (2%) TU |

Part 2 - Assessment Policy

3. Does your Institution administer internal assessments for dyslexia?

> 195 responded to this question (0% no response):
>
> | **92 (47%) Yes** | **103 (53%) No** |
> |---|---|
> | 17 (41%) TU | 24 (59%) TU |
> | 20 (44%) NU | 25 (56%) NU |
> | 55 (51%) Col | 54 (49%) Col |

4. If "Yes" then how are such assessments funded?

> 92 (out of 92) responded to this question (0% no response):
>
> | 69 (59%) Institution | 14 (61%) TU; 18 (58%) NU; 37 (60%) Col |
> |---|---|
> | 13 (11%) DSA | 2 (9%) TU; 3 (10%) NU; 8 (13%) Col |
> | 13 (11%) Student | 3 (13%) TU; 4 (13%) NU; 6 (10%) Col |
> | 7 (6%) ASU (FEFC) | 7 (11%) Col |
> | 7 (6%) ACCESS funds | 2 (9%) TU; 3 (10%) NU; 2 (3%) Col |
> | 5 (4%) LEA | 2 (9%) TU; 2 (6%) NU; 1 (2%) Col |
> | 2 (2%) Other | 1 (3%) NU; 1 (2%) Col |

5. If "No" then where does a student get an assessment?

> 97 (out of 103) responded to this question (6% no response):
>
> | 85 (83%) Psychologist | 23 (85%) TU; 24 (92%) NU; 38 (78%) Col |
> |---|---|
> | 10 (10%) Other Institution | 2 (7%) TU; 2 (8%) NU; 6 (12%) Col |
> | 3 (3%) Access Centre | 1 (4%) TU; 2 (4%) Col |
> | 4 (4%) Other | 1 (4%) TU; 3 (6%) Col |

6. What are the qualifications of the person(s) who carry out dyslexia assessments for you?

> 160 responded to this question (18% no response):

> 134 (77%) Psychologist   31 (89%) TU; 38 (84%) NU; 65 (69%) Col
> 29 (17%) Dip.SpLD   1 (3%) TU; 6 (13%) NU; 22 (23%) Col
> 9 (5%) SpLD Assessment Cert. 2 (6%) TU; 1 (2%) NU; 6 (6%) Col
> 2 (1%) Med. MRCSLT   1 (3%) TU; 1 (1%) Col

7. Does your Institution carry out a screening or preliminary assessment before students are referred for a full psychological assessment?

> 185 responded to this question (5% no response):
> **130 (70%) Yes**   **55 (30%) No**
> 24 (62%) TU   15 (38%) TU
> 37 (84%) NU   7 (16%) NU
> 69 (68%) Col   33 (32%) Col

8. Do you find, in general, that your assessments are accepted by LEA's for DSA purposes?

> 150 responded to this question (23% no response):
> **87 (58%) Yes**   **13 (9%) No**   **50 (33%) Sometimes**
> 20 (61%) TU   2 (6%) TU   11 (33%) TU
> 24 (56%) NU   4 (9%) NU   15 (35%) NU
> 43 (58%) Col   7 (10%) Col   24 (32%) Col

Part 3 - Incidence

9. What is the total number of current students at your Institution who have declared themselves to be dyslexic on the UCAS form?

> 112 responded to this question (43% no response):
> Min = 0   Max = 225   Mean = 51
>   TU = 63 (n = 29)
>   NU = 83 (n = 33)
>   Col = 22 (n = 50)

10. What is the total number of current students at your Institution who have been identified or diagnosed as dyslexic **after** admission?

> 135 responded to this question (31% no response):
> Min = 0   Max = 375   Mean = 38
>   TU = 27 (n = 30)
>   NU = 88 (n = 32)
>   Col = 21 (n = 73)

11. What is the total student population at your Institution?

> 161 responded to this question (17% no response):
> Min = 100   Max = 40,000   Mean = 7916
>   TU = 9480 (n = 36)
>   NU = 13155 (n = 39)
>   Col = 4885 (n = 86)

Number of dyslexic students as a percentage of the total student population:

> Min = 0   Max = 10*   Mean = 1.35
>   TU = 0.95 (n = 31)
>   NU = 1.31 (n = 38)
>   Col = 1.54 (n = 73)

> *excludes one college which claims 35% incidence of dyslexia.

12. As far as you know, are these dyslexic students distributed about equally across different subject areas, or unequally?

167 responded to this question (14% no response):

95 (57%) Equally	72 (43%) Unequally
22 (58%) TU	16 (42%) TU
15 (36%) NU	27 (64%) NU
58 (67%) Col	29 (33%) Col

Part 4 - Support

13. Does your Institution have a support service for dyslexic students?

189 responded to this question (3% no response):

138 (73%) Yes	**51 (27%) No**
28 (68%) TU	13 (32%) TU
34 (79%) NU	9 (21%) NU
76 (72%) Col	27 (28%) Col

14. If "Yes", approximately how many dyslexic students currently use that service on a regular basis?

95 (out of 138) responded to this question (31% no response):

Min = 0	Max = 604	Mean = 34
		TU = 61 (n = 19)
		NU = 42 (n = 26)
		Col = 19 (n = 50)

15. Do dyslexic students have access to a dyslexia-trained tutor at your Institution?

191 responded to this question (2% no response):

87 (45%) Yes	**104 (55%) No**
11 (27%) TU	29 (73%) TU
25 (57%) NU	19 (43%) NU
51 (48%) Col	56 (52%) Col

16. If "Yes", is that tutor **employed** by your Institution?

102 responded to this question (0% no response):

74 (73%) Yes	**28 (27%) No**
9 (53%) TU	8 (47%) TU
16 (57%) NU	12 (43%) NU
49 (86%) Col	8 (14%) Col

17. Does your Institution organise any group activities for dyslexic students, such as special courses, modules or workshops?

190 responded to this question (3% no response):

76 (40%) Yes	**114 (60%) No**
16 (39%) TU	25 (61%) TU
29 (64%) NU	16 (36%) NU
31 (30%) Col	73 (70%) Col

18. Does your Institution provide any **special** support for dyslexic students to help them use Library facilities?

187 responded to this question (4% no response):

78 (42%) Yes	**109 (58%) No**
15 (37%) TU	26 (63%) TU
24 (55%) NU	20 (45%) NU
39 (38%) Col	63 (62%) Col

19. Does your Institution permit dyslexic students to use tape-recorders in lectures?

188 responded to this question (4% no response):

185 (98%) Yes	**3 (2%) No**

                    40 (100%) TU
                    44 (98%) NU   1 (2%) NU
                    101 (98%) Col   2 (2%) Col

Part 5 - Counselling

20. Does your Institution provide any **specialist** counselling facilities for dyslexic students?

    190 responded to this question (3% no response):

74 (39%) Yes	**116 (61%) No**
13 (32%) TU	27 (68%) TU
18 (41%) NU	26 (59%) NU
43 (41%) Col	63 (59%) Col

Part 6 - Staff Development

21. Does your Institution give all academic staff information on dyslexia?

    192 responded to this question (2% no response):

99 (52%) Yes	**93 (48%) No**
22 (54%) TU	19 (46%) TU
24 (55%) NU	20 (45%) NU
53 (49%) Col	54 (51%) Col

22. Does your Institution run staff development courses on dyslexia?

    191 responded to this question (2% no response):

88 (46%) Yes	**103 (54%) No**
16 (39%) TU	25 (61%) TU
26 (59%) NU	18 (41%) NU
46 (43%) Col	60 (57%) Col

Part 7 - General Awareness

23. Does your Institution display posters to raise general awareness of dyslexia among students?

    190 responded to this question (3% no response):

64 (34%) Yes	**126 (66%) No**
11 (27%) TU	29 (73%) TU
20 (45%) NU	24 (55%) NU
33 (31%) Col	73 (69%) Col

24. Does your Institution make available to students any special information about dyslexia support services?

    190 responded to this question (3% no response):

112 (59%) Yes	**78 (41%) No**
24 (62%) TU	15 (38%) TU
31 (69%) NU	14 (31%) NU
57 (54%) Col	49 (46%) Col

25. If "Yes" please give brief details:

    97 (out of 112) responded to this question (13% no response):

37% Support Service Info	7 (23%) TU; 23 (40%) NU; 25 (42%) Col
33% General Dyslexia Info	13 (43%) TU; 16 (28%) NU; 20 (33%) Col
9% Lit. from other Organisations	3 (10%) TU; 2 (4%) NU; 8 (13%) Col

9% Videos on dyslexia   2 (7%) TU; 7 (12%) NU; 4 (7%) Col
6% Students and disabilities   3 (10%) TU; 4 (7%) NU; 2 (3%) Col
5% Audio tapes on dyslexia   2 (7%) TU; 5 (9%) NU; 1 (2%) Col

Part 8 - Computer / Technology Support

26. Are there any **special** computer facilities in your Institution to which dyslexic students have open access?

     192 responded to this question (2% no response):

88 (46%) Yes	**104 (54%) No**
17 (41%) TU	24 (59%) TU
25 (56%) NU	20 (44%) NU
46 (43%) Col	60 (57%) Col

27. If "Yes" please give brief details:

     80 (out of 88) responded to this question (9% no response):

41% Scanners	9 (41%) TU; 20 (42%) NU; 25 (40%) Col
27% Talking WP's	3 (14%) TU; 14 (29%) NU; 19 (31%) Col
23% PC software for dyslexics	8 (36%) TU; 10 (21%) NU; 13 (21%) Col
5% Laptops	1 (2%) NU; 5 (8%) Col
2% Tape-recorders	1 (5%) TU; 2 (4%) NU
1% Magnification systems	1 (2%) NU
1% Spellmasters	1 (5%) TU

28. Does your Institution have any tutors or technicians who have special responsibility for advising or assisting dyslexic students in the use of computer technology?

     192 responded to this question (2% no response):

61 (32%) Yes	131 (68%) No
12 (30%) TU	28 (70%) TU
18 (40%) NU	27 (60%) NU
31 (29%) Col	76 (71%) Col

Part 9 - Disabled Students Allowance

29. Do you know how many dyslexic students at your Institution are currently in receipt of the DSA?

     190 responded to this question (3% no response):

55 (29%) Yes	**135 (71%) No**
11 (27%) TU	29 (73%) TU
11 (24%) NU	34 (76%) NU
33 (31%) Col	72 (69%) Col

30. If "Yes", how many?

     49 (out of 55) responded to this question (11% no response):

Min = 0	Max = 152	Mean = 18
		TU = 24 (n = 8)
		NU = 35 (n = 10)
		Col = 11 (n = 31)

31. Does your Institution help students to apply for the DSA?

     181 responded to this question (7% no response):

165 (91%) Yes	**16 (9%) No**
36 (95%) TU	2 (5%) TU

44 (100%) NU
85 (86%) Col   14 (14%) Col

32. How do you view the DSA system with respect to dyslexic students?

155 responded to this question (21% no response):

48 (31%) Satisfactory   **107 (69%) Unsatisfactory**
14 (36%) TU   25 (64%) TU
3 (7%) NU   40 (93%) NU
31 (42%) Col   42 (58%) Col

33. If "Unsatisfactory", briefly outline your dissatisfactions:

104 (out of 107) responded to this question (3% no response):
39% Inconsistencies between LEA's
20 (51%) TU;   27 (40%) NU;   19 (31%) Col
20% Time-consuming and difficult to obtain / delay in allocation
5 (13%) TU;   13 (19%) NU;   16 (26%) Col
9% DSA doesn't cover initial assessment
5 (13%) TU;   6 (9%) NU;   4 (7%) Col
7% Various students excluded
2 (5%) TU;   6 (9%) NU;   4 (7%) Col
6% Assessments are not standardised
1 (3%) TU;   4 (6%) NU;   5 (8%) Col
4% DFE guidelines are unclear
2 (5%) TU;   2 (3%) NU;   3 (5%) Col
4% Little knowledge of dyslexia in LEA's
1 (3%) TU;   3 (4%) NU;   2 (3%) Col
11% Other
3 (8%) TU;   7 (10%) NU;   8 (13%) Col

Part 10 - Examinations

34. Does your Institution have a general policy on provision for dyslexic students in examinations, or is policy delegated to the examination boards for different subjects?

169 responded to this question (13% no response):
117 (69%) General policy   52 (31%) Subject area policy
31 (86%) TU   5 (14%) TU
36 (86%) NU   6 (14%) NU
50 (55%) Col   41 (45%) Col

35. Does your Institution allow extra time for dyslexic students in examinations?

181 responded to this question (7% no response):
180 (99%) Yes   **1 (1%) No**
39 (100%) TU
44 (100%) NU
97 (99%) Col   1 (1%) Col

36. If "Yes", is this provision **standard** for all dyslexic students or does provision vary from student to student?

178 (out of 180) responded to this question (1% no response):
69 (39%) Standard   109 (61%) Varies
13 (34%) TU   25 (66%) TU
16 (36%) NU   28 (64%) NU
40 (42%) Col   56 (58%) Col

37. If "Standard", please specify the standard arrangements:

82 responded to this question (0% no response)
      39 (48%) 10 minutes / hour   13 (72%) TU; 8 (30%) NU; 18 (49%) Col
      40 (49%) 15 minutes / hour   5 (28%) TU; 17 (63%) NU; 18 (49%) Col
      2 (2%) 20 minutes / hour   1 (4%) NU; 1 (3%) Col
      1 (1%) 30 minutes / hour   1 (4%) NU

38. If "Varied", please explain briefly:

104 (out of 109) responded to this question (5% no response):
    86 (83%) According to assessment report
        22 (88%) TU; 28 (90%) NU; 36 (75%) Col
    12 (11%) Negotiated by Student and Department
        3 (12%) TU; 3 (10%) NU; 6 (12%) Col
    6 (6%) Depends on Examination Board 6 (12%) Col

39. Does your Institution permit the use of an amanuensis for dyslexic students in examinations?

165 responded to this question (15% no response):
144 (87%) Yes	**21 (13%) No**
31 (82%) TU	7 (18%) TU
39 (91%) NU	4 (9%) NU
74 (88%) Col	10 (12%) Col

40. Does your Institution permit the use of a reader for dyslexic students in examinations?

160 responded to this question (18% no response):
137 (86%) Yes	**23 (14%) No**
28 (76%) TU	9 (24%) TU
36 (90%) NU	4 (10%) NU
73 (88%) Col	10 (12%) Col

41. Does your Institution permit dyslexic students to use Word Processors in examinations?

159 responded to this question (18% no response):
136 (86%) Yes	**23 (14%) No**
33 (92%) TU	3 (8%) TU
40 (93%) NU	3 (7%) NU
63 (79%) Col	17 (21%) Col

42. Does your Institution permit dyslexic students to tape-record examination answers?

142 responded to this question (27% no response):
92 (65%) Yes	**50 (35%) No**
17 (53%) TU	15 (47%) TU
26 (68%) NU	12 (32%) NU
49 (68%) Col	23 (32%) Col

43. Does your Institution permit dyslexic students to have an oral examination instead of a written examination?

153 responded to this question (22% no response):
89 (58%) Yes	**64 (42%) No**
13 (37%) TU	22 (63%) TU
24 (62%) NU	15 (38%) NU
52 (66%) Col	27 (34%) Col

44. If your Institution makes any other special examination provision for dyslexic students not covered above, please outline briefly:

46 responded to this question (76% no response):
    31% Separate room provided
        7 (27%) TU; 7 (28%) NU; 8 (38%) Col
    21% Examination questions enlarged / Coloured paper / Overlays

5 (19%) TU;   5 (20%) NU;   5 (24%) Col
10% Use of Dictionary / Thesaurus / Hand-held Spellchecker
3 (12%) TU;   2 (8%) NU;   2 (10%) Col
8% Rest break during examination
3 (12%) TU;   3 (14%) Col
10% Labels on scripts so dyslexia taken into account by examiners
5 (19%) TU;   2 (8%) NU
7% Taped questions
1 (4%) TU;   3 (12%) NU;   1 (5%) Col
4% Scripts transcribed by a secretary
2 (8%) NU;   1 (5%) Col
3% Same time as other candidates but fewer questions
1 (4%) TU;   1 (5%) Col
3% Take home photocopy of script to Word Process
2 (8%) NU
3% Checker for multiple choice questions
1 (4%) TU;   1 (4%) NU
1% Take list of key points into examination (if STM problem)
1 (4%) NU

Part 11 - General

45. Please outline any provision your Institution makes for dyslexic students which you feel is not covered above:

32 respnded to this question (84% no response):
24 % Study practice assessment / Study skills work
4 (36%) TU;   6 (25%) NU;   1 (9%) Col
9% Links with local BDA or DI
2 (18%) TU;   1 (4%) NU;   1 (9%) Col
4% Extention of deadlines
2 (8%) NU
7% Regular mailing of information / Information access service
2 (18%) TU;   1 (4%) NU
4% Dyslexic Society in SU
1 (4%) NU;   1 (9%) Col
4% Work labelled for sympathetic marking
2 (8%) NU
4% Optometrist advice
1 (9%) TU;   1 (9%) Col
4% Equipment on loan
1 (9%) TU;   1 (4%) NU
4% Directions to students departments on provisions / course delivery
1 (9%) TU;   1 (4%) NU
4% Quiet rooms for working in
1 (4%) NU;   1 (9%) Col
4% Photocopy card
1 (4%) NU;   1 (9%) Col
28 % Other provision, including:
Varying length of assessment work
Record reading material
Proof-reading
Filter sheets
Extra computer paper
Module for dyslexic students in better thinking skills (credited)

> Overheads copied / enlarged
> Training on use of WP's
> Advice on admission
> Equal Opportunities Policy
> Premises with computers / printers just for dyslexics

46. In your experience, what is the biggest problem confronting your Institution at the present time in relation to dyslexic students?

> 165 responded to this question (15% no response):
>
> 22% Funding for assessments, equipment and support
> > 11 (19%) TU;   20 (24%) NU;   28 (22%) Col
>
> 18% Lack of knowledge / understanding among staff / students
> > 13 (22%) TU;   17 (21%) NU;   18 (14%) Col
>
> 16% Lack of qualified staff for specialist help / limited time
> > 12 (21%) TU;   11 (13%) NU;   20 (16%) Col
>
> 11% Increasing number of dyslexic students
> > 8 (14%) TU;   9 (11%) NU;   11 (9%) Col
>
> 10% Getting students to come forward / identifying dyslexic students
> > 2 (3%) TU;   3 (4%) NU;   21 (17%) Col
>
> 6% DSA provision
> > 2 (3%) TU;   6 (7%) NU;   7 (6%) Col
>
> 3% Lack of money for students not eligible for DSA
> > 1 (2%) TU;   5 (6%) NU;   2 (2%) Col
>
> 14% Other problems, including:
> > Standard provision not suitable for all dyslexic students
> > No overall policy
> > Exam concessions / marking work
> > Creation of a supportive framework for dyslexic students
> > Need for a pre-assessment screening test
> > Teaching organisational skills to dyslexic students
> > Liasing with subject tutors
> > Split-site - support only available on one campus
> > Getting students to take advantage of support
> > Inappropriate admissions (NU)
> > Variation in assessment reports (TU)
> > Worries about academic standards (NU)
> > Lack of literature re dyslexia in HE / Adults (NU)
> > Possible outcome of DFEE review (NU)
> > Need to improve library service (Col)
> > Persuading schools that dyslexics can teach (Col)

14.4   Addresses of organisations and suppliers

Academic Therapy Publications, 20 Commercial Boulevard, Novato, California 94941–6191, US.

Adult Development and Skills Centre, 5 Tavistock Place, London WC1H 9SN. Tel: 0171 388 8744. Fax: 0171 387 7968.

Adult Dyslexia Organisation, 336 Brixton Road, London SW9 7AA. Tel: 0171 924 9559. Fax: 0171 274 7840. [*www.futurenet.co.uk/charity/ado*]

Association of Educational Psychologists, c/o David Webster (Association Secretary), 26 The Avenue, Durham DH1 4ED.

British Association for Counselling, 1 Regent Place, Rugby CV21 2PJ. Tel: 01788 578328.

British Association of Behavioural Optometrists (BADO), 72 High Street, Billericay, Essex CM12 9BS. Tel: 01277 624916.

British Computer Society Disability Group, c/o Room C126, EASAMS Ltd., West Hanningfield Road, Great Baddow, Chelmsford CM2 8HN. Tel: 01245 242950. Fax: 01245 478317. [*www.bcs.org.uk*]

British Dyslexia Association, 98 London Road, Reading RG1 5AU. Tel: 0118 966 8271. Fax: 0118 935 1927. [*www.bda-dyslexia.org.uk*]

British Psychological Society, St Andrews House, 48 Princess Road East, Leicester LE1 7DR. Tel: 0116 254 9568. Fax: 0116 247 0887. [*www.bps.org.uk*]

Committee of Vice-Chancellors and Principals (CVCP), 20 Tavistock Square, London WC1H 9HQ. Tel: 0171 419 4111. Fax: 0171 388 8649.

Computability Centre, P.O. Box 94, Warwick CV34 5WS. Tel: 01926 312847 / 0800 269545. Fax: 01926 311345.

Computer Centre for People with Disabilities, University of Westminster, 72 Great Portland Street, London W1N 5AL. Tel: 0171 911 5000. Fax: 0171 911 5162. [*www.wmin.ac.uk/ccpd/*]

Department for Education and Employment, Sanctuary Buildings, Great Smith Street, Westminster, London SW1P 3BT. Tel: 0171 925 5000. Fax: 0171 925 6000.

Disability Action, 2 Annandale Avenue, Belfast BT7 3JH, Northern Ireland. Tel: 01232 491011.

Disability Scotland, Princes House, 5 Shandwick Place, Edinburgh EH2 4RG, Scotland. Tel: 0131 229 8632. Fax: 0131 229 5168.

Disability Wales/Anabledd Cymru, Llys Ifor, Crescent Road, Caerphilly CF83 1XL, Wales. Tel: 01222 887325. Fax: 01222 888702.

Dis-Forum. *dis-forum@mailbase.ac.uk* This is an e-mail discussion network for disability advisers and coordinators. For instructions on how to join see *www.mailbase.ac.uk/lists/dis-forum/join.html*

DIS in HE Support Centre, Department of Applied Computing, University of Dundee, DUNDEE, DD1 4HN, Scotland.   Tel: 01382   345050.   Fax: 01382   345509.   E-mail: *enquiries@disinhe.ac.uk* [*www.disinhe.ac.uk*]

Dyslexia Archive, HENSA Computing Laboratory, University of Kent, Canterbury, Kent CT2 7NF. Tel: 01227 823784. Fax: 01227 762811. [*www.hensa.ac.uk/dyslexia.html*]

Dyslexia Forum. *dyslexia@mailbase.ac.uk.* This is an e-mail discussion network concerning dyslexia. For further details refer to *www.mailbase.ac.uk/lists/dyslexia/join.html*

Dyslexia Institute, 133 Gresham Road, Staines, TW18 2AJ. Tel: 01784 463851 Fax: 01784 460747. [*www.dyslexia-inst.org.uk*]

Dyslexia Unit, University of Wales, Bangor, Gwynedd LL57 2DG, Wales. Tel: 01248 383843. Fax: 01248 382599.

Employers' Forum on Disability, Nutmeg House, 60 Gainsford Street, London SE1 2NY. Tel: 0171 403 3020. Fax: 0171 403 0404.

Helen Arkell Dyslexia Centre, Frensham, Farnham, Surrey GU10 3BW. Tel: 01252 792400. Fax: 01252 795669.

Higher Education Funding Council for England (HEFCE), Northavon House, Coldharbour Lane, Bristol BS16 1QD. Tel: 0117 931 7317. Fax: 0117 931 7203.

Higher Education Funding Council for Wales / Cyngor Cyllido Cymru, Lambourne House, Cardiff Business Park, Llanishen, Cardiff CF4 5GL, Wales. Tel: 01222 761861. Fax: 01222 763163.

Higher Education Statistics Agency (HESA), 18 Royal Crescent, Cheltenham GL50 3DA. Tel: 01242 255577. Fax: 01242 232648.

Hodder and Stoughton Educational, c/o Bookpoint Ltd., Direct Services, 78 Milton Park, Abingdon, Oxon OX14 4TD. Fel: 01235 400477. Fax: 01235 821511,

Hornsby International Dyslexia Centre, 261 Trinity Road, London SW18 3SN. Tel: 0181 874 1844. Fax: 0181 877 9737.

iANSYST Ltd., The White House, 72 Fen Road, Cambridge, CB4 1UN. Tel: 01223 420101. Fax: 01223 426644. Email: *sales@dyslexic.com*

Irlen Institute, 123 High Street, Chard, Somerset TA20 1QT. Tel/Fax: 01460 65555.

Joint Forum for GCSE and GCE, 1, Regent Street, Cambridge CB2 1GG. Tel: 01223 553425. Fax: 01223 354274.

London Language and Literacy Unit, Southwark College, St Mary's Road, London SE15 2EA. Tel: 0171 639 9512.

Moray House Centre for Specific Learning Difficulties (Dyslexia), Heriot-Watt University, Holyrood Campus, Holyrood Road, Edinburgh EH8 8QA, Scotland Tel: 0131 556 8455. Fax: 0131 557 3458.

National Federation of Access Centres, The ACCESS Centre, Hereward College of Further Education, Branston Crescent, Tile Hill Lane, Coventry CV4 9SW. Tel: 01203 461231. Fax: 01203 694305. [*www.wmin.ac.uk/ccpd/*]

NFER–NELSON, Darville House, 2 Oxford Road East, Windsor, Berks. SL4 1DF. Tel: 01753 858961. Fax: 01753 856830. E-mail: *edu&hsc@nfer-nelson.co.uk* [www.*nfer-nelson.co.uk*]

Psychological Corporation, 24-28, Oval Road, London NW1 1YA. Tel: 0171 424 4456. Fax: 0171 424 4515.

RNIB (Royal National Institute for the Blind), 224 Great Portland Street, London W1N 6AA. Tel: 0171 388 1266. Fax: 0171 388 2034.

Scottish Dyslexia Association, Unit 3, Stirling Business Centre, Wellgreen Place, Stirling FK8 2DZ. Tel: 01786 446650.

Scottish Higher Education Funding Council (SHEFC), Donaldson House, 97 Haymarket Terrace, Edinburgh EH12 5HD. Tel: 0131 313 6500. Fax: 0131 313 6501.

Skill (The National Bureau for Students with Disabilities), 336 Brixton Road, London SW9 7AA. Tel: 0171 978 9890. Fax: 0171 274 7840.

14.5 Educational and psychological tests

This list includes a broad selection of those tests that personnel working in the field of disability/dyslexia in higher education are most likely to encounter. Tests that are not recommended have been included as well as those that it is possible to recommend for use with students in higher education. The main limitations of each test are also mentioned and sources of reviews or comments on the use of these tests are given. For addresses of suppliers, see Section 14.4. Tests marked **R** in the third column are resticted to use by qualified psychologists. The table is dividec in to two parts: the first part deals with tests of reading and spelling, the second part with other tests, including arithmetic, intelligence and dyslexia screening.

The fundamental problem in this field is the lack of tests specifically designed for use within higher education. UK tests available for the adult age range have been designed to assess *functional literacy* within the general population or of neurological patients, rather than being standardised for the assessment of the full range of literacy abilities. Functional literacy tests such as the *National Adult Reading Test* (NART) and the *Basic Skills Test* are consequently insufficiently sensitive to be of use when assessing higher education students.

For the time being, at least, the use of US tests that are suitable for the age-range, and which have been well-standardised for the full range of literacy abilities, is generally preferable to the use of UK tests designed for younger children, because the latter will lack the sensitivity for the higher education population. Where some tests have norms for students in the 16–18 years range, a case can be made for their extension to slightly older students *for diagnostic purposes only*, but this practice should not be encouraged. Tests designed for students under 16 will rarely have much applicability to the higher education population because almost all higher education students will score at the ceiling of such tests. Educational, linguistic and cultural changes will have rendered largely obsolete those tests with norms dating from earlier than 1980.

READING AND SPELLING

Test name and publication date	Brief description, comments, main limitations and references where reviews and further comments can be found	Publisher or Supplier
Wide Range Achievement Test **(WRAT –3).** (1993)	Tests of single word oral reading, spelling [and mathematics]. Age range 5–75 years. Alternate forms for re-test purposes. Approx. administration time: 10 minutes (reading); 10 minutes (spelling). Good standards of validity and reliability. **Recommended.** *Limitations:* US norms only. *Reviews and comments:* Beech and Singleton (1997a) pp. 227, 329-330; McLoughlin, Fitzgibbon and Young (1993) pp. 41-3; Turner (1997) pp. 271, 275, 282 .	UK Supplier: **Psychological Corporation** [Published by Jastak Associates, Delaware, US]
Woodcock Reading Mastery Tests (1987).	Tests of non-word reading and single oral word reading, plus three tests of single word comprehension and one test of passage comprehension. Age range 5–75 years. Approx. administration time: 30+ minutes. Alternate forms for re-test purposes. Good standards of validity and reliability. **Recommended.** *Limitations:* US norms only. *Reviews and comments:* Beech and Singleton (1997a) pp. 331-3; Turner (1997) pp. 106-112, 205.	UK Supplier: **Dyslexia Institute** [Published by American Guidance Service, Minnesota, US]

WORD **(Wechsler Objective Reading Dimensions)**. (1993)	Tests of single word oral reading, spelling and oral/silent reading comprehension. Age range 5–16 years. Approx. administration time: 10–20 minutes per subtest. Good standards of validity and reliability. UK norms. When used with WISC-III, discrepancies between literacy achievement and ability can be assessed. Can only be purchased by educational psychologists, but can be used by suitably trained personnel under supervision of an educational psychologist. *Limitations:* 16 years upper age limit. No alternate forms for re-test purposes. Lacks sensitivity at upper age range. Not recommended for higher education students. *Reviews and comments:* Beech and Singleton (1997a) pp. 325-6, 336-8; Turner (1997) pp. 105-112.	**Psychological Corporation** **R**
Spadafore Diagnostic Reading Test (1983)	Tests of single word oral reading, prose reading, reading comprehension and listening comprehension. Age range: school age to adult. Approx. administration time: 10+ minutes per subtest. Recommended by McLoughlin et al (1994) for its rating of professional, technical, vocational and functional levels. *Limitations:* Criterion-referenced. US spellings. *Reviews and comments:* Beech and Singleton (1997a) pp. 227-8, 322-3; McLoughlin, Fitzgibbon and Young (1993) p. 42.	**Academic Therapy Publications, US**
British Ability Scales (BAS-II) Reading and Spelling Scales. (1996)	Tests of single oral word reading and spelling. Age range: 5–18 years. Approx. administration time: 10 minutes per subtest. Good standards of validity and reliability. UK norms. When used with BAS-II, discrepancies between literacy achievement and ability can be assessed. *Limitations:* 18 years upper age limit. *Reviews and comments:* Beech and Singleton (1997a) pp. 294-8, 334-5; Turner (1997) pp. 32-4, 106.	**NFER– NELSON** **R**
Differential Ability Scales (DAS) Word Reading Test (1990).	A US/international version of the BAS-II. Age up to 17:11. *Limitations:* 18 years upper age limit. *Reviews and comments:* Beech and Singleton (1997a) pp.334-5; Turner (1997) pp. 72-9.	**Psychological Corporation** **R**
NFER Reading Comprehension Test EH2 (1975)	Test of silent reading comprehension involving seven passages of text and multiple-choice questions. Can be group-administered. Reasonable validity and reliability. UK norms. Untimed (average range 15–45 minutes). Age range: 11:0–15:11, but sometimes used for HE students with a 15 minutes time limit; no norms for this group available. *Limitations:* 15 years 11 months upper age limit. Norms now rather dated. *Reviews and comments:* Pumfrey (1985) p. 170.	**NFER– NELSON**

British Spelling Tests (BST) (1998)	BST Level 4: 12:6–17:5 years. BST Level 5: 15:6–24+ years. Alternate forms for re-testing. Approx. administration time: 30–40 minutes. UK norms. **BST Level 5 recommended.** *Limitations:* Rather lengthy assessment. *Reviews and comments:* None as the test has only been available very recently.	**NFER–NELSON**
National Adult Reading Test (NART) (1982)	A list of irregular words that predicts adult intelligence. Age range 20–70 years. *Limitations:* Designed for use in neuropsychological assessment (generally for estimating pre-morbid intelligenec in cases of dementia) rather than for educational assessment. Not recommended for use with higher education students. *Reviews and comments:* Beech and Singleton (1997) pp. 19, 227, 312-3; Pumfrey (1985) pp. 145; Turner (1997) p. 294.	**NFER–NELSON**
Neale Analysis of Reading (Revised) (1989)	Progressive passages of text read aloud, with measures of reading accuracy, reading rate and reading comprehension. Age range: 6–13. UK norms. Good validity and reliability. *Limitations:*13 years upper age limit. Not recommended for higher education students. *Reviews and comments:* Beech and Singleton (1997a) pp. 312-3; Turner (1997) pp. 105-111.	**NFER–NELSON**
Schonell Graded Word Reading and Spelling Tests (1955)	Single word oral reading and spelling. Age range: 5–15. UK norms. *Limitations:*15 years upper age limit. Seriously outdated norms (revised in 1972 for children 6–11 years). Not recommended for higher education students. *Reviews and comments:* Beech and Singleton (1997a) pp. 18-9; Pumfrey (1985) p. 189 ; Turner (1997) pp. 198, 205.	Oliver and Boyd, Edinburgh (now out of print).
Burt Word Reading Test (1974 Revision)	Single word oral reading. Age range: 6–12. UK norms. *Limitations:*12 years upper age limit. Seriously outdated norms. Not recommended for higher education students. *Reviews and comments:* Pumfrey (1985) p. 108; Turner (1997) p. 198.	Hodder and Stoughton (now out of print).
Graded Word Reading Test (Vernon) (1938)	Single word oral reading. Age range: 6–18. UK norms. Approx. administration time: 15 minutes. *Limitations:*18 years upper age limit. Seriously outdated and doubtful norms, especially at the upper range. Scores available in reading ages only. Not recommended for higher education students. *Reviews and comments:* Pumfrey (1985) p. 126.	Hodder and Stoughton (now out of print).

Graded Word Spelling Test (Vernon) (1977/1983)	80 item spelling test, arranged in order of difficulty. Age range: 5–17:6. UK norms. Approx. administration time: 30 minutes. *Limitations:*17½ years upper age limit. Rather outdated and norms no longer reliable. Scores available in spelling quotients. Not recommended for higher education students. *Reviews and comments:* Pumfrey (1985) p. 127; Turner (1997) p. 206.	**Hodder and Stoughton**
Basic Skills Test (1988)	Designed to measure functional literacy skills of individuals aged 16 to adult. Can be used individually or as a group assessment. Examinees read a 'newspaper' and answer questions in a test booklet. This is a criterion test to determine basic adequacy for clerical work. Approx. administration time: 30 minutes. *Limitations:* Unsuitable for higher education assessment. Has no diagnostic value. *Reviews and comments:* Beech and Singleton (1997a) pp. 19, 292-3.	**NFER–NELSON**

OTHER TESTS

Test name and publication date	Brief description, comments, main limitations and review references	Publisher or Supplier
Wide Range Achievement Test (WRAT –3) (Arithmetic) (1993)	Test of arithmetic for age range 5–75 years [also comprise single word oral reading and spelling]. Alternate forms for re-test purposes. Approx. administration time: 15 minutes. Good standards of validity and reliability. **Recommended.** *Limitations:* US norms only. *Reviews and comments:* Turner (1997) p. 209, 275-6.	**Psychological Corporation**
Standard Progressive Matrices (SPM) (Raven) (1958 / 1979)	A set of matrix problems of increasing difficulty. Assumed by many to be a test of non-verbal intelligence, although verbal reasoing can be used to solve the problems. Also *Advanced Progressive Matrices* (1947). *Limitations:* Original norms now very old. Newer norms have been produced (1979), although these have been criticised. *Reviews and comments:* McLoughlin, Fitzgibbon and Young (1993) pp. 29; Thomson (1993), p.157; Turner (1997) pp. 210-213.	**NFER–NELSON**
Mill Hill Vocabulary Scale (Senior Form) (1943/1994)	Designed to complement the *Standard Progressive Matrices*, this test of word definitions and synonyms has a form that is suitable for adults. *Limitations:* Original norms now very old, but new norms have been produced. Reliability has been questioned. Very few items cover an enormous range of vocabularies. Not recommended for higher education assessment. *Reviews and comments:* Pumfrey (1985) p.58.	**NFER-NELSON**

British Picture Vocabulary Scale (BPVS) (1982)	A test of receptive vocabulary using pictures. Age range: 3–17:11. UK norms. Untimed; approx. administration time: 20 minutes (short form); 40 minutes (long form). Reasonable reliability (less at upper age range); validity has been questioned, but generally assumed to give a fair estimate of verbal intelligence. *Limitations:*17:11 years upper age limit. Not recommended for higher education students. *Reviews and comments:*Pumfrey (1985) p.54.	**NFER–NELSON**
Bangor Dyslexia Test (1982/1997)	Age range 7–18 years. Individually administered. Approx. administration time: 40 minutes. Some validity data is given in the manual. Comprises 10 sub-tests of characteristics that provide 'positive signs' of dyslexia. *Limitations:* Not fully standardised but useful in screening and counselling. *Reviews and comments:* Beech and Singleton (1997a) pp. 290-1; McLoughlin, Fitzgibbon and Young (1993) pp.28-9; Thomson (1993), p. 175.	**LDA** Duke Street, Wisbech, Cambs. PE13 2AE.
Dyslexia Adult Screening Test (DAST) (1998)	A new screening test comprising 11 subtests, including one-minute reading, two-minute spelling, verbal and semantic fluency. Adminstration time about 30 minutes. See Nicolson and Fawcett (1997). Standardisation recently completed. *Limitations:* Not likely to be suitable for diagnostic purposes, but promises to be useful for adult screening purposes. *Reviews and comments:* None as the test has only been available very recently.	**Psychological Corporation**
Wechsler Adult Intelligence Test (Revised) (WAIS–R) (1981)	The most widely used adult (age 16+) intelligence assessment instrument in the world. Eleven sub-tests of verbal and non-verbal ('performance') IQ. Provides a cognitive profile that can be checked for dyslexic characteristics, including the 'A-C-I-D profile'. Extremely well-researched and of high technical quality. *Limitations:* IQ calculation includes some dyslexia-sensitive subtests (e.g. Digit Span). Weak on assessment of visual memory. *Reviews and comments:* McLoughlin, Fitzgibbon and Young (1993) pp. 31-9; Turner (1997) pp. 262-93.	**Psychological Corporation** **R**
Wechsler Intelligence Scale for Children (3rd Edition, UK) (WISC–III[UK]**)** (1981)	Designed for use with children aged 6:0 to 16:11. Provides a similar profile of cognitive skills and IQ scales as WAIS–R. Extremely well-researched and of high technical quality. Replaced WISC–R. *Limitations:* Unsuitable for use with higher education population, although if IQ scores have been obtained using WISC–III or WISC–R when the student was aged 14–16, then these may be considered to give a reasonable estimate of the individual's intelligence. *Reviews and comments:* Thomson (1993) pp. 150-164; Turner (1997) pp. 40-69.	**Psychological Corporation** **R**

| British Ability Scales (2nd edition)

(BAS-II)

(1996) | Formerly BAS (Elliott, Murray and Pearons, 1979). Also found in the version *Differential Ability Scales* (DAS) (Elliott, 1990).

A comprehensive set of cognitive and attainment tests for use up to 17 years. Produces various IQ measures.

Reviews and comments: Beech and Singleton (1997a) pp. 334-5; Thomson (1993) pp. 150-3; Turner (1997) pp. 40-69. | **NFER-NELSON**

R |

14.6 British Dyslexia Association's Criteria for Accreditation of Training Courses for Dyslexia Teaching in Further and Higher Education

The target group with which this document is concerned is primarily those staff in Further and Higher Education institutions who are involved in the identification and support of students with Specific Learning Difficulties/ Dyslexia.[62]

The BDA have considered several examples of 'best practice' in Learning Support and in consultation with experienced tutors, have formulated these Criteria. Where training of learning support staff includes all the elements following, the BDA feels that training will efficiently equip staff to identify and support dyslexic learners at all stages of their lifelong learning.

Although in this document the word 'learner' is used broadly to refer to learners with Specific Learning Difficulty/Dyslexia, many other students will benefit from the approaches to learning detailed here.

Learning support teams in Further and Higher Education feel that there is a genuine need for specific training of staff supporting dyslexic learners. The BDA hopes that, by identifying criteria to be met by such training, courses will be established to meet these needs, upon successful completion of which participants will be recognised by the award of AMBDA(FE/HE).[63] Such an award would identify those with specialist knowledge of dyslexia who could advise administrative and academic staff, examining bodies and training organisations on the special strengths and special needs of individual students as well as supporting and advising individual learners.

Specific courses of training to meet the needs of staff in Further and Higher Education are rare and the BDA would hope to encourage the establishment of such courses to meet the increasing demand for individual guidance in the growing field of post-16 education and training.

Any training course that is developed to meet these criteria should include at every stage opportunities for the student to demonstrate practical application and practical ability. Assessment of such practical skills should be an essential part of any course.

Criteria for Learning Support Training to Meet the Needs of Dyslexic Learners

THE FOLLOWING CRITERIA ARE DESIGNED IN THREE SECTIONS, BUT EACH SECTION IS INTENDED TO INFORM AND SUPPORT THE OTHER TWO.

Section 1. Basic support

Students should:

1.1   Understand the theoretical bases for adult learning

1.2   Conduct a practical exploration with adult learners of preferences in learning styles and strategies

1.3   Analyse individual differences in learning styles and strategies. (Comparison of dyslexic and non-dyslexic styles)

1.4   Understand the current research into the biological bases of dyslexia (eg in neurology, genetics, etc).

---

[62] Source: *British Dyslexia Association FE/HE Criteria*, May 1998. This document is reproduced verbatim and there has been no attempt by the Working Party to consider the suitability of its contents.

[63] AMBDA (Associate Member of the British Dyslexia Association) is an accredited teaching diploma.

1.5   Analyse the cognitive aspects of the above

- information processing

- memory

- spatial skills, etc.

1.6   Understand how SpLD modifies learning, matching different teaching styles and learning environments in relation to individual learning goals.

1.7   Analyse the strengths and weaknesses of dyslexic learners.

1.8   Establish a profile of relative strengths and weaknesses including the impact on life choices; eg career choices, employment.

1.9   Understand the theory and application of counselling skills.

1.10   Understand the principles of stress management.

1.11   Demonstrate practical counselling skills to include:

- facilitating dialogue

- self-awareness - enabling tutors to deal with feelings of frustration and failure

- enabling students to deal with feelings of frustration and failure

- recognition of need for involvement of other agencies

- facilitating communication with staff, parents or other appropriate agencies.

1.12   Recognise the social/economic/and educational contexts which define dyslexia SpLD as problematic.

1.13   Recognise the different aims and outcomes of Further Education and Higher Education, and the implications for the style of support.

Section 2. Assessment and analysis

Students should demonstrate the following:

2.1   Interview Techniques

- and appropriate techniques of asking questions

- informal discussion

- informal assessment and analysis of options

- a practical exploration with an individual student

- a formal assessment

2.2   Analysis of interview and identifying learning goals demonstrating the ability to draw appropriate conclusions.

2.3   Choice of assessment procedures

- to identify the most appropriate learning styles, learning environments and learning goals

- to identify needs in relation to course and curriculum

- to help the learner understand his needs

2.4   Selection of assessment methods

- Understanding of appropriate informal and formal test materials

- Selection of appropriate diagnostic approaches

- Effective diagnostic assessment

- Understanding the different requirements of FE and HE with respect to diagnostic assessment criteria

2.5   Analysis of assessment
- specific needs of the individual learner
- analysis of multidisciplinary communications - including psychological and medical reports
- writing diagnostic reports
- analysis and interpretation of Education Psychologist's report:
  - ♦ to staff
  - ♦ to learner
- analysis of appropriate teaching/learning environments
- identification of specific provision to meet needs

2.6   Recognition of the relationship between assessment and learning

2.7   Analytical, systematic and continuing assessment of progress toward learning goals
- measuring progress in small steps
- continuing revision of learning styles and teaching styles

2.8   Record keeping
- for learner information
- for tutor information
- writing diagnostic reports – consideration of issues of confidentiality and appropriateness for differing purposes and differing audiences
- recording for systematic and continuing assessment for learner progress towards his specified learning goals.

NB: Course input on cognitive assessment must be delivered by a Chartered Psychologist with relevant training or experience.

Section 3. Implementing strategies: Designing and implementing an individualised learning programme

3.1   Analysis of learner's course requirements including curriculum content, delivery and assessment

3.2   Identifying assessment requirements of course

3.3   Analysis of the needs of the learner for success, e.g.
- literacy, numeracy
- training in organisation and memory skills
- Information Technology
- study skills
- higher level reading and writing skills
- problem solving
- metacognition
- thinking skills
- self advocacy

3.4   Demonstrate the ability to implement a range of teaching methods appropriate to dyslexic learners
- trialling, delivery, monitoring of individual strategies appropriate to the learner's strengths and weaknesses
- ongoing evaluation of methods

- ongoing reviewing of progress

- making appropriate adjustments to encourage independent learning

3.5 Formative and summative assessments, including formal examinations analysis of course requirements for examinations - GCSE, NVQ,GNVQ,

- Degree, Diploma, others

- what kind of assessment/examination?

- examination regulations

- preparation for examinations
  - ♦ revision techniques
  - ♦ strategies
  - ♦ stress management

- timetabling

- special examination provisions

- assessment for examination boards - timing

3.6 Implications for college policy

- developing learning support (principles, policy and practice)

- implementing staff development and liaison

- ensuring communication throughout whole college

- implications for college funding

- understanding funding mechanisms for students with learning difficulties and disabilities

- relationships with employers and trainers

N.B. Tutors will be expected to assess their students' grasp of the course as a whole, and of each section element. Adequate methods of assessment of individual student's practical ability must be specified. In addition, evidence must be provided, as appropriate, with the approval of the BDA, by means of essays, presentations, material design, record keeping.

14.7 Professional courses for dyslexia support in higher education

The following list (which is not necessarily comprehensive) is a selection of professional training courses in the UK that either (i) have been specifically designed to provide training for individuals intending to work with dyslexic students in higher or further education, or (ii) include significant coverage of this aspect of training.

Evaluation of these courses was outside the remit of the Working Party, and consequently no recommendations are made regarding their suitability, and no assuarnces are given regarding their content or accredited status. Most courses will require prior qualifications (e.g. a degree and/or accredited teaching qualification). Further information can be obtained from the contact names and addresses given in each case.

In 1998 the British Dyslexia Association published *Criteria for Learning Support Training to meet the Needs of Dyslexia Learners in Further and Higher Education* (see Secton 14.6). At the time of going to press, some of the courses listed below are in the process of gaining accreditation under these BDA Criteria. For further information regarding this, contact the BDA (address in Section 14.4).

DE MONTFORT UNIVERSITY

M.A and Postgraduate Diploma in Dyslexia Studies

Noreen Walker, Learning and Training Support Service, De Montfort University, Lincoln City Campus, 3 Lindum Road, Lincoln LN2 1NN. Tel: 01522 5673 54. Fax: 01522 528793.

[*www.lincolnshire.net/dmu/Student_Info/LTSS/dyslexia.htm*]

HELEN ARKELL DYSLEXIA CENTRE

Postgraduate Certificate and Diploma in Specific Learning Difficulties in Further and Higher Education

Anne Simmons, Helen Arkell Dyslexia Centre, Frensham, Farnham, Surrey GU10 3BW. Tel: 01252 792400.

KINGSTON UNIVERSITY

Postgraduate Certificate and Diploma in Professional Studies in Education (Specific Learning Difficulties Post-16)

Sylvia Mullett, INSET Office, School of Education, Kingston University, Kingston Hill, Surrey KT2 7LB. Tel: 0181 547 2000 Ext 5073.

MANCHESTER METROPOLITAN UNIVERSITY

Diploma in Teaching in Specific Learning Difficulties (HE and FE)

Mrs Marian Kelly, Course Development Officer, Faculty of Community Studies Law and Education, 799 Wilmslow Road, Didsbury, Manchester M20 2RR. Tel: 0161-247-2004.

MORAY HOUSE INSTITUTE OF EDUCATION, EDINBURGH

Postgraduate Diploma and M.Ed. in Specific Learning Difficulties (Dyslexia)

Dr Gavin Reid, Moray House Institute of Education, Heriot-Watt University, Holyrood Campus, Holyrood Road, Edinburgh EH8 8QA. Tel: 0131 556 8455.

OXFORD BROOKES UNIVERSITY

M.A., Postgraduate Diploma and Certificate in Dyslexia Studies (FE/HE/Adult Education /Employment)

Dr Ginny Stacey, Student Services, Helena Kennedy Student Centre, Oxford Brookes University, Headington Hill Campus, Headington, Oxford OX3 0BP. Tel: 01865 484659.

UNIVERSITY OF BANGOR

Diploma, Advanced Diploma and M. Ed. in Learning Difficulties (specialising in Dyslexia/Specific Learning Difficulties)

Gwen Hughes, School of Education, University of Wales, Bangor, Gwynedd LL57 2DG. Tel: 01248 382932.

Certificate of Further Professional Studies in Specific Learning Difficulties

Mrs C Coker, School of Education, University of Wales, Bangor, Gwynedd LL57 2DG. Tel: 01248 382938.

14.8   Basic reading list

The following is a recommended basic reading list intended for dyslexia support tutors, disability officers or other individuals who wish to improve their understanding of dyslexia, how it affects students in higher education, and how such students can be supported effectively.

1. Research background

Hulme, C. and Snowling, M. (Eds.) (1997) *Dyslexia: Biology, Cognition and Intervention.* London: Whurr.

Miles, T. (1993) *Dyslexia: the pattern of difficulties* (Second edition). London: Whurr.

Pumfrey, P.D. and Reason, R. (Eds.) (1991) *Specific learning difficulties (Dyslexia): challenges and responses.* London: Routledge.

West, T.G. (1997) *In the Mind's Eye.* (Updated edition) New York: Prometheus Books.

2. General policy and practice

Closs, A., Lannen, S. and Reid, G. (1996) Dyslexia in Further and Higher Education: a framework for practice. In G. Reid (Ed.) *Dimensions of Dyslexia.* Vol. 1. Edinburgh: Moray House, pp. 447-467.

Gilroy, D. E. (1993) *Dyslexia and Higher Education.* Bangor: Dyslexia Unit, University of Bangor.

Pumfrey, P.D. (1998) Reforming policy and provision for dyslexic students in higher education: Towards and national code of practice. *Support for Learning,* **13**, 87-90.

Reid, G. (1998) *Dyslexia: a practitioner's handbook.* Chichester: Wiley.

Skill (National Bureau for Students with Disabilities) (1997) *The Coordinator's Handbook.* London: Skill.

Stephens, C. (Ed.) (1996) *Dyslexic Students in Higher Education.* Huddersfield: University of Huddersfield with Skill (National Bureau for Students with Disabilities).

Waterfield, J. (Ed.) (1995) *Dyslexia in Higher Education: Learning along the continuum.* (Proceedings of the 1st International Conference on Dyslexia in Higher Education) Plymouth: University of Plymouth.

Waterfield, J. (Ed.) (1998) *Dyslexia in Higher Education: Learning along the continuum.* (Proceedings of the 2nd International Conference on Dyslexia in Higher Education) Plymouth: University of Plymouth.

3. Identification and assessment

Beaton, A., McDougall, S. and Singleton, C.H. (Eds.) (1997) *Dyslexia in literate adults.* (Special issue of the *Journal of Research in Reading,* **20**, 1). Oxford: Blackwell.

Beech, J. and Singleton, C.H. (Eds.) (1997) *The Psychological Assessment of Reading.* London: Routledge,

McGuire, J.M., Madaus, J.W., Litt, V. and Ramirez, M.O. (1996) An investigation of documentation submitted by university students to verify their learning disabilities. *Journal of Learning Disabilities,* 29, 297-304.

McLoughlin, D., Fitzgibbon, G. and Young, V. (1994) *Adult dyslexia: assessment, counselling and training.* London: Whurr.

Turner, M. (1997) *Psychological Assessment of Dyslexia.* London: Whurr.

4. Student support

Gilroy, D. E. and Miles, T. R. (1996) *Dyslexia at college.* Second edition. London: Routledge.

Goodwin, V. and Thomson, B. (1991) *Adult student and dyslexia: a resource book for adult students and staff.* Milton Keynes: The Open University.

Krupska, M. and Klein, C. (1995) *Demystifying Dyslexia.* London: London Language and Literacy Unit.

Matty, J. (1995) *Dyslexia: signposts to success. a guide for dyslexic adults.* Reading: British Dyslexia Association.

Stacey, G. (1997) A dyslexic mind a-thinking. *Dyslexia*, **3**, 111-119.

Williams, L.V. (1986) *Teaching for the Two-Sided Mind.* New York: Simon and Schuster.

Wolfendale, S. and Corbett, J. (1996) *Learning Support in Higher Education.* London: Cassell.

5. *Counselling issues*

Edwards, J. (1994) *The Scars of Dyslexia.* London: Cassell.

Miles, T. and Varma, V. (Eds.) (1995) *Dyslexia and Stress.* London: Whurr.

Riddick, B., Farmer, M. and Sterling, C. (1997) *Students and Dyslexia: Growing up with a specific learning difficulty.* London: Whurr.

6. *Technology support*

Kaufman, C. (with C.H Singleton and J. Hutchins) (1998) *IT for dyslexic adults.* Reading: British Dyslexia Association.

Kaufman, C. and Singleton, C.H. (1998) *Study skills with ICT.* Reading: British Dyslexia Association.

Nisbet, P and Poon, P. (1998) *Special Access Technology.* Edinburgh: CALL Centre, University of Edinburgh.

INDEX